# THE ULTIMATE HUNTERS

## WILD GAME COOKBOOK GUIDE

200+ MOUTH-WATERING RECIPES TO MASTER THE ART OF COOKING POPULAR NORTH AMERICAN ANIMALS WITH FACTS AND STATS

## PAT GATZ

© **Copyright 2023 - All rights reserved.**

The content contained within this book may not be reproduced, duplicated, or transmitted without direct written permission from the author or the publisher.

Under no circumstances will any blame or legal responsibility be held against the publisher, or author, for any damages, reparation, or monetary loss due to the information contained within this book, either directly or indirectly.

Legal Notice:
This book is copyright protected. It is only for personal use. You cannot amend, distribute, sell, use, quote, or paraphrase any part, or the content within this book, without the author's or publisher's consent.

Disclaimer Notice:
Please note the information contained within this document is for educational and entertainment purposes only. All effort has been executed to present accurate, up-to-date, reliable, and complete information. No warranties of any kind are declared or implied. Readers acknowledge that the author is not engaged in rendering legal, financial, medical, or professional advice. The content within this book has been derived from various sources. Please consult a licensed professional before attempting any techniques outlined in this book.

By reading this document, the reader agrees that under no circumstances is the author responsible for any losses, direct or indirect, that are incurred as a result of the use of the information contained within this document, including, but not limited to, errors, omissions, or inaccuracies.

Interior Design by FormattedBooks

# CONTENTS

Introduction ................................................................. xiii

## CHAPTER 1: SIMPLE SMALL GAME .................................. 1

### BREAKFAST
Scrumptious Small Game Burritos ............................... 4
Remarkable Rabbit Kebab ........................................ 6
Sneaky Snake Meat Egg Rolls .................................... 8
Simple Small Game Scramble ................................... 10

### LUNCH
Savoury Sautéed Muskrat ....................................... 14
Delicious Deep-Fried Rabbit ................................... 16
Favourite Fried Squirrel ....................................... 18

### DINNER
Classic Oven-Fried Game ....................................... 22
Saporous Small Game Potpie .................................... 24
Satisfying Small Game Dumpling Soup ........................... 26

## CHAPTER 2: BIRD BUFFET ........................................ 28

### BREAKFAST
Perfect Parmesan Turkey Scramble .............................. 32
Wild Turkey and Parmesan Salad ................................ 34
Sour Partridge Salad .......................................... 36
Minty and Lemon Zest Dove Scramble ............................ 38
Heavenly Honey and Sage Quail Toast ........................... 40
Sweet and Sour Grouse Sandwich ................................ 42
Powerful Partridge Salad Toast ................................ 44
Wine-Infused Crispy Duck ...................................... 46

Beautiful Breakfast Goose Omelet . . . . . . . . . . . . . . . . . . . . . . . . . . . . . . . . . . . . 48
Crispy Pheasant Egg Rolls. . . . . . . . . . . . . . . . . . . . . . . . . . . . . . . . . . . . . . . . . 50

## LUNCH

Bashful Breaded Grouse . . . . . . . . . . . . . . . . . . . . . . . . . . . . . . . . . . . . . . . . . . 54
Grateful Grouse Macaroni Salad . . . . . . . . . . . . . . . . . . . . . . . . . . . . . . . . . . . 56
Greatness Grouse Sandwich Salad . . . . . . . . . . . . . . . . . . . . . . . . . . . . . . . . . 58
Caribbean Coconut Grouse . . . . . . . . . . . . . . . . . . . . . . . . . . . . . . . . . . . . . . 60
Peaceful Ptarmigan Mini Pie . . . . . . . . . . . . . . . . . . . . . . . . . . . . . . . . . . . . . . 62
Pretty Pigeon Quiche. . . . . . . . . . . . . . . . . . . . . . . . . . . . . . . . . . . . . . . . . . . . 64
Spicy Toast Turkey Sandwich . . . . . . . . . . . . . . . . . . . . . . . . . . . . . . . . . . . . . 66
Saline Snipe Salad . . . . . . . . . . . . . . . . . . . . . . . . . . . . . . . . . . . . . . . . . . . . . . 68
Whisper Woodcock Wrap . . . . . . . . . . . . . . . . . . . . . . . . . . . . . . . . . . . . . . . 70
Dainty Dove Kebab . . . . . . . . . . . . . . . . . . . . . . . . . . . . . . . . . . . . . . . . . . . . . 72
Quick Quail and Potatoes in Mushroom Sauce . . . . . . . . . . . . . . . . . . . . . . 74
Golden Grouse Pie. . . . . . . . . . . . . . . . . . . . . . . . . . . . . . . . . . . . . . . . . . . . . . 76
Sour Partridge Soup. . . . . . . . . . . . . . . . . . . . . . . . . . . . . . . . . . . . . . . . . . . . 78

## DINNER

Wicked Wild Duck Fillets in Raspberry Sauce . . . . . . . . . . . . . . . . . . . . . . . 82
Quick Goose Roast . . . . . . . . . . . . . . . . . . . . . . . . . . . . . . . . . . . . . . . . . . . . 84
Pleasant Pheasant With Mushroom Sauce . . . . . . . . . . . . . . . . . . . . . . . . . 86
Breaded Ptarmigan With Wine and Blueberry Sauce . . . . . . . . . . . . . . . . 88
Friendly Fried Pigeon in Sweet Potato Applesauce. . . . . . . . . . . . . . . . . . . 90
Dodging Dove Risotto Roast . . . . . . . . . . . . . . . . . . . . . . . . . . . . . . . . . . . . 92
Wonderful Wild Turkey Stew . . . . . . . . . . . . . . . . . . . . . . . . . . . . . . . . . . . . 94
Quaint Quail Vegetable Roast . . . . . . . . . . . . . . . . . . . . . . . . . . . . . . . . . . . 96
Sweety Potato Grouse Stew. . . . . . . . . . . . . . . . . . . . . . . . . . . . . . . . . . . . . 98
Particular Partridge Stew . . . . . . . . . . . . . . . . . . . . . . . . . . . . . . . . . . . . . .100
Dipping Duck and Rice Stir-Fry . . . . . . . . . . . . . . . . . . . . . . . . . . . . . . . . .102
Down Deep-Fried Goose Fillets . . . . . . . . . . . . . . . . . . . . . . . . . . . . . . . . .104
Special Stuffed Pheasants. . . . . . . . . . . . . . . . . . . . . . . . . . . . . . . . . . . . . .106
Whole Ptarmigan Risotto Roast . . . . . . . . . . . . . . . . . . . . . . . . . . . . . . . . .108
Delight Deep-Fried Turkey . . . . . . . . . . . . . . . . . . . . . . . . . . . . . . . . . . . . 110
Sensible Snipe Pie . . . . . . . . . . . . . . . . . . . . . . . . . . . . . . . . . . . . . . . . . . . 112
Panfried Woodcock Risotto. . . . . . . . . . . . . . . . . . . . . . . . . . . . . . . . . . . . 114
Perky Pesto Pigeon Tarts . . . . . . . . . . . . . . . . . . . . . . . . . . . . . . . . . . . . . . 116
Witty Wild Turkey and Mushroom Risotto . . . . . . . . . . . . . . . . . . . . . . . . 118

# CHAPTER 3: DELICIOUS DEER . . . . . . . . . . . . . . . . . . . . . . . . . . . . . . . . . . . . . . . . . . . . . . . . . . . .120

## BREAKFAST

Deer Egg Rolls . . . . . . . . . . . . . . . . . . . . . . . . . . . . . . . . . . . . . . . . . . . . . . . . . . . . . . . . . . . . 124

Venison Liver Pate . . . . . . . . . . . . . . . . . . . . . . . . . . . . . . . . . . . . . . . . . . . . . . . . . . . . . . . 126

Creamy Venison Salad . . . . . . . . . . . . . . . . . . . . . . . . . . . . . . . . . . . . . . . . . . . . . . . . . . . 128

Creamy Venison Salad Sandwich . . . . . . . . . . . . . . . . . . . . . . . . . . . . . . . . . . . . . . . . . 130

Delicious Venison Wrap . . . . . . . . . . . . . . . . . . . . . . . . . . . . . . . . . . . . . . . . . . . . . . . . . . 132

Panfried Venison With Veggies . . . . . . . . . . . . . . . . . . . . . . . . . . . . . . . . . . . . . . . . . . . 134

Venison Morning Hash . . . . . . . . . . . . . . . . . . . . . . . . . . . . . . . . . . . . . . . . . . . . . . . . . . 136

Venison Breakfast Fried Egg Toast . . . . . . . . . . . . . . . . . . . . . . . . . . . . . . . . . . . . . . . . 138

Fried Egg and Venison Patties . . . . . . . . . . . . . . . . . . . . . . . . . . . . . . . . . . . . . . . . . . . .140

Venison Breakfast Sausage . . . . . . . . . . . . . . . . . . . . . . . . . . . . . . . . . . . . . . . . . . . . . . 142

Venison Breakfast Pie . . . . . . . . . . . . . . . . . . . . . . . . . . . . . . . . . . . . . . . . . . . . . . . . . . .144

Venison Mini Quiche . . . . . . . . . . . . . . . . . . . . . . . . . . . . . . . . . . . . . . . . . . . . . . . . . . . . 146

## LUNCH

Venison Roast Sandwich. . . . . . . . . . . . . . . . . . . . . . . . . . . . . . . . . . . . . . . . . . . . . . . . . 150

Venison Pasta Salad. . . . . . . . . . . . . . . . . . . . . . . . . . . . . . . . . . . . . . . . . . . . . . . . . . . . . 152

Venison Kebab . . . . . . . . . . . . . . . . . . . . . . . . . . . . . . . . . . . . . . . . . . . . . . . . . . . . . . . . .154

Ground Breaded Venison Kebab. . . . . . . . . . . . . . . . . . . . . . . . . . . . . . . . . . . . . . . . . . 156

Light Venison Stew . . . . . . . . . . . . . . . . . . . . . . . . . . . . . . . . . . . . . . . . . . . . . . . . . . . . . 158

Venison and Wild Mushroom Medley . . . . . . . . . . . . . . . . . . . . . . . . . . . . . . . . . . . . .160

Venison Pie . . . . . . . . . . . . . . . . . . . . . . . . . . . . . . . . . . . . . . . . . . . . . . . . . . . . . . . . . . . . 162

Light Dumpling Venison Broth. . . . . . . . . . . . . . . . . . . . . . . . . . . . . . . . . . . . . . . . . . . .164

Venison Bites in Blueberry Sauce . . . . . . . . . . . . . . . . . . . . . . . . . . . . . . . . . . . . . . . . . 166

Spaghetti in Venison Sauce . . . . . . . . . . . . . . . . . . . . . . . . . . . . . . . . . . . . . . . . . . . . . . 168

Spaghetti Mushrooms and Venison . . . . . . . . . . . . . . . . . . . . . . . . . . . . . . . . . . . . . . 170

## DINNER

Venison Medallions in Mushroom Sauce . . . . . . . . . . . . . . . . . . . . . . . . . . . . . . . . . .174

Deer Stew . . . . . . . . . . . . . . . . . . . . . . . . . . . . . . . . . . . . . . . . . . . . . . . . . . . . . . . . . . . . . 176

Deer Pepper Stew . . . . . . . . . . . . . . . . . . . . . . . . . . . . . . . . . . . . . . . . . . . . . . . . . . . . . . 178

Deer and Broccoli Risotto . . . . . . . . . . . . . . . . . . . . . . . . . . . . . . . . . . . . . . . . . . . . . . .180

Venison Steak Tartare. . . . . . . . . . . . . . . . . . . . . . . . . . . . . . . . . . . . . . . . . . . . . . . . . . . 182

Venison in Garlic Sauce. . . . . . . . . . . . . . . . . . . . . . . . . . . . . . . . . . . . . . . . . . . . . . . . . .184

Fried Venison With Sweet Potatoes. . . . . . . . . . . . . . . . . . . . . . . . . . . . . . . . . . . . . . . 186

Breaded Venison With White Mushroom Sauce . . . . . . . . . . . . . . . . . . . . . . . . . . . . 188

Fried Venison Chops With Tomato Sauce . . . . . . . . . . . . . . . . . . . . . . . . . . . . . . . . . .190

Venison Roast . . . . . . . . . . . . . . . . . . . . . . . . . . . . . . . . . . . . . . . . . . . . . . . . . . . . . 192

Easy Venison Wellington With Blueberry Sauce . . . . . . . . . . . . . . . . . . . . . . . . . 194

Baked Venison Pasta . . . . . . . . . . . . . . . . . . . . . . . . . . . . . . . . . . . . . . . . . . . . . 196

Mouth-Watering Whitetail Axis Bacon Grilled Cheeseburger . . . . . . . . . . . . . . . 198

## CHAPTER 4: ELECTRIFYING ELK . . . . . . . . . . . . . . . . . . . . . . . . . . . . . . . . . 200

### BREAKFAST

Spinach and Mushrooms Elk Omelet . . . . . . . . . . . . . . . . . . . . . . . . . . . . . . . . 204

Panfried Elk Pate . . . . . . . . . . . . . . . . . . . . . . . . . . . . . . . . . . . . . . . . . . . . . . . 206

Elk Breakfast Casserole . . . . . . . . . . . . . . . . . . . . . . . . . . . . . . . . . . . . . . . . . . 208

Delicious Elk Pie Wraps . . . . . . . . . . . . . . . . . . . . . . . . . . . . . . . . . . . . . . . . . . 210

Elk Breakfast Quiche . . . . . . . . . . . . . . . . . . . . . . . . . . . . . . . . . . . . . . . . . . . . 212

Simple Elk and Spinach Scramble . . . . . . . . . . . . . . . . . . . . . . . . . . . . . . . . . . 214

Elk Breakfast Tart . . . . . . . . . . . . . . . . . . . . . . . . . . . . . . . . . . . . . . . . . . . . . . 216

Elk Bacon Breakfast Wraps . . . . . . . . . . . . . . . . . . . . . . . . . . . . . . . . . . . . . . . 218

Oven-Baked Grilled Elk and Cheese Sandwich . . . . . . . . . . . . . . . . . . . . . . . . 220

Elk and Bacon With Fried Eggs . . . . . . . . . . . . . . . . . . . . . . . . . . . . . . . . . . . . 222

### LUNCH

Apple and Elk Salad . . . . . . . . . . . . . . . . . . . . . . . . . . . . . . . . . . . . . . . . . . . . 226

Roasted Elk and Leek Risotto . . . . . . . . . . . . . . . . . . . . . . . . . . . . . . . . . . . . . 228

Oven-Roasted Elk Sandwich . . . . . . . . . . . . . . . . . . . . . . . . . . . . . . . . . . . . . . 230

Elk Macaroni Salad . . . . . . . . . . . . . . . . . . . . . . . . . . . . . . . . . . . . . . . . . . . . . 232

Tortilla Elk Salad (Gyros) . . . . . . . . . . . . . . . . . . . . . . . . . . . . . . . . . . . . . . . . . 234

Cool Elk Spaghetti Salad . . . . . . . . . . . . . . . . . . . . . . . . . . . . . . . . . . . . . . . . . 236

Fried Elk Mini Kebabs . . . . . . . . . . . . . . . . . . . . . . . . . . . . . . . . . . . . . . . . . . . 238

Elk Burger With Fries . . . . . . . . . . . . . . . . . . . . . . . . . . . . . . . . . . . . . . . . . . . . 240

### DINNER

Elk Wellington Steak . . . . . . . . . . . . . . . . . . . . . . . . . . . . . . . . . . . . . . . . . . . . 244

Elk Fillet in Blackberry Brandy Sauce . . . . . . . . . . . . . . . . . . . . . . . . . . . . . . . . 246

Fried Elk With Veggie Mash . . . . . . . . . . . . . . . . . . . . . . . . . . . . . . . . . . . . . . . 248

Elk Cheese and Veggie Soup . . . . . . . . . . . . . . . . . . . . . . . . . . . . . . . . . . . . . . 250

White Elk and Mushroom Macaroni . . . . . . . . . . . . . . . . . . . . . . . . . . . . . . . . 252

Elk Meatballs . . . . . . . . . . . . . . . . . . . . . . . . . . . . . . . . . . . . . . . . . . . . . . . . . . 254

Sweet Elk Shepherd's Pie . . . . . . . . . . . . . . . . . . . . . . . . . . . . . . . . . . . . . . . . 256

Elk Meat Loaf in Cherry Sauce . . . . . . . . . . . . . . . . . . . . . . . . . . . . . . . . . . . . 258

## CHAPTER 5: MARVELOUS MOOSE . . . . . . . . . . . . . . . . . . . . . . . . . . . . . . . . . . . . . . . . . . . . . . . . . . . . . . . . . . . . .262

### BREAKFAST

- Scrumptious Moose Scramble . . . . . . . . . . . . . . . . . . . . . . . . . . . . . . . . . . . . . . . . . . . . . . . . . . . . . . . . . . . . . . . . .266
- Cheesy Moose Breakfast Casserole . . . . . . . . . . . . . . . . . . . . . . . . . . . . . . . . . . . . . . . . . . . . . . . . . . . . . . . . . . .268
- Moose Spring Salad . . . . . . . . . . . . . . . . . . . . . . . . . . . . . . . . . . . . . . . . . . . . . . . . . . . . . . . . . . . . . . . . . . . . . . . . . . .270
- Cesar Moose Salad . . . . . . . . . . . . . . . . . . . . . . . . . . . . . . . . . . . . . . . . . . . . . . . . . . . . . . . . . . . . . . . . . . . . . . . . . . .272
- Easy Moose Scramble . . . . . . . . . . . . . . . . . . . . . . . . . . . . . . . . . . . . . . . . . . . . . . . . . . . . . . . . . . . . . . . . . . . . . . . .274
- Moose Morning Toast With Cherry Sauce . . . . . . . . . . . . . . . . . . . . . . . . . . . . . . . . . . . . . . . . . . . . . . . . . . . . .276

### LUNCH

- Moose Sandwich . . . . . . . . . . . . . . . . . . . . . . . . . . . . . . . . . . . . . . . . . . . . . . . . . . . . . . . . . . . . . . . . . . . . . . . . . . . . . 280
- Cool Moose Bacon Salad Toast . . . . . . . . . . . . . . . . . . . . . . . . . . . . . . . . . . . . . . . . . . . . . . . . . . . . . . . . . . . . . . . .282
- Breaded and Stuffed Moose Fillet . . . . . . . . . . . . . . . . . . . . . . . . . . . . . . . . . . . . . . . . . . . . . . . . . . . . . . . . . . . . 284
- Moose Omelet . . . . . . . . . . . . . . . . . . . . . . . . . . . . . . . . . . . . . . . . . . . . . . . . . . . . . . . . . . . . . . . . . . . . . . . . . . . . . . .286
- Munching Moose Taco Salad . . . . . . . . . . . . . . . . . . . . . . . . . . . . . . . . . . . . . . . . . . . . . . . . . . . . . . . . . . . . . . . . . 288
- Moose Burritos . . . . . . . . . . . . . . . . . . . . . . . . . . . . . . . . . . . . . . . . . . . . . . . . . . . . . . . . . . . . . . . . . . . . . . . . . . . . . . 290

### DINNER

- Moose Kebab . . . . . . . . . . . . . . . . . . . . . . . . . . . . . . . . . . . . . . . . . . . . . . . . . . . . . . . . . . . . . . . . . . . . . . . . . . . . . . . .294
- Moose Carbonara . . . . . . . . . . . . . . . . . . . . . . . . . . . . . . . . . . . . . . . . . . . . . . . . . . . . . . . . . . . . . . . . . . . . . . . . . . . .296
- Veggie Moose Soup . . . . . . . . . . . . . . . . . . . . . . . . . . . . . . . . . . . . . . . . . . . . . . . . . . . . . . . . . . . . . . . . . . . . . . . . . .298
- Moose Moussaka . . . . . . . . . . . . . . . . . . . . . . . . . . . . . . . . . . . . . . . . . . . . . . . . . . . . . . . . . . . . . . . . . . . . . . . . . . . . 300
- Moose Ragu–Goulash . . . . . . . . . . . . . . . . . . . . . . . . . . . . . . . . . . . . . . . . . . . . . . . . . . . . . . . . . . . . . . . . . . . . . . . .302
- Algonquin Moose Stew . . . . . . . . . . . . . . . . . . . . . . . . . . . . . . . . . . . . . . . . . . . . . . . . . . . . . . . . . . . . . . . . . . . . . . 304
- Moose Meat One Dish . . . . . . . . . . . . . . . . . . . . . . . . . . . . . . . . . . . . . . . . . . . . . . . . . . . . . . . . . . . . . . . . . . . . . . . 306
- Moose Whispers Marvel Fast Fry . . . . . . . . . . . . . . . . . . . . . . . . . . . . . . . . . . . . . . . . . . . . . . . . . . . . . . . . . . . . . 308
- Gammy's Crazy Lasagna . . . . . . . . . . . . . . . . . . . . . . . . . . . . . . . . . . . . . . . . . . . . . . . . . . . . . . . . . . . . . . . . . . . . . .310
- Mandy's Moose Death Row Soup . . . . . . . . . . . . . . . . . . . . . . . . . . . . . . . . . . . . . . . . . . . . . . . . . . . . . . . . . . . . . .312

## CHAPTER 6: BLISSFUL BEAR . . . . . . . . . . . . . . . . . . . . . . . . . . . . . . . . . . . . . . . . . . . . . . . . . . . . . . . . . . . . . . . . . . .314

### BREAKFAST

- Bear Liver Pate . . . . . . . . . . . . . . . . . . . . . . . . . . . . . . . . . . . . . . . . . . . . . . . . . . . . . . . . . . . . . . . . . . . . . . . . . . . . . . .318
- Bear Breakfast Casserole . . . . . . . . . . . . . . . . . . . . . . . . . . . . . . . . . . . . . . . . . . . . . . . . . . . . . . . . . . . . . . . . . . . . .320
- Cheesy Arugula Bear Salad . . . . . . . . . . . . . . . . . . . . . . . . . . . . . . . . . . . . . . . . . . . . . . . . . . . . . . . . . . . . . . . . . . .322
- Bear-Stuffed Zucchinis With Cheesy Eggs . . . . . . . . . . . . . . . . . . . . . . . . . . . . . . . . . . . . . . . . . . . . . . . . . . . . .324
- Cheesy Bear-Stuffed Paprika Slices . . . . . . . . . . . . . . . . . . . . . . . . . . . . . . . . . . . . . . . . . . . . . . . . . . . . . . . . . . . .326

## LUNCH

Bear Quiche . . . . . . . . . . . . . . . . . . . . . . . . . . . . . . . . . . . . . . . . . . . . . . . . . . . . . . . . . . . . . . . . . . . . . . . . . . . . . . . . . .330

Bear Cheese and Veggie Rolls . . . . . . . . . . . . . . . . . . . . . . . . . . . . . . . . . . . . . . . . . . . . . . . . . . . . . . . . . . . .332

Light Bear Burgers . . . . . . . . . . . . . . . . . . . . . . . . . . . . . . . . . . . . . . . . . . . . . . . . . . . . . . . . . . . . . . . . . . . . . .334

Bear Stew . . . . . . . . . . . . . . . . . . . . . . . . . . . . . . . . . . . . . . . . . . . . . . . . . . . . . . . . . . . . . . . . . . . . . . . . . . . . . .336

Roasted Bear Risotto . . . . . . . . . . . . . . . . . . . . . . . . . . . . . . . . . . . . . . . . . . . . . . . . . . . . . . . . . . . . . . . . . . . .338

Ground Bear Salad . . . . . . . . . . . . . . . . . . . . . . . . . . . . . . . . . . . . . . . . . . . . . . . . . . . . . . . . . . . . . . . . . . . . .340

## DINNER

Bear-Stuffed Paprika Stew . . . . . . . . . . . . . . . . . . . . . . . . . . . . . . . . . . . . . . . . . . . . . . . . . . . . . . . . . . . . . .344

Bear Moussaka . . . . . . . . . . . . . . . . . . . . . . . . . . . . . . . . . . . . . . . . . . . . . . . . . . . . . . . . . . . . . . . . . . . . . . . 346

Bear and Bean Stew . . . . . . . . . . . . . . . . . . . . . . . . . . . . . . . . . . . . . . . . . . . . . . . . . . . . . . . . . . . . . . . . . . . 348

Bear Veggie Roast . . . . . . . . . . . . . . . . . . . . . . . . . . . . . . . . . . . . . . . . . . . . . . . . . . . . . . . . . . . . . . . . . . . . . .350

Bear Steak in Wine Sauce . . . . . . . . . . . . . . . . . . . . . . . . . . . . . . . . . . . . . . . . . . . . . . . . . . . . . . . . . . . . . . .352

Bear in White Sauce With Mushrooms . . . . . . . . . . . . . . . . . . . . . . . . . . . . . . . . . . . . . . . . . . . . . . . . . . .354

Bear Goulash With Sweet Potato Mash . . . . . . . . . . . . . . . . . . . . . . . . . . . . . . . . . . . . . . . . . . . . . . . . . .356

## CHAPTER 7: WONDERFUL WILD BOAR . . . . . . . . . . . . . . . . . . . . . . . . . . . . . . . . . . . . . . . . . . . . . . .358

## BREAKFAST

Wild Boar Medley . . . . . . . . . . . . . . . . . . . . . . . . . . . . . . . . . . . . . . . . . . . . . . . . . . . . . . . . . . . . . . . . . . . . . .362

Wild Boar Breakfast Sausage With Pound Cakes . . . . . . . . . . . . . . . . . . . . . . . . . . . . . . . . . . . . . . . . . 364

Woody Wild Boar Breakfast Burgers . . . . . . . . . . . . . . . . . . . . . . . . . . . . . . . . . . . . . . . . . . . . . . . . . . . . .366

Wild Boar Grilled Cheese Sandwich . . . . . . . . . . . . . . . . . . . . . . . . . . . . . . . . . . . . . . . . . . . . . . . . . . . . .368

Wild Boar Breakfast Tortillas . . . . . . . . . . . . . . . . . . . . . . . . . . . . . . . . . . . . . . . . . . . . . . . . . . . . . . . . . . . .370

Fried Boar in Rice Tarts . . . . . . . . . . . . . . . . . . . . . . . . . . . . . . . . . . . . . . . . . . . . . . . . . . . . . . . . . . . . . . . . .372

Wild Boar and Fried Egg Delight . . . . . . . . . . . . . . . . . . . . . . . . . . . . . . . . . . . . . . . . . . . . . . . . . . . . . . . .374

Wild Boar Breakfast Quiche . . . . . . . . . . . . . . . . . . . . . . . . . . . . . . . . . . . . . . . . . . . . . . . . . . . . . . . . . . . . .376

Nutty Wild Boar and Mushroom Medley . . . . . . . . . . . . . . . . . . . . . . . . . . . . . . . . . . . . . . . . . . . . . . . . .378

## LUNCH

Wicked Wild Boar in Mushroom Sauce and Potatoes . . . . . . . . . . . . . . . . . . . . . . . . . . . . . . . . . . . . .382

Wild Boar Pesto Spaghetti . . . . . . . . . . . . . . . . . . . . . . . . . . . . . . . . . . . . . . . . . . . . . . . . . . . . . . . . . . . . . 384

Hearty Tomato Boar and Bean Stew . . . . . . . . . . . . . . . . . . . . . . . . . . . . . . . . . . . . . . . . . . . . . . . . . . . . .386

Wild Boar Bacon and Sweet Potato Chips . . . . . . . . . . . . . . . . . . . . . . . . . . . . . . . . . . . . . . . . . . . . . . . 388

Wilderness Wild Boar Risotto With Mushrooms . . . . . . . . . . . . . . . . . . . . . . . . . . . . . . . . . . . . . . . . . .390

Wild Boar Moussaka . . . . . . . . . . . . . . . . . . . . . . . . . . . . . . . . . . . . . . . . . . . . . . . . . . . . . . . . . . . . . . . . . . .392

Wild Boar Pasta With Cauliflower and Cheese . . . . . . . . . . . . . . . . . . . . . . . . . . . . . . . . . . . . . . . . . . . .394

## DINNER

Smokey Wild Boar Rib Roast . . . . . . . . . . . . . . . . . . . . . . . . . . . . . . . . . . . . . . . . . . . . . . .398

Wild Boar Risotto Roast . . . . . . . . . . . . . . . . . . . . . . . . . . . . . . . . . . . . . . . . . . . . . . . . . 400

Wild Boar Steak With Sweet Potato Mash . . . . . . . . . . . . . . . . . . . . . . . . . . . . . . . . . 402

Wild Boar and Pumpkin Pie . . . . . . . . . . . . . . . . . . . . . . . . . . . . . . . . . . . . . . . . . . . . . 404

Beautiful Boar and Sweet Potato Stew . . . . . . . . . . . . . . . . . . . . . . . . . . . . . . . . . . . 406

Cauliflower and Mozzarella Wild Boar Risotto Roast . . . . . . . . . . . . . . . . . . . . . . . . 408

Wonderful Wild Boar and Sweet Potato Salad. . . . . . . . . . . . . . . . . . . . . . . . . . . . . .410

# CHAPTER 8: GOODNESS GAME FISH . . . . . . . . . . . . . . . . . . . . . . . . . . . . . . . . . . . . . . .412

## BREAKFAST

Tuna Corn and Tomato Scramble . . . . . . . . . . . . . . . . . . . . . . . . . . . . . . . . . . . . . . . .416

Fried Shrimp . . . . . . . . . . . . . . . . . . . . . . . . . . . . . . . . . . . . . . . . . . . . . . . . . . . . . . . . .418

Tunas in Blankets . . . . . . . . . . . . . . . . . . . . . . . . . . . . . . . . . . . . . . . . . . . . . . . . . . . . 420

Almond and Shrimp. . . . . . . . . . . . . . . . . . . . . . . . . . . . . . . . . . . . . . . . . . . . . . . . . . .422

Potato Tuna Salad Toast . . . . . . . . . . . . . . . . . . . . . . . . . . . . . . . . . . . . . . . . . . . . . . .424

Tuna Pate Toast. . . . . . . . . . . . . . . . . . . . . . . . . . . . . . . . . . . . . . . . . . . . . . . . . . . . . .426

Herring Scramble . . . . . . . . . . . . . . . . . . . . . . . . . . . . . . . . . . . . . . . . . . . . . . . . . . . .428

Fishy Deviled Wild Game Eggs. . . . . . . . . . . . . . . . . . . . . . . . . . . . . . . . . . . . . . . . . . 430

Boiled Egg Tuna Salad . . . . . . . . . . . . . . . . . . . . . . . . . . . . . . . . . . . . . . . . . . . . . . . . .432

Fish Fillet and Rice Tarts . . . . . . . . . . . . . . . . . . . . . . . . . . . . . . . . . . . . . . . . . . . . . . 434

Fish and Corn Salad in Buns . . . . . . . . . . . . . . . . . . . . . . . . . . . . . . . . . . . . . . . . . . . 436

## LUNCH

Fried Fish and Veggies . . . . . . . . . . . . . . . . . . . . . . . . . . . . . . . . . . . . . . . . . . . . . . . . 440

Fish Pesto Pasta . . . . . . . . . . . . . . . . . . . . . . . . . . . . . . . . . . . . . . . . . . . . . . . . . . . . . 442

Wild Game Seafood Spaghetti in Tomato Sauce . . . . . . . . . . . . . . . . . . . . . . . . . . . 444

Wild Fish and Cauliflower Cheese Sauce Mini Pies . . . . . . . . . . . . . . . . . . . . . . . . . 446

Herring Grilled Cheese Sandwich . . . . . . . . . . . . . . . . . . . . . . . . . . . . . . . . . . . . . . . 448

Fancy Fishy Tuna Sandwich . . . . . . . . . . . . . . . . . . . . . . . . . . . . . . . . . . . . . . . . . . . . 450

Fabulous Fishy Tuna Salad. . . . . . . . . . . . . . . . . . . . . . . . . . . . . . . . . . . . . . . . . . . . . .452

Shrimp Spaghetti . . . . . . . . . . . . . . . . . . . . . . . . . . . . . . . . . . . . . . . . . . . . . . . . . . . . 454

## DINNER

Fish Sandwich . . . . . . . . . . . . . . . . . . . . . . . . . . . . . . . . . . . . . . . . . . . . . . . . . . . . . . . 458

Breaded Fish Fillets With Fried Vegetables. . . . . . . . . . . . . . . . . . . . . . . . . . . . . . . . 460

Fish and Veggie Roast . . . . . . . . . . . . . . . . . . . . . . . . . . . . . . . . . . . . . . . . . . . . . . . . 462

Fried Fish With Pesto Sauce . . . . . . . . . . . . . . . . . . . . . . . . . . . . . . . . . . . . . . . . . . . 464

- Breaded Fish With Risotto . . . . . . . . . . . . . . . . . . . . . . . . . . . 466
- Drunken Catfish in Pie Crust . . . . . . . . . . . . . . . . . . . . . . . . . 468
- Breaded Fish With Veggie Salad . . . . . . . . . . . . . . . . . . . . . . .470
- Wild Fish With Cooked Veggies . . . . . . . . . . . . . . . . . . . . . . . .472
- Sautéed Fish With Lima Beans in Red Sauce . . . . . . . . . . . . . . . .474
- Grandpa's Easy Fish Batter . . . . . . . . . . . . . . . . . . . . . . . . . .476

Conclusion . . . . . . . . . . . . . . . . . . . . . . . . . . . . . . . . . . . . . .481

References . . . . . . . . . . . . . . . . . . . . . . . . . . . . . . . . . . . . . . 485

## A SPECIAL GIFT TO OUR READERS!

Included with your purchase of this book is our Field Dressing Starters Guide. This guide will prepare you with some essential critical tips to remember when you start field dressing small game. It has a secret golden nugget at the end, too!

### Click the link below and let us know which
### email address to deliver it to.

www.patgatz.com

# INTRODUCTION

Are you interested in hunting? If you're anything like me, you are thrilled by the idea of hunting your food on your own, scouring isolated marshes and forests for the best game. Although many people get excited by the idea of hunting, this excitement is often subdued by the notion that there's only a little you can do with game meat. You wouldn't be the first soon-to-be hunter to feel like there's little use of wild game meat unless you're hosting a large feast right after the hunt.

While this isn't necessarily true, it's understandable, considering just how many popular misconceptions there are about hunting. They almost make a person feel like hunting isn't for them if they don't want to roast the meat on an open campfire in the middle of a desolate forest. As an experienced hunter who grew up in Northern Ontario, I learned firsthand that hunting for wild game is as much about the art of cooking as it is about self-sufficiency and a healthy, fulfilled lifestyle that's aligned with nature. Not to say that field trips like those aren't memorable and enjoyable, but that's a topic for a different book.

Believe it or not, hunters get excited about different recipes. We experiment with seasoning and sauces, and we love to treat our friends and family to a delicious meal. Our game is far from being just for show. It's sustenance for our families and a healthier way to eat for a year. In my previous two books, The Simple Hunting Guide: Beginners Quick Start Into The Sport With Ease - Tracking, Scouting, And Survival Skills and Eat My Meat: A Beginners Field Dressing Guide For Small Game, I wrote in more detail about hunting for beginners, and I recommend checking out those books if you haven't yet!

In this cookbook, I will give you simple lessons in hunting and cooking various types of large and small wild game. However, if your one obstacle with taking up hunting is not knowing what to do with all the game meat or you fear that game meat is somehow more complicated, this book is for you! With this in mind, my goal is to show you what kind of meals are best and most easily made with wild game, which seasoning, and sauces go best with them, and the best ways to cook game meat.

By the end of reading this cookbook, I hope you'll feel convinced you can make delicious game meals with ingredients you already have at home! In this book, I'm focusing on the following:

- Economical. Get as much as you can out of your game meat. We'll make breakfast, lunch, and dinner with over a dozen wild game varieties! Your precious game deserves to be well used and honored, and what better way to do it than include it in each of your meals?
- Practicality. I aimed to simplify the cooking process to use your time and food the best way and focus more on building different flavors than combining dozens of ingredients or preparing 10 pots and pans. In this cookbook, I'm mainly focusing on two types of meals: those that you can make quickly and easily and those that are more elaborate but are not so much hands-on as to keep you tied to the stove for hours. You may put in more work to make a wild game steak Wellington, pate, or a roast, but you can let your meal simmer or roast while tending to your other chores. Aside from that, I aimed to make the steps and ingredients as simple and common as possible so that you wouldn't have to run out to the grocery store for each new recipe. Regardless of the simplicity, the recipes you'll find in this book will be delicious, and many might look fancier than they are.
- Familiarity. Wild game meat puts many people off since they think it tastes worse than a domesticated pig, chicken, or veal. Indeed, the taste of game meat reflects the animal's diet and surroundings, but it's far from being its only component. If you learn to work with the "gamey" flavor and complement it with carefully chosen toppings, sauces, and seasoning, you'll benefit from its other aspects. Game meat is often said to taste "clean" and sweet and have a more tender texture than you could ever achieve with domesticated meat. I designed the recipes so that these aspects of the game are at the forefront, so you don't have to worry about being overwhelmed with the types of smells and tastes you don't usually appreciate.
- Health. Last but not least, this cookbook focuses on health. From the fats used for cooking to the number of vegetables and herbs, the recipes in this cookbook will further emphasize the already existing nutritional richness of game meat.

Now, you could be wondering who I am. Why should you trust me and take my advice? My name is Pat Gatz, and I am from Northern Ontario's Eagle Village First Nation-Kipawa Indian Reserve. I've been hunting since I was six years old and have been in the profession for over 30 years. Over time, I learned to make plenty of versatile recipes without much hustle and bustle—just everyday cooking that you can do in real life.

My books aim to bring the hunting lifestyle closer to an average purpose and revive the innate hunting skills as part of a peaceful lifestyle in harmony with Mother Nature. Hunting for

Greatness is about connecting humans back to mother nature! This is the secret of true happiness, a philosophy that I wish to honor by passing down my knowledge and experience.

With this in mind, it's time to start your journey! Before you begin cooking your game meat, I recommend getting the following basic supplies just so that you have everything you need in place:

- Saucepan, frying pan, stockpot, baking dish, and salad bowl (prepare one of each). These dishes will suffice for most recipes. You also need basic utensils like forks, knives, wooden spoons, and cutting boards.
- Meat grinder. If you ever thought about getting some new appliances for your game meat, it should be a grinder. This little machine that comes in a variety of capacities and features enables you to make your favorite ground meat recipes and, with that, some of the easiest and most common daily meals.
- Butter, olive oil, chicken, beef, or vegetable stock. These ingredients ensure your meals are healthy, delicious, and quick to cook.
- Heavy cream, sour cream, and cream cheese. You'll find that these ingredients earn a spot in soups, stews, sauces, roasts, and salads, making them lighter and more flavorful.
- Your favorite seasoning. I use salt, pepper, garlic powder, cumin, ginger, cinnamon, nutmeg, dill, celery, parsley leaf, cilantro, and sage in this cookbook. If you feel like stocking up, the best time is now!
- Wine, sherry, rum, and regular and balsamic vinegar. A little bit goes a long way when using alcoholic drinks and vinegar in cooking. Their addition doesn't change the volume or texture of the food, but as little as a tablespoon can make the flavor sweeter or more savory. You'll also use these in marinades and sauces, so give yourself a head start and stock up as soon as possible.
- Dough and batter. Bread crumbs, flour, milk, and baking powder will all be needed to follow the recipes found in this book.
- Berries and apples. Believe it or not, game meat goes great with various fruit sauces! Stock up on fresh or frozen berries, and you'll quickly learn to whip up a delicious fruit sauce for your elk, deer, or bear steaks.

Now, you're ready to start! You can move on to Chapter 1, where you'll learn the simplest recipes to cook small games.

# HUNTING FOR GREATNESS
# KITCHEN CONVERSIONS

## WEIGHT EQUIVALENTS
### U.S STANDARD-METRIC (APPROX)

- ½ oz
- 1 oz
- 2 oz
- 4 oz
- 8 oz
- 12 oz
- 16 oz or 1 lb

- 15 g
- 30 g
- 60 g
- 115 g
- 225 g
- 340 g
- 455 g

## OVEN TEMPERATURES
### FAHRENHEIT - CELSIUS

- 250 F
- 300 F
- 325 F
- 350 F
- 375 F
- 400 F
- 425 F

- 120 C
- 150 C
- 165 C
- 180 C
- 190 C
- 200 C
- 220 C

## LIQUID VOLUME EQUIVALENTS
### U.S STANDARD-METRIC (APPROX)

- 2 tbs - 30 mL
- ¼ cup - 60 mL
- ½ cup - 120 mL
- 1 cup - 240 mL

- 1 ½ cups - 355 mL
- 2 cups - 475 mL
- 4 cups - 1 L
- 1 gallon - 4 L

## DRY VOLUME EQUIVALENTS
### U.S STANDARD-METRIC (APPROX)

- ⅛ tsp - 0.5 mL
- ¼ tsp - 1 mL
- ½ tsp - 2 mL
- ¾ tsp - 4 mL
- 1 tsp - 5 mL
- 1 tbs - 15 mL
- ¼ cup - 59 mL
- ⅓ cup - 79 mL

- ½ cup - 118 mL
- ⅔ cup - 156 mL
- ¾ cup - 177 mL
- 1 cup - 235 mL
- 2 cups - 475 mL
- 4 cups - 1 L
- ½ gallon - 2 L
- 1 gallon - 4 L

# CHAPTER 1
# Simple Small Game

If you are new to hunting or want to get your children out of the house and connect with mother nature, small game hunting is a great place to start. Small game hunting teaches you outdoor skills, gun safety, accurate shooting, and woodsmanship. Popular small game in North America is rabbits, squirrels, goats, beavers, snakes, opossums, beavers, and muskrats. Small game is fun to hunt and provides many delicious dishes. Lessons learned from small game last a lifetime, and the quarry here provides wonderful table fare the entire family will enjoy!

### Breakfast
Scrumptious Small Game Burritos
Remarkable Rabbit Kebab
Sneaky Snake Meat Egg Rolls
Simple Small Game Scramble

### Lunch
Savoury Sautéed Muskrat
Delicious Deep-Fried Rabbit
Favourite Fried Squirrel

### Dinner
Classic Oven-Fried Game
Saporous Small Game Potpie
Satisfying Small Game Dumpling Soup

# BREAKFAST

# SCRUMPTIOUS SMALL GAME BURRITOS

This is a quick & simple recipe for the ones that need to get back out to the woods. It is a high-protein breakfast that will give you the fuel to keep you going all day! You can substitute any small game in the freezer with this recipe.

## SERVING SIZE: 1 (2 BURRITOS)

### INGREDIENTS:

- 1 cup cooked game meat (rabbit, squirrel, snake, beaver, or goat), shredded
- 1 cup of canned beans
- 1 tbsp garlic, minced
- 1 cup cooked rice
- ½ tbsp salt
- ½ tbsp pepper
- 1 dried chili, chopped
- ½ tsp parsley
- ½ tsp thyme
- ½ tsp cumin powder
- ½ tsp dill, chopped
- ½ cup vegetable broth
- 2 tortillas
- 2 tbsp olive oil
- 2 tbsp heavy cream

### DIRECTIONS:

1. Pour the olive oil into a saucepan and add all ingredients except the tortillas and heavy cream.
2. Heat up to medium temperature and let simmer for 10–15 minutes with constant stirring. Allow excess liquid to evaporate.
3. Top the tortillas with the heavy cream and the wild game topping.
4. Wrap and enjoy!

# FACTS AND STATS:

*Small game is hunted throughout the year, depending on the species. Theirs over twenty species of small game in North America, like rabbits, hares, squirrels, muskrats, beavers, and many more. Small game can be easily found in fields, thickets, bushes, and gardens. You can hunt small game in various ways like snares, slingshots, bow and arrow, traps, and firearms. If you want to see if hunting is for you, start with a small game.*

# REMARKABLE RABBIT KEBAB

Rabbit and hare are one of the healthiest small game meats to eat. It is lean, high in protein, and very low in calories compared to other meats like chicken. Rabbit does taste a little like chicken with a bit of earthiness. Rabbit and hare taste a bit different. Rabbit meat is almost all white, has a fine texture, and has a similar appearance and flavor to chicken. Hare meat is darker in color and has a stronger taste. Hare resembles dark meat.

## SERVING SIZE: 4

## INGREDIENTS:

- 3–4 rabbits, deboned and cut into 9–12 pieces
- 1 tsp ground turmeric
- 1 tbsp parsley
- 1 tbsp celery
- 1 tbsp dill, chopped
- 1 tbsp red pepper powder
- 2 cups potatoes, diced
- 3–4 kebab skewers
- 2 tbsp olive oil

## DIRECTIONS:

1. Grab a large saucepan and heat the olive oil on low heat.
2. Mix the spices in a large bowl.
3. While the oil is heating up, dredge the rabbits and potatoes into the spices.
4. Skewer pieces of meat topped with chunks of potatoes.
5. Brown on olive oil until cooked and soft.

# FACTS AND STATS:

*Rabbits have powerful hind legs and raise up on their toes to run. Some species of rabbit can run up to 45 mph or 72 kph in brief spurts. Rabbits run if you get too close, but they usually try to blend into their surroundings. The difference between rabbits and hares is that rabbits have smaller, shorter ears and are born bald and blind. Hares are born with hair and open eyes and can even somewhat fend for themselves right after birth. Rabbits breed like crazy, making rabbit hunting the number#1 small game for hunters everywhere. Rabbits and hares can be hunted in various ways with minimum equipment.*

# SNEAKY SNAKE MEAT EGG ROLLS

Yes, you can eat snake meat! Snake meat is rich in magnesium and calcium. It exists in the form of protein fusion, and the human body absorbs it very well. It has been known to prevent osteoporosis and cardiovascular diseases. It is a light color meat with a texture between chicken and fish. Snake has a unique flavor, not similar to any other meat. Snake is enjoyed by frying in butter with a light batter, just like how you would cook fish.

## SERVING SIZE: 4

## INGREDIENTS:

- 1 lb snake meat
- 2 cups cabbage, chopped
- 1 cup carrots, chopped
- ½ cup onions, chopped
- 1 tbsp garlic, minced
- 1 tbsp brown rice, soaked or cooked
- 2 tbsp soy sauce
- 2 tbsp olive oil
- egg roll wrappers

## DIRECTIONS:

1. Grab a saucepan and pour all of the ingredients except for the wrappers.
2. Brown on medium heat until all of the ingredients are cooked through.
3. Take the filling out of the saucepan.
4. Grab your egg rolls and fill each with up to 4 tbsp of the filling. Roll the dough over the filling, fold the sides, and fry for up to 2 minutes. Flip your rolls to make sure they're fried evenly on each side.

## FACTS AND STATS:

*North America has about 150 species of snake. Over 90% are non-venomous, and rattlesnakes, copperheads, cottonmouths, and coral snakes are native to the U.S. and are venomous. One reliable method to hunt snakes is cruising paved roads at dusk. Reptiles are cold-blooded, which means they cannot generate their own body heat and uses outside sources like asphalt roads because they retain heat from the day. If you hunt without paved roads, you can find snakes slithering through the grass, hiding under logs, or sunbathing on a rock. On very hot days, you will discover them buried in manure piles, under tarps, or rocks.*

# SIMPLE SMALL GAME SCRAMBLE

Small game can be field dressed into five pieces: the shoulders, saddles, loins, ribs, and legs. The legs of most small game animals carry most of the meat. When you are field dressing small game, make sure to remove the silverskin and sinew because it is like chewing rubber. You want to remove as much fat as possible because it is disgusting. You can substitute any small game meat with this delicious dish.

## SERVING SIZE: 6

## INGREDIENTS:

- 1 lb of small game meat cut into cubes
- 8 Eggs
- 2 Each - vegetables of your choice, like mushrooms, red/green/yellow peppers, onions, carrots
- Garlic cloves

## DIRECTIONS:

1. Preheat the frying pan with butter on medium heat.
2. Cut and boil vegetables of your choice.
3. When the frying pan is hot, cook the wild meat to a golden brown.
4. Mix eggs and vegetables of your choice in the frying pan.
5. Fry it all up and watch it disappear!

## FACTS AND STATS:

*Food safety is the most important part of healthy eating. Practice these easy steps. Wash your hands and surfaces regularly with disinfectant. Separate your raw meat from other foods to prevent cross-contamination. Ensure all wild game meat is cooked at recommended temperatures to kill harmful bacteria. The proper way to tell temperature is to use an instant food thermometer by placing it in the thickest part of the meat without touching fat, bone, or gristle.*

# LUNCH

# SAVOURY SAUTÉED MUSKRAT

Muskrat is good to eat. Muskrat's primary food source are plants, but eats other small animals such as snails, insects, small fish, and frogs. Believe it or not, it is one of the healthiest foods available. Muskrat meat is an excellent source of niacin, thiamine, riboflavin, and is loaded with b vitamins. B vitamins are important for healthy skin, hair, nerves, and muscle growth.

## SERVING SIZE: 4

## INGREDIENTS:

**FOR BRINE**

- 1 cup salt
- 1 cup sugar
- 1 gallon of water

**FOR COOKING**

- ¼ cup olive oil
- 1 cup white wine
- 2 cups vegetable broth
- 2 garlic cloves, minced
- pepper and salt, to taste
- 4 muskrats, prepped
- 1 bay leaf
- fresh herbs to taste

## DIRECTIONS:

1. Soak the muskrats into the brine and let them sit for 12 hours in the fridge.
2. Pat dry with a cloth before cooking.
3. Either remove the meat from the bones or cut the muskrats into smaller pieces.
4. Drizzle with olive oil and season with herbs, pepper, and salt.
5. Heat the olive oil over the medium temperature in a large skillet and brown the meat evenly for up to 15 minutes.
6. Add the minced onion, broth, garlic, and wine. Let simmer after a short boil for up to 3 hours.

## FACTS AND STATS:

*The muskrat is the most common furbearer in North America. It has contributed more income for North American trappers than any other animal. The muskrat is a rotund creature with a pointed head with small ears hidden beneath the fur. The average adult weighs 1 kg (2.2 lbs) and measures about 50 cm (20 in) from nose to tail. The muskrats range from the Arctic Ocean to the Gulf of Mexico and from the Atlantic to Pacific Oceans. They were introduced in Europe and Asia in 1905. The greatest numbers of muskrats reside in southern Ontario.*

# DELICIOUS DEEP-FRIED RABBIT

It's imperative to cool your wild game as quickly as possible especially small game because it spoils quickly. You want to get your meat under refrigeration to preserve quality and taste. Wild game will keep in your freezer for over a year if packaged right. I recommend the best way to package your wild game meat to prevent freezer burnt & last the longest is to wrap it first with saran wrap, taking out all the air, then wrap it with wax paper or butcher wrap. Always label the cut of meat and date, so you can keep track of what to eat first and never waste any of mother nature's gifts of life.

## SERVING SIZE: 4

## INGREDIENTS:

**FOR BRINE**

- 1 ½ cups milk
- ½ cup vinegar
- ½ tsp mustard
- ½ tsp pepper powder
- ½ tsp ground black pepper
- 4 tbsp thyme, chopped
- 1 tbsp rosemary, chopped
- 1 tbsp onion, chopped
- 2 tsp salt
- ½ tsp garlic, minced

**FOR COOKING**

- 1 medium-large rabbit, prepped
- 2 cups flour
- 1 tbsp salt
- ½ tsp ground black pepper
- 4 cups vegetable oil

## DIRECTIONS:

1. Mix the brine ingredients together in a bowl.
2. Cut the rabbit into small to medium chunks or separate the meat from the bones.
3. Soak the rabbit and let it sit in the fridge for 8–12 hours.
4. Drain before cooking.
5. Mix the flour, salt, and pepper in a bowl.
6. Heat the olive oil.
7. Cover the rabbit meat with the flour mixture and fry in olive oil until crisp.

## FACTS AND STATS:

*The late season is a great time to hunt rabbits. You will usually find rabbits on the sunny leeward sides of ridges, forests, and brush piles on cold and windy mornings after a cold winter night. The most important considerations in finding late-season rabbits are to find raspberry & blackberry bushes, pine saplings, clover fields, and deer hunter food plots.*

# FAVOURITE FRIED SQUIRREL

**Squirrel tastes like a milder version of rabbit. The flavor resembles the taste between chicken and rabbit with a hint of nuts, depending on their primary food source. Squirrel meat is light in color, has a fine texture, and has a sweet taste. The great thing about squirrel meat is it goes well with various flavors, from berries and nuts to bold, creamy sauces, making it a versatile wild game meat.**

### SERVING SIZE: 4

### INGREDIENTS:

- 4 squirrels, cut into pieces
- ½ tsp salt
- ½ tsp pepper
- 1 tbsp garlic, minced
- 3 tbsp onion, chopped
- ¼ cup flour
- 1 tbsp celery, chopped
- 1 tbsp rosemary leaves, chopped
- 2 tbsp lemon juice
- 2 cups vegetable broth
- 4 cups potatoes, cubed
- 2 cups olive oil

### DIRECTIONS:

1. Mix flour with garlic, celery, and rosemary.
2. Dredge the squirrel pieces in the mixture.
3. Brown on olive oil over medium heat until cooked.
4. Remove from the skillet and add potatoes, vegetable broth, and onions.
5. Simmer until potatoes are cooked.
6. Serve drizzled with lemon juice.

## FACTS AND STATS:

*Stay put in a good spot and wait for squirrels to show themselves. Take your time with the first two or three down and wait for others to show. When a squirrel hugs the trunk high in the tree, usually facing up, you want to hug the tree yourself, and the squirrel will think the coast is clear. It will make its move giving you a shot at the fast little tree huggers. Throw something over to the squirrel's side, and he will often circle around, giving you a perfect shot. If a squirrel is on the opposite side of the tree playing hide-and-seek with you, and you can't get a clean shot.*

# DINNER

# CLASSIC OVEN-FRIED GAME

Small game hunting is popular worldwide, with millions participating every year. Small game hunting is a popular outdoor activity in the United States. According to the U.S. Fish and Wildlife Service, there were approximately 2.3 million small game hunters in the U.S. in 2016. Small game hunting involves hunting animals such as rabbits, squirrels, quail, pheasants, and other small game animals. Small game hunting has many health benefits. Small game hunting involves a lot of physical activity, including walking, hiking, and carrying equipment, which provides an excellent cardiovascular workout and helps improve overall physical fitness.

## SERVING SIZE: 2

## INGREDIENTS:

- 2 squirrel meats, deboned
- 6 eggs
- 2 cups potatoes, cubed
- 5 tbsp of your favorite seasoning mix
- 2 tbsp flour
- 2 tbsp olive oil
- 1 cup vegetable broth
- 2 tbsp butter

## DIRECTIONS:

1. Preheat your oven to 375 °F.
2. Begin prepping your squirrel meat. Mix in the seasoning with the flour and set aside.
3. Whisk the eggs and fully soak the meat in them. Dredge the meat in the seasoned flour and place in a baking dish drizzled with olive oil.
4. Add the potatoes and pour in the broth toward the bottom of the dish so that you're not rinsing off the flour.
5. Bake for an hour.

## FACTS AND STATS:

*The most popular small game animals hunted in the U.S. are rabbits, squirrels, and quail. Small game hunting can be done with various weapons, including shotguns, rifles, and bows. Small game hunting is typically done in the fall and winter when the animals are most active. Many states & provinces require hunters to have a valid hunting license and complete a hunter education course before going small game hunting.*

# SAPOROUS SMALL GAME POTPIE

There are many health benefits of small game hunting. Some Health benefits are mental health, fresh air, and sunshine. Spending time outdoors and engaging in a challenging activity like hunting can help reduce stress and improve mental health tremendously. Everything on mother earth is connected. We need nature just as much as nature requires us to flourish and survive. Small game hunting takes place outdoors, which means hunters are exposed to fresh air and sunshine, both of which have been shown to have numerous health benefits.

## SERVING SIZE: 4

## INGREDIENTS:

- 3 cups shredded quail meat (or any small game of your choice), cooked
- 2 tbsp butter
- 1 pie crust, homemade or frozen
- 1 cup carrots, chopped
- 1 cup potato, cubed
- ½ cup peas
- ½ cup onion, chopped
- 10 oz mushroom soup
- 3 tbsp celery, chopped
- salt and pepper, to taste

## DIRECTIONS:

1. Melt the butter in a large skillet for up to 10 minutes.
2. Add potatoes, peas, celery, and onion, and simmer for 5 more minutes.
3. Once the vegetables are tender, mix in the quail.
4. Pour the filling into a casserole dish and top with a pie crust.
5. Cut slits into the crust and bake for 35 minutes at 375 °F.

## FACTS AND STATS:

*Small game hunting can be an affordable way to provide food for your family, connect with nature, and enjoy the outdoors to the fullest. Small game hunting can offer health benefits by keeping you fit. Hunting can be a great way to get exercise and fresh air and help reduce stress levels. Consuming wild game can provide a lean source of protein and essential nutrients. Small game hunting can also be an important tool for wildlife management. Hunting helps to control animal populations and can help prevent overgrazing and damage to natural habitats.*

# SATISFYING SMALL GAME DUMPLING SOUP

Small game hunting can be a rewarding and beneficial activity for those participating. As with any outdoor activity, following safety guidelines and regulations is important to ensure a safe and enjoyable experience. Hunting for Greatness offers an outdoors mentoring program to allow you to learn one-on-one about the outdoors from Pat Gatz, a First Nation Algonquin Native with over 30 years of hunting experience. If you want to experience the native way, go to www.patgatz.com.

## SERVING SIZE: 4

## INGREDIENTS:

- 1 lb goat meat (or beaver, muskrat, squirrel), shredded
- 1 cup onions, chopped
- 4 tbsp olive oil
- 1 tbsp garlic, minced
- ½ tsp parsley
- ½ tsp rosemary
- ½ tsp dill
- ½ tsp salt
- ½ tsp pepper
- 1 cup chicken broth
- 1 cup carrots, chopped
- 1 cup celery, chopped
- 1 cup corn flour
- 1 whole egg
- 1 tsp baking soda

## DIRECTIONS:

1. Cook the meat in a large pot with the vegetables and spices until cooked.
2. Grab a small bowl and whisk an egg. Add the corn flour and baking soda and mix.
3. Use a teaspoon to section off small pieces of dumpling dough and pop them into the soup.
4. Bring to a soft boil and let cook for 10–15 minutes.

# FACTS AND STATS:

*Small game hunting can be done using a variety of weapons, including shotguns, rifles, and bows and arrows. Shooting a gun or a bow and arrow requires good hand-eye coordination, and practicing these skills can help improve coordination and dexterity. Small game hunting requires a lot of movement, which can help improve balance. Overall, small game hunting can be a rewarding and beneficial activity for those who participate in it. What are you waiting for?*

# CHAPTER 2
# Bird Buffet

Nothing is better than a coffee in one hand, a shotgun on the side, sitting and listening to mother nature come alive! Upland bird hunting includes pheasant, quail, grouse, partridge, dove, and wild turkey. Duck, Duck, Goose, your it! I'm 37 years old, and it's one of my favorite games, except the adult version ends with a yummy meal. Bird buffet has many recipes making your tastebuds excited with every dish. Bird hunting is a fast-action activity bringing fun for the whole family. Good food and good friends keep me bird hunting year after year.

### Breakfast
Perfect Parmesan Turkey Scramble
Wild Turkey and Parmesan Salad
Sour Partridge Salad
Minty and Lemon Zest Dove Scramble
Heavenly Honey and Sage Quail Toast
Sweet and Sour Grouse Sandwich
Powerful Partridge Salad Toast
Wine-Infused Crispy Duck
Beautiful Breakfast Goose Omelet
Crispy Pheasant Egg Rolls

### Lunch
Bashful Breaded Grouse
Grateful Grouse Macaroni Salad
Greatness Grouse Sandwich Salad
Caribbean Coconut Grouse
Peaceful Ptarmigan Mini Pie
Pretty Pigeon Quiche

## Lunch Continued

Spicy Toast Turkey Sandwich
Saline Snipe Salad
Whisper Woodcock Wrap
Dainty Dove Kebab
Quick Quail and Potatoes in Mushroom Sauce
Golden Grouse Pie
Sour Partridge Soup

## Dinner

Wicked Wild Duck Fillets in Raspberry Sauce
Quick Goose Roast
Pleasant Pheasant With Mushroom Sauce
Breaded Ptarmigan With Wine and Blueberry Sauce
Friendly Fried Pigeon in Sweet Potato Applesauce
Dodging Dove Risotto Roast
Wonderful Wild Turkey Stew
Quaint Quail Vegetable Roast
Sweety Potato Grouse Stew
Particular Partridge Stew
Dipping Duck and Rice Stir-Fry
Down Deep-Fried Goose Fillets
Wild Turkey Potato Soup
Special Stuffed Pheasants
Whole Ptarmigan Risotto Roast
Delight Deep-Fried Turkey
Sensible Snipe Pie
Panfried Woodcock Risotto
Perky Pesto Pigeon Tarts
Witty Wild Turkey and Mushroom Risotto

# BREAKFAST

# PERFECT PARMESAN TURKEY SCRAMBLE

There is a big difference between wild and store-bought turkey, but not for what you think. Wild turkey is so much more nutritious than store-bought turkey. There are several benefits to eating wild turkey. Wild turkey is an excellent source of lean protein, essential for building and repairing muscle tissue, and can help you feel full and satisfied. Wild turkey is low in fat, particularly saturated fat, which can help lower your risk of heart disease and other health problems. Wild turkeys feed on a natural diet of seeds, nuts, and insects, resulting in healthier and more nutritious meat than commercially-raised turkeys. Commercial turkeys live in unsanitary living conditions. They are raised with hormones, fed unnutritional feed, and overpopulated areas make folks unhealthy store-bought turkeys. Make sure you look at how it's fed, and you would like grass-fed is the best, in my opinion.

## SERVING SIZE: 4-6

## INGREDIENTS:

- 1 lb wild turkey meat, chopped
- 8 whole eggs
- ½ cup fresh tomatoes, chopped
- ½ cup bell peppers, chopped
- ½ tbsp garlic, minced
- ½ cup shredded Parmesan
- salt and pepper, to taste
- 2 tbsp olive oil

## DIRECTIONS:

1. Brown the turkey meat, peppers, garlic, and tomatoes in olive oil over medium heat.
2. Break the eggs, whisk, and mix in half of the Parmesan.
3. Pour the eggs over the turkey, tomatoes, and peppers.

## FACTS AND STATS:

*Wild turkeys are native to North America and are found in the United States and parts of Mexico and Canada. They are a popular game bird hunted by humans and predators such as foxes, coyotes, and bobcats. The male wild turkey is called a tom, while the female is called a hen. Toms are larger than hens and have more colorful plumage. Wild turkeys are omnivorous and feed on various foods, including nuts, seeds, fruits, insects, and small animals.*

# WILD TURKEY AND PARMESAN SALAD

**Field-dressing is the first thing you want to do when you harvest a turkey. It's easier right away to pluck the turkey because if you wait too long, it becomes more difficult. The best two things you can do is brine your bird and baste the bugger as much as possible! Turkeys taste best the day or two after harvest, depending on if you will brine it first or deep fry it that day.**

## SERVING SIZE: 4

## INGREDIENTS:

- 1 lb ground turkey meat
- 1 cup tomato puree
- 1 cup chopped cabbage
- 3 oz ground Parmesan cheese
- 1 cup salsa of your choosing
- 1 tbsp lemon juice or vinegar
- 1 cup sour cream
- salt and pepper, to taste
- 1 tbsp celery leaf, chopped
- 2 tbsp butter

## DIRECTIONS:

1. Brown the turkey meat in butter for 10 minutes.
2. Add seasoning and a drizzle of water, and fry for another 10 minutes.
3. Chop the cabbage and mix it with shredded Parmesan in a separate salad dish.
4. Mix the taco meat with cabbage and Parmesan.
5. Grab a small bowl or a cup and mix vinegar or lemon juice with sour cream and celery to make a dressing.
6. Top the salad with the dressing, mix carefully, and enjoy!

## FACTS AND STATS:

*They have excellent eyesight and hearing and can run up to 25 miles per hour. During mating season, toms display their feathers and strut around in a stud manner to attract hens. This display is known as "strutting." Wild turkeys can fly short distances but usually prefer to walk or run. They roost in trees at night to avoid predators and can fly up to their roosts using powerful wings.*

# SOUR PARTRIDGE SALAD

Partridge is a type of game bird that tastes similar to chicken or turkey. Here are some potential health benefits of consuming partridge. Partridge is a good source of protein, with approximately 26 grams of protein per 100 grams of cooked meat. Protein is vital for building and repairing muscle tissue and can help keep you full and satisfied. Partridge is low in fat compared to other meats like beef or pork. This can make it a good choice for people trying to reduce their overall calorie intake. Rich in vitamins and minerals, partridge is a good source of vitamins B6 and B12, which are important for maintaining healthy nerve function and producing red blood cells.

## SERVING SIZE: 4

## INGREDIENTS:

- 2 cans (6 oz) partridge
- 3 oz canned black beans
- 4 tbsp sour cream
- 1 tbsp mayonnaise
- 1 tbsp lemon juice
- 1 tsp dill
- 1 tsp celery leaf
- ½ tsp garlic powder
- sliced tomato
- fresh buns

## DIRECTIONS:

1. Mix partridge, black beans, sour cream, mayo, herbs, and spices in a salad bowl.
2. Top fresh buns with tomato slices and the salad, and serve.

## FACTS AND STATS:

*Partridges are ground-dwelling birds typically found in grasslands, woodlands, and agricultural fields. Partridges are game birds found throughout Europe, Asia, Africa, and the Americas. Several species of partridge exist, including the grey partridge, red-legged partridge, chukar partridge, and rock partridge.*

# MINTY AND LEMON ZEST DOVE SCRAMBLE

**Doves, also known as pigeons, are a type of game bird consumed in many parts of the world. Dove meat is a good source of protein, with approximately 23 grams of protein per 100 grams of cooked meat. Protein is essential for building and repairing muscle tissue and can help keep you full and satisfied. Compared to beef or pork, dove meat is relatively low in fat. This can make it a good choice for people trying to reduce their overall calorie intake.**

## SERVING SIZE: 4

## INGREDIENTS:

- 2 cups dove meat, chopped
- 6–8 eggs
- 2 tbsp flour
- 1 tbsp mint, chopped
- lemon zest, to taste
- 1 tsp garlic, minced
- 4 tbsp ground Parmesan cheese
- 2–3 tbsp butter
- salt and pepper, to taste

## DIRECTIONS:

1. Brown the dove meat with garlic in butter until ready.
2. Add the mint, salt, pepper, and lemon zest after 10–15 minutes.
3. Add a bit of water to prevent burning and sticking.
4. Whisk the eggs and mix in the flour.
5. Pour the batter over the fried meat.
6. You can fry it into an omelet or split up the mixture and stir for a scramble.
7. Serve sprinkled with Parmesan or any cheese you like.

## FACTS AND STATS:

*Doves are small to medium-sized birds, with a length ranging from 15 to 75 cm (6 to 30 inches) and a weight ranging from 30 to 1200 grams (1 to 42 ounces), depending on the species. Doves are part of the pigeon family and are found throughout the world, with over 300 species in existence. The most common dove species is the rock dove, also known as the city pigeon or the common pigeon.*

# HEAVENLY HONEY AND SAGE QUAIL TOAST

Quail meat is a good source of protein, with approximately 22 grams of protein per 100 grams of cooked meat. Protein is important for building and repairing muscle tissue and can help keep you full and satisfied. Quail meat is relatively low in fat compared to other meats like beef or pork. This can make it a good choice for people trying to reduce their overall calorie intake. Rich in vitamins and minerals, quail meat is a good source of vitamins B6 and B12, which are important for maintaining healthy nerve function and producing red blood cells. It contains healthy fats like omega-3 fatty acids. These fats are important for maintaining heart health and reducing inflammation in the body.

## SERVING SIZE:

## INGREDIENTS:

- 1 lb quail meat
- 1 tbsp honey
- 2 tbsp butter
- 1 pureed avocado
- 1 tbsp chopped sage
- salt and pepper, to taste
- ½ cup white wine
- 1 tbsp Dijon mustard
- slices of toast

## DIRECTIONS:

1. Sauté the quail meat with butter, white wine, mustard, and seasoning on low-medium heat until ready.
2. Let all the liquid evaporate before removing off the heat without the meat sticking or burning.
3. Grab a small bowl and mix the honey with the avocado.
4. Top toast slices with the honey–avocado mix and either top with the meat or serve the meat separately.

## FACTS AND STATS:

*Quail are small game birds that are found throughout the world, with over 130 species in existence. They are known for their plump bodies and small size, with most species ranging from 12 to 25 cm (4.7 to 9.8 inches) in length. Quail are ground-dwelling birds often found in grasslands, forests, and agricultural areas. They are omnivores and feed on various foods, including seeds, insects, and small animals. Quail are often raised for their meat and eggs, which are considered a delicacy in many cultures.*

# SWEET AND SOUR GROUSE SANDWICH

Grouse makes low, deep belly calls. Grouse are little fat birds with a similar look to quail and lean meat. I recommend marinating it in different sauces. Whatever your favorite sauce is, try it out! Grouse meat is a good source of protein, with approximately 22 grams of protein per 100 grams of cooked meat. Protein is vital for building and repairing muscle tissue.

### SERVING SIZE: 4-6

### INGREDIENTS:

- 1 lb grouse meat, chopped
- 1 tbsp mayonnaise
- 1 tbsp Dijon mustard
- 1 tbsp sour cream
- 1 tsp cayenne pepper
- 1 tsp sage
- 1 tsp fresh mint, chopped
- 1 tsp basil
- 2-3 tbsp butter
- buns, as needed

### DIRECTIONS:

1. Brown the grouse meat in butter with Dijon mustard, cayenne pepper, sage, mint, and basil until ready.
2. Top the buns with mayonnaise and sour cream.
3. Add the meat to make a sandwich, and enjoy!

## FACTS AND STATS:

*Grouse are medium-sized game birds in many parts of the world, including North America, Europe, and Asia. There are several species of grouse, including the ruffed grouse, spruce grouse, and sharp-tailed grouse. Grouse are known for their distinctive mating displays, in which the males puff up their feathers and make a drumming sound by beating their wings. They are also known for their camouflaging ability, which allows them to blend in with their surroundings and avoid predators.*

# POWERFUL PARTRIDGE SALAD TOAST

Partridge supports heart health by the omega-3 fatty acids found in partridge to help reduce the risk of heart disease by lowering cholesterol levels and reducing inflammation. A 100-gram serving of partridge contains around 130 calories, making it a good option for people trying to lose weight. It has anti-inflammatory properties. Some research suggests that game meat, including partridge, may have anti-inflammatory properties due to its high levels of omega-3 fatty acids. It's important to note that the health benefits of partridge can vary depending on how it is cooked and prepared. If you are considering adding partridge to your diet, it's best to prepare it healthily, such as grilling, baking, or roasting, and to eat it in moderation as part of a balanced diet.

## SERVING SIZE: 4

## INGREDIENTS:

- 1 lb partridge meat, chopped
- 2 tsp garlic, minced
- 1 tsp mint, chopped
- 1 tsp basil, chopped
- salt and pepper, to taste
- 3–4 cups sweet potatoes, diced
- 1 cup sour cream
- 1 tsp honey
- 1 tbsp ground Parmesan
- slices of toast

## DIRECTIONS:

1. Brown the partridge meat in butter with garlic, mint, basil, salt, and pepper.
2. Mix the honey with sour cream and top the slices of toast.
3. Add 2–3 tbsp of fried meat between two toast slices, make a sandwich, and enjoy!

## FACTS AND STATS:

*They are omnivores and feed on a variety of foods, including seeds, insects, and small animals. Partridges are known for their distinctive calls, often used to attract mates or communicate with other members of their flock.*

# WINE-INFUSED CRISPY DUCK

Duck meat can be a good source of nutrients and has potential health benefits. Duck meat is a good source of protein, which is important for building and repairing muscles and other tissues in the body. Duck meat is rich in vitamin B12, essential for nerve function and the production of red blood cells. It also contains iron for healthy blood cells and zinc, which is necessary for a healthy immune system.

## SERVING SIZE: 4

## INGREDIENTS:

- 1 lb duck meat, chopped or cubed
- 1 egg
- 1 cup flour
- salt and pepper, to taste
- 1 tbsp celery leaf, chopped
- 1 tbsp basil
- 1 tsp garlic powder
- 1 tbsp red wine
- 3–4 tbsp butter

## DIRECTIONS:

1. Mix the batter with egg, flour, wine, and seasoning.
2. Dredge the duck meat in the batter.
3. Fry in butter until ready.

## FACTS AND STATS:

*Duck hunting has been practiced for thousands of years and was an important food source for many indigenous cultures. My people First Nation Algonquins, eat duck regularly. In many countries, duck hunting is a popular recreational activity regulated by laws and regulations to ensure sustainability and safety. Hunting ducks can be done using a variety of methods, including using decoys to lure them in, using trained hunting dogs to retrieve them, and stalking them in wetlands or other habitats. Different species of ducks have different migratory patterns and hunting seasons, so hunters need to know the regulations and rules in their area.*

# BEAUTIFUL BREAKFAST GOOSE OMELET

Goose meat is a good source of protein, which is essential for building and repairing muscles and other tissues in the body. Goose meat is also high in iron, which is vital for healthy red blood cells and oxygen transport in the body. Vitamins and minerals in goose meat are vitamin B12, which is essential for nerve function and the production of red blood cells. It also contains vitamins and minerals, including vitamin D, zinc, and selenium.

## SERVING SIZE: 4-6

## INGREDIENTS:

- 1 lb wild goose meat, ground
- 2 tbsp butter
- 1 cup of beer
- 1 tbsp mustard
- 1 tbsp basil
- 1 tsp oregano
- 1 tsp garlic powder or minced garlic
- 4–6 eggs
- 1 cup of milk
- 1 tsp baking soda
- 2–3 tbsp flour

## DIRECTIONS:

1. Sauté ground goose meat in butter, beer, mustard, and seasoning for up to 20 minutes. Make sure all of the liquid is gone before proceeding.
2. Whisk the eggs with flour, milk, and baking soda.
3. In another pan, fry separate servings of omelet on one side and top one side with a couple of tablespoons of goose filling.
4. Fold the omelet over the meat to create a wrap, turn, and fry evenly on both sides until ready.

## FACTS AND STATS:

*Geese are waterfowl that belong to the family Anatidae, which also includes ducks and swans. There are several species of geese, including the Canada goose, snow goose, and domesticated goose, among others. Geese are known for their distinctive honking call, used to communicate with other flock members. Geese are highly social birds and typically mate for life, forming strong pair bonds with their partners.*

# CRISPY PHEASANT EGG ROLLS

While pheasant meat may be less common than other types of meat, it can provide a range of nutrients and potential health benefits when consumed as part of a balanced diet. Pheasant meat is a good source of vitamins B6 and B12, which are essential for nerve function and the production of red blood cells. It also contains other vitamins and minerals, including zinc and selenium. Pheasant meat is a good source of omega-3 fatty acids, which are important for heart health and may also have other health benefits. Free-range pheasant meat is hormone-free and antibiotic-free. Pheasant meat is lean and tender with a mild flavor, making it a versatile ingredient for various recipes.

## SERVING SIZE: 4–6

## INGREDIENTS:

- 1 lb pheasant meat, ground
- ½ cup white wine
- 1 tbsp rosemary
- 1 tbsp lemon zest
- 1 tbsp Parmesan cheese, ground
- salt and pepper, to taste
- 4–6 eggs
- 1 cup of milk
- 2 tbsp flour
- 1 tsp baking powder

## DIRECTIONS:

1. Sauté ground pheasant meat in butter, wine, and seasoning for 15–20 minutes.
2. Whisk eggs with flour, milk, lemon zest, and baking powder.
3. Grab a separate pan, top it with butter, and fry small omelet pieces. Pour a tablespoon of the mix into several places in the pan, and top with some ground meat and Parmesan.
4. Cover with another layer of egg batter.
5. Fry for a minute or two on both sides.

## FACTS AND STATS:

*Pheasants are native to Asia but have been introduced to other parts of the world, including Europe, Africa, and North America. The scientific name for the common pheasant is Phasianus colchicus. Pheasants are game birds that are hunted for sport and their meat. The male pheasant is known for its brightly colored plumage, which includes a long, colorful tail. The female pheasant, on the other hand, is more drab in coloration. Pheasants are ground-dwelling birds that can fly short distances.*

# LUNCH

# BASHFUL BREADED GROUSE

Grouse meat is known for its distinctive flavor, ranging from slightly gamey to rich and earthy. It is best cooked quickly over high heat, such as on a grill or in a hot skillet. Grouse meat can be dry and tough if overcooked, so consider brining it before cooking. A simple brine of water, salt, and sugar can help to tenderize the meat and add flavor. This helps seal the juices and preserve the taste of the meat.

## SERVING SIZE: 4-6

## INGREDIENTS:

- 6 grouse chunks
- 1 egg
- ½ cup flour
- ½ cup bread crumbs
- ½ tbsp celery
- ½ tbsp dill
- 1 tsp garlic powder
- 2 tbsp ground nuts (peanuts, almonds, hazelnuts, etc.)
- ¼ tsp baking soda or powder
- ½ cup white wine
- 2 tbsp lemon juice
- olive oil, as needed

## DIRECTIONS:

1. Mix the batter ingredients (egg, bread crumbs, flour, wine, seasoning, and nuts) in a bowl.
2. Soak the grouse pieces in the wine batter for 15 minutes.
3. Fry the grouse in olive oil evenly on each side until ready.

## FACTS AND STATS:

*Grouse feed on various foods, including leaves, berries, and insects. Grouse are considered a delicacy in many cultures. They are also important indicators of ecosystem health, as their populations are sensitive to changes in habitat and climate. Some grouse species, such as the sage grouse in North America, are threatened or endangered due to habitat loss and other factors.*

# GRATEFUL GROUSE MACARONI SALAD

Grouse have a plump, flavorful meat that is high in protein and low in fat, making it a healthy and nutritious food source. Use savory marinades to add extra flavor to your grouse meat. Consider marinating it in a flavorful mixture of herbs, spices, and acidic ingredients like vinegar or citrus juice. Keep it moist because grouse meat can be dry. It's important to keep it moist during cooking by basting the meat with butter or oil can help to keep it juicy and flavorful. Grouse meat is best served rare to medium rare, as this helps preserve the meat's natural flavor and tenderness.

## SERVING SIZE: 4-6

## INGREDIENTS:

- 6 oz grouse, chopped
- 3 oz dry macaroni
- ½ cup sour cream
- ½ cup of your favorite salsa
- 1 tbsp lemon juice
- 1 tbsp butter
- 1 tbsp olive oil
- 1 tsp garlic powder
- 2 tbsp ground Parmesan
- 1 tsp thyme
- 1 tsp basil
- 1 tsp oregano
- salt and pepper to taste

## DIRECTIONS:

1. Start cooking the macaroni according to package instructions in a regular pot.
2. Fry the grouse in butter with thyme, basil, oregano, and garlic powder.
3. Transfer the macaroni from the pot into a larger salad bowl.
4. Top with fried fish.
5. Make a salad dressing by mixing sour cream with salsa, lemon juice, olive oil, and Parmesan.
6. Mix and serve.

## FACTS AND STATS:

*Scout the area before you go hunting. It's a good idea to scout the area to know where the grouse will likely be. Look for areas with a lot of cover, such as thickets or brushy fields, as grouse tend to hide in these areas. Grouse feed on various plant and insect matter, so look for areas with abundant food sources like berries, buds, and insects.*

# GREATNESS GROUSE SANDWICH SALAD

When cooked properly, grouse meat can be a delicious and flavorful addition to your meals. Pair it with bold flavors like mushrooms, red wine, and hearty herbs like rosemary and thyme. This helps to balance out the gamey flavor of the meat. Following these cooking tips, you can help ensure that your grouse meat will be tender, juicy, and full of flavor!

### SERVING SIZE: 4

### INGREDIENTS:

- 1 lb grouse meat, cooked and chopped
- ½ cup sour cream
- ½ cup mayonnaise
- 1 tsp oregano
- 1 tsp garlic powder
- 1 tsp basil
- 1 tsp dill
- 1 tbsp butter
- 1 sliced pickle
- 1 lettuce leaf
- slices of toast or buns, as needed

### DIRECTIONS:

1. Briefly brown the grouse meat with the seasoning.
2. Mix with sour cream and mayonnaise.
3. Serve as a sandwich on buns or slices of toast.

## FACTS AND STATS:

*Hunt early in the morning or late in the afternoon: Grouse tends to be most active early in the morning and late in the afternoon, so plan your hunt accordingly. A well-trained hunting dog can help you locate and flush out grouse, making it easier to get a clear shot. Be patient and quiet because grouse can be easily spooked, so it's important to move quietly and be patient when waiting for them to appear. (A SECRET TIP - GO TO BACK GRAVEL ROADS OR TRAILS AS THE SUN IS RISING AND BEATING DOWN BECAUSE, MOST LIKELY, GROUSE WILL BE EATING STONES TO HELP THEM DIGEST THEIR FOOD EASIER.)*

# CARIBBEAN COCONUT GROUSE

**The grouse population in North America varies depending on the specific species and geographic region. Several species of grouse are found in North America, including the spruce grouse, ruffed grouse, and sage grouse. According to data from the North American Breeding Bird Survey, which monitors bird populations across the continent, the populations of some grouse species have declined in recent years. For example, the spruce grouse has declined by about 3% per year since 1966, while the sage grouse has declined by an estimated 80% since the early 20th century due to habitat loss and other factors.**

### SERVING SIZE: 4-6

### INGREDIENTS:

- 6 grouse fillets
- 1 egg
- 1 cup coconut flour
- ½ tbsp celery
- 1 tsp garlic powder
- ½ tbsp dill
- 2 tbsp tomato puree
- ¼ tsp baking soda or powder
- ½ cup red wine
- 2 tbsp lemon juice
- olive oil, as needed

### DIRECTIONS:

1. To make the batter, mix and whisk together all ingredients except the fillets.
2. Soak the fillets in the batter and let them sit for up to half an hour.
3. Fry the grouse fillets in a skillet until both sides are as crispy as you want.

## FACTS AND STATS:

*Practice good gun safety procedures when hunting, including keeping your firearm pointed in a safe direction and never firing unless you know your target. Use a shotgun when hunting grouse because they are small, fast-moving birds, so using a shotgun with a modified or improved cylinder choke is recommended. Aim for the head or neck when shooting at grouse. You want to aim for the head or neck to ensure a clean kill. Always follow local hunting regulations and obtain necessary permits or licenses before going on a grouse hunt. With these tips, patience, and persistence, you can increase your chances of having a successful and enjoyable grouse hunting trip.*

# PEACEFUL PTARMIGAN MINI PIE

Wild ptarmigan is a rich source of lean protein, which is important for building and repairing muscle tissue. A 3.5-ounce serving of cooked ptarmigan provides around 24 grams of protein. Wild ptarmigan is also relatively low in fat, with a 3.5-ounce serving containing only about 2 grams of fat. This can make it a good option for those watching their fat intake.

### SERVING SIZE: 4-6

### INGREDIENTS:

- 1 lb ptarmigan meat, ground
- 2–3 tbsp butter
- 1 cup shallots, chopped
- 1 cup carrots, chopped
- 1 tsp garlic powder
- 1 cup of wine
- 1 cup sour cream
- 1 tbsp mustard
- ½ tbsp honey
- 1 tsp cumin powder
- ½ tbsp thyme
- ½ tbsp oregano
- ½ tbsp cilantro
- 1 tbsp lemon zest
- salt and pepper, to taste
- 2–3 store-bought pie crusts

### DIRECTIONS:

1. Sauté the ptarmigan meat in butter, wine, sour cream, mustard, and seasoning for 15–20 minutes.
2. Preheat your oven to 390 °F.
3. Grab a baking dish and glaze the bottom with butter.
4. Cut the pie crusts into circles, triangles, or any shape you like.
5. Add a bit of the ptarmigan filling and either wrap the crust or cover it with a second layer of crust to create mini pies.
6. Bake for up to 30 minutes or as needed.

# FACTS AND STATS:

*Ptarmigans are a bird in the grouse family, found primarily in the Arctic and sub-Arctic regions of North America, Europe, and Asia. There are three species of ptarmigans: the willow ptarmigan, the rock ptarmigan, and the white-tailed ptarmigan. Ptarmigans are well-adapted to cold environments and have several physical and behavioral adaptations that help them survive in snowy, icy habitats. For example, their feet are covered in feathers to help them stay warm, and they can change the color of their plumage to blend in with their surroundings.*

# PRETTY PIGEON QUICHE

Pigeon meat is relatively low in calories, with a 3.5-ounce serving containing around 160 calories. This is a good option for those trying to manage their weight. Sustainable and free-range pigeons are typically raised in free-range environments, which means they have not been raised with antibiotics or hormones. Additionally, some populations of pigeons are considered pests, and hunting them can help control and prevent damage to crops and buildings. However, it's worth noting that the nutritional content of pigeon meat can vary depending on factors like age, sex, and diet. It's very important to follow safe food handling and cooking practices when preparing pigeon meat to reduce the risk of foodborne illness.

## SERVING SIZE: 4-6

## INGREDIENTS:

- 1 lb pigeon meat, cooked and shredded
- 6-8 eggs
- 3 oz hard cheese, chopped
- 1 cup paprika, chopped
- 1 cup mushrooms, chopped
- 1 cup sour cream
- 2 cups flour
- 2 tsp baking powder
- salt and pepper, to taste
- 2-3 tbsp butter
- quiche molds for frying or baking

## DIRECTIONS:

1. If baking, preheat your oven to 350 °F.
2. Brown the pigeon meat with the seasoning for 15-20 minutes.
3. Mix all the remaining ingredients in a bowl and stir until the veggies, meat, and cheese are distributed evenly.
4. Pour in the quiche molds.
5. If baking, leave it in the oven for 20-30 minutes.
6. If frying, do so in butter for a couple of minutes on both sides.

## FACTS AND STATS:

*Pigeons have been domesticated for thousands of years and used for various purposes, including as messengers, racing birds, and food sources. Pigeons are known for their homing abilities and have been used as messengers throughout history. During both World Wars, pigeons were used to carry messages across enemy lines. Pigeons are highly intelligent and capable of complex problem-solving and pattern recognition. They can also recognize themselves in a mirror, a sign of self-awareness.*

# SPICY TOAST TURKEY SANDWICH

Wild turkeys can live for up to 10 years in the wild. There are six subspecies of wild turkey in North America, each with unique characteristics and range. Wild turkeys are found throughout North America and can be found in a variety of habitats. The specific habitat requirements of wild turkeys can vary depending on the subspecies, but in general, they require a mix of forested and open areas. Wild turkeys are typically found in forests that have a mix of mature trees and open understory.

## SERVING SIZE: 4-6

## INGREDIENTS:

- 1 lb wild turkey meat, cooked and shredded
- 2 tbsp butter
- chili sauce, as needed
- 1 tbsp pepper powder
- salt and pepper, to taste
- 1 cup tomato sauce
- 1 tbsp parsley
- 1 tbsp cilantro
- slices of toast or buns, as needed

## DIRECTIONS:

1. Brown the turkey meat in butter for 5-10 minutes.
2. Add the seasoning, chili sauce, and tomato sauce and simmer until the excess liquid has evaporated.
3. Serve between buns or toast slices.
4. You can serve it with tea, juice, yogurt, and salad. Don't forget that you can swap the tomato sauce with any sauces!

## FACTS AND STATS:

*Field dressing a turkey is an important step in preparing the bird for cooking. Remove feathers right away. Use a sharp knife to remove the feathers from the bird carefully. Make sure to remove all of the feathers and any remaining down. Remove the head and neck using a sharp knife to cut through the skin and flesh around the base of the neck. Pull the head and neck away from the body and set them aside. Make the initial incision by shallow incision through the skin and flesh from the breastbone down to the vent. Remove the innards by reaching into the cavity and removing the organs, including the heart, liver, and gizzard. Set these aside if you plan to use them later. Cut away any excess fat or tissue.*

# SALINE SNIPE SALAD

Snipe meat is a good source of protein, which is essential for building and repairing tissues in the body. Protein is also vital for maintaining muscle mass, supporting the immune system, and providing energy. Snipe meat is relatively low in fat, benefiting those trying to maintain a healthy weight or reduce their intake. The taste of snipe meat can vary depending on factors such as the bird's diet and the preparation method, but it is generally described as having a rich and gamey flavor. The meat is often compared to other game birds like grouse or woodcock. It has a tender and slight texture and can be cooked in various ways, including roasting, grilling, or pan-frying. Some people also describe the taste of snipe as slightly sweet or nutty, which may be influenced by the bird's diet of seeds, insects, and other small prey. Snipe is considered a delicacy by many hunters and chefs.

### SERVING SIZE: 4-6

### INGREDIENTS:

- 1 lb snipe meat, cooked and shredded
- 3-4 cups sweet potato, cubed
- 2 cups onions, sliced
- barbecue sauce, as needed
- 2 tbsp butter
- 2 tbsp red pepper powder
- 1 tbsp cilantro
- 1 tsp thyme
- 1 tsp garlic powder

### DIRECTIONS:

1. Grab a frying pan and melt the butter.
2. Pop in the meat and sweet potato.
3. Fry until the potatoes are tender.
4. Grab a salad bowl and mix the meat and potato with the sauce and seasoning.

# FACTS AND STATS:

*Snipes are small, long-beaked birds that belong to the family Scolopacidae. Several species of snipes are found around the world, including the common snipe, Wilson's snipe, and the pin-tailed snipe. Snipes are typically found in wetland habitats, such as marshes, bogs, and wet meadows. Snipes are known for their distinctive aerial displays, flying high in the sky and making a series of zigzagging maneuvers.*

# WHISPER WOODCOCK WRAP

Woodcock is a small game bird that has tender and flavorful meat. Woodcock is a small bird, so be careful not to overcook it, as it can become dry and tough. Additionally, woodcock is often served with a side of sautéed mushrooms, roasted potatoes, or a simple green salad to balance the flavors.

## SERVING SIZE: 4-6

## INGREDIENTS:

- 1 lb woodcock meat, cooked and shredded
- 4-6 tortillas
- 1 cup onions, sliced
- 3-4 tomatoes, sliced
- 3-4 paprikas, sliced
- Barbecue sauce, as needed
- sour cream or mayonnaise, as needed
- 2 tbsp butter
- salt and pepper, to taste

## DIRECTIONS:

1. Sauté the woodcock meat in butter and barbecue sauce for 10-15 minutes, then season with salt and pepper.
2. Heat the tortillas as per package instructions.
3. Top the tortillas with sour cream and mayonnaise.
4. Add the meat and slices of onion, paprika, and tomatoes.
5. Wrap and enjoy!

## FACTS AND STATS:

*Woodcocks have a unique feeding behavior called "roding." This involves males flying in a zigzag pattern at dusk, making a distinctive nasal call as they search for mates and food. Woodcocks are excellent fliers and can fly up to 50 mph despite their plump and round appearance. Woodcocks have large eyes on their heads, giving them a 360-degree view of their surroundings and helping them avoid predators. The male woodcock performs a unique courtship display during mating season, known as the "sky dance," where he flies up high and then spirals to the ground while making a series of musical sounds.*

# DAINTY DOVE KEBAB

There are many delicious ways to prepare dove, and the best method for cooking depends on personal preference. You can grill the dove by marinating the dove breasts in your favorite marinade for a few hours, then grill over medium-high heat until cooked through. This method is simple and allows the natural flavor of the dove to shine. Cover the dove breasts in seasoned flour for fried dove, then fry in hot oil until crispy and cooked through. This method is classic and adds a crispy texture to the meat. Bacon-wrapped dove is the dove breasts wrapped in bacon and grilled or baked until the bacon is crisp and the dove is cooked through. This method adds a smoky, savory flavor to the meat. Bacon makes everything delicious!

### SERVING SIZE: 4

### INGREDIENTS:

- 1 lb dove meat, chopped
- 4–6 eggs
- 1 cup flour
- 1 tsp baking powder
- salt and pepper, to taste
- 1 tbsp lemon zest
- 1 tbsp dried mint
- 3 zucchinis, sliced
- 2 cups mozzarella cheese, diced
- 1 eggplant, sliced
- 3–4 cups bread crumbs
- 3–4 tbsp butter
- kebab sticks

### DIRECTIONS:

1. Mix the eggs with flour, baking powder, salt, pepper, lemon zest, and dry mint.
2. Take 6–8 kebab picks and line slices of meat, followed by slices of zucchini, mozzarella cheese, and eggplant.
3. Soak the kebabs in the batter and sit for 15–20 minutes so the batter sticks well.
4. Pour the bread crumbs onto a larger flat plate.
5. Take out the kebabs one by one and dredge in bread crumbs.
6. Heat plenty of butter in a larger frying pan.
7. Fry the kebabs evenly, around 5–10 minutes on each side or until ready.

## FACTS AND STATS:

*One method of hunting doves involves setting up decoys, such as plastic or wooden birds, in a field or on a branch to attract doves. Once the doves are lured in, hunters can take aim. Pass shooting involves positioning yourself along the flight path of the doves and waiting for them to fly overhead. It requires good shooting skills and the ability to identify doves quickly in flight. Still-hunting involves stalking the doves on foot or using a hunting dog to flush them out of cover. It requires patience and stealth.*

# QUICK QUAIL AND POTATOES IN MUSHROOM SAUCE

Quail is a delicious and versatile meat that can be prepared in many ways. Here are some popular methods for cooking quail. Pan-roasted quail is seasoned with salt, pepper, and herbs, then seared in a hot skillet with butter and oil until browned on all sides. Finish cooking in the oven until the internal temperature reaches 165°F (74°C). This method creates crispy skin and tender, juicy meat. You can grill quail by marinating the quail in your favorite marinade for a few hours, then grill over medium-high heat until cooked through. This method adds a smoky flavor to the meat and is great for entertaining.

## SERVING SIZE: 4

## INGREDIENTS:

- 1 lb quail meat, cut into slices
- 2–3 whole leeks, chopped
- 6–8 whole potatoes, halved or cut into thick slices
- 1 tbsp sage
- 1 tbsp basil
- 1 tsp garlic powder
- 5–6 cups mushrooms, sliced
- 3–5 cups sour cream
- 1–2 cups of white wine

## DIRECTIONS:

1. Sauté the quail meat, leeks, and halved potatoes gently in butter with a drizzle of water for 15–20 minutes.
2. Turn sides as needed so that the food is cooked evenly.
3. Pour the white wine and sprinkle it with sage, basil, and garlic powder.
4. Continue simmering until there's just a bit of "juice" at the bottom of the pan.
5. Take the meat and potatoes out and add mushrooms and sour cream. If more liquid is needed, pour some more wine.
6. Simmer until the mushrooms are cooked, and you've achieved the desired thickness.
7. Serve the quail and potatoes in a large dish, plate, or bowl.
8. Pour the sauce over and enjoy!

## FACTS AND STATS:

*Several hunting techniques can be used to hunt quail effectively. Flushing involves walking through the brush and flushing out the quail with a dog. The dog's job is to scare the quail from their hiding places, causing them to fly into the air where they can be shot. Stationary hunting involves setting up in a good location near a known water source or feeding area and waiting for the quail to come to you. This can be done on foot or from a blind or stand.*

# GOLDEN GROUSE PIE

Canada is home to a wide variety of grouse species, each with their unique habitats and ranges. Some of the best places to hunt grouse in Canada is Ontario. Ontario has several grouse species, including ruffed, spruce, and sharp-tailed grouse. The northern and central regions of the province are particularly good for grouse hunting. Quebec is known for its dense forests and abundant wildlife, making it an excellent place to hunt ruffed and spruce grouse. British Columbia is home to several grouse species, including ruffed, spruce, and blue grouse. The province's mountainous terrain and dense forests provide excellent habitats for grouse.

### SERVING SIZE: 4

### INGREDIENTS:

- 1 lb wild grouse meat, ground
- 1 cup onions, chopped
- 1 cup carrots, chopped
- 1–2 cups sour cream
- 1–2 cups spinach, chopped
- 2–3 tbsp butter
- pie crust, as needed

### DIRECTIONS:

1. Preheat your oven to 350 °F.
2. Sauté the ground grouse meat with onions and carrots in butter for 15–20 minutes.
3. Pour the sour cream in and add spinach.
4. Stir and bring to a soft boil.
5. Let simmer until the excess liquid has evaporated.
6. Take a baking dish and glaze the bottom and the sides with butter.
7. Spread the pie crust or dough across the bottom and sides.
8. Pour in the filling and top with the crust.
9. Bake for 10–20 minutes and enjoy.

# FACTS AND STATS:

*Field dressing grouse is a straightforward process that can be completed in just a few steps:*

1. *Remove the feathers by plucking them feathers from the bird. This can be done by hand. Be sure to remove all feathers, including the ones on the wings and tail.*

2. *Remove the head using a sharp knife to cut off the head of the bird just below the neck.*

3. *Cut open the bird making a small incision in the skin near the base of the breastbone. Carefully cut through the skin and muscle, careful not to puncture any internal organs.*

4. *Remove the entrails by reaching into the body cavity and carefully remove the organs. This includes the heart, liver, lungs, and intestines. Be sure to remove everything in one piece without puncturing any organs.*

5. *Rinse the inside and outside of the bird thoroughly with cold water.*

6. *Chill the bird in a cooler with ice before cooking.*

# SOUR PARTRIDGE SOUP

**Canada is home to several species of partridge, including the gray partridge and the Hungarian partridge. Saskatchewan is known for its excellent partridge hunting opportunities. The province's prairies and grasslands provide ideal gray and Hungarian partridge habitats. Alberta is home to gray and Hungarian partridge, and the province's grasslands and parklands offer excellent hunting opportunities. Manitoba is another great place to hunt gray and Hungarian partridge. The province's agricultural areas and grasslands provide ideal habitats for these birds.**

### SERVING SIZE: 4

### INGREDIENTS:

- 1 lb partridge meat, chopped
- 2 whole leeks, sliced
- 1 tbsp parsley, chopped
- 4–5 potatoes, cubed
- 2 cups peas
- 2 cups cauliflower, chopped
- 2 tbsp butter
- 1–2 cups sour cream
- 1 tbsp basil
- 1 tsp garlic powder
- 1 cup of wine
- 2 tbsp vinegar or lemon juice

### DIRECTIONS:

1. Sauté the partridge meat with leeks, potatoes, peas, and cauliflower in butter for about 10–15 minutes.
2. Add the broth and bring it to a slow boil.
3. Pour the sour cream in and let simmer for 15–20 minutes.
4. Before taking the soup off the heat, add the basil, parsley, garlic powder, and wine.
5. Ensure the soup simmers for another 10 minutes for the wine to cook fully.
6. Once the soup has cooled down slightly, add the vinegar or lemon juice.

# FACTS AND STATS:

*Quebec is known for its excellent hunting opportunities, and the province is home to gray and Hungarian partridge. The province's forests and agricultural areas provide excellent habitats for these birds. British Columbia is home to the gray partridge, and the province's grasslands and agricultural areas provide excellent habitats for these birds. It's important to note that hunting regulations and seasons may vary by province/state and species, so it's essential to check with local hunting and wildlife authorities before planning a hunt.*

# DINNER

# WICKED WILD DUCK FILLETS IN RASPBERRY SAUCE

Cooking wild ducks can be challenging due to the leaner and tougher nature of the meat compared to farm-raised ducks. Before cooking, it is important to prepare the duck properly. Remove the feathers, clean and gut the duck, and remove any excess fat. You can also brine the duck to help tenderize the meat and remove any gamey flavor. The best cooking methods for wild duck are roasting, grilling, or pan-searing. Avoid overcooking the duck, as it can become tough and dry. Aim for a medium-rare to medium doneness to keep the meat tender and juicy.

## SERVING SIZE: 4

## INGREDIENTS:

- 1 lb duck meat, filleted
- ½ cup red wine
- 1 tsp garlic powder
- 3 cups raspberries
- 1 tsp cinnamon
- 2 tbsp cornstarch
- 2 cups heavy cream
- 2 tbsp butter

## DIRECTIONS:

1. Sauté the wild duck fillets in butter and red wine for 15–20 minutes. Toward the end, add garlic powder.
2. Once the meat is finished, take it off the heat and set it aside.
3. Pour the raspberries into the remaining juice and add more wine if needed.
4. Bring to a soft boil and simmer at a desired thickness. Add cinnamon, heavy cream, and cornstarch for 5–10 minutes before taking off the heat.
5. Top the duck with the sauce, and enjoy!

# FACTS AND STATS:

*Scout the area before going duck hunting. Scout the area for potential hotspots where ducks are likely to be found. You want to look for feeding areas, nesting grounds, and water sources. Using decoys increases your odds tremendously. Set up decoys in the water or on the ground to attract ducks. Make sure to use a mix of different species and positions, such as floating decoys, standing decoys, and even motion decoys. Build or set up a blind to conceal yourself from the ducks. The blind should be positioned in a spot that offers a clear line of sight to the decoys and the incoming ducks.*

# QUICK GOOSE ROAST

Cooking geese can be challenging due to their larger size and stronger flavor than other poultry. Sous vide is a modern cooking technique involving the goose in a vacuum-sealed bag in a water bath. This method can help ensure the goose is cooked evenly and moist. Cook the goose at 140°F for 4-6 hours, then sear the skin in a hot pan before serving. The key to cooking geese is to avoid overcooking, which can result in dry, tough meat. Use a meat thermometer to check the internal temperature, and let the goose rest for a few minutes before carving to allow the juices to redistribute.

### SERVING SIZE: 4

### INGREDIENTS:

- 1 lb goose meat, cut into larger chunks
- salt and pepper, to your taste
- 2 tbsp butter
- ½ cup olive oil
- 1 tbsp turmeric
- 1 tbsp red pepper powder
- 2 tsp lemon zest
- 1 tsp thyme
- 4–6 cups potatoes, cubed

### DIRECTIONS:

1. Preheat your oven to 390 °F.
2. Grab a larger baking dish and glaze the bottom and sides with butter.
3. Mix the turmeric, red pepper powder, salt, pepper, lemon zest, and thyme in a separate dish.
4. Glaze the meat and potatoes with olive oil and dredge in the spices.
5. Pour in the baking dish and bake for 20–30 minutes at 390 °F.

## FACTS AND STATS:

*Two main species of geese are hunted in the United States: Canadian geese and snow geese. Canadian geese are the most common goose hunted in the United States. They are found throughout North America and are known for their distinctive honking calls. Snow geese are another popular species of goose hunted in the United States. They are known for their white plumage and distinctive black wingtips. Hunting geese is regulated by state and federal laws in the United States. Hunters must obtain the proper licenses and follow regulations on bag limits, hunting seasons, and hunting methods.*

# PLEASANT PHEASANT WITH MUSHROOM SAUCE

**Grilling is an excellent option for cooking pheasant. Preheat the grill to medium-high heat, brush the bird with oil, and grill for 6-8 minutes per side or until the internal temperature reaches 165°F. Slow cooking can be a great way to keep the pheasant moist and tender. Place the bird in a slow cooker with vegetables, herbs, broth, or wine, and cook on low for 6-8 hours. Cut the bird into pieces and simmer in a flavorful broth with vegetables and spices until tender. Pheasant is also great for use in stews or casseroles. Remember always to use a meat thermometer to check the internal temperature of the pheasant to ensure it is fully cooked before serving your fantastic dish that will have your friends coming back for seconds.**

### SERVING SIZE: 4

### INGREDIENTS:

- 1 lb pheasant, legs or breasts (or both)
- 2–3 tbsp butter
- 1–2 cups chicken broth
- 2 cups leeks, sliced
- salt and pepper, to taste
- 3–4 cups sweet potatoes, cubed
- 1 tbsp parsley leaf
- 1 tsp garlic powder
- 1 tsp thyme
- 1 tbsp cilantro
- 1 cup of wine
- 4–5 cups mushrooms, sliced
- 1–2 cups sour cream
- ½ cup cornstarch

### DIRECTIONS:

1. Brown pheasant slices in butter for 5 minutes on each side.
2. Add half of the broth, boil, and let sauté on low heat for 30–45 minutes.
3. Add the leeks, salt, pepper, sweet potatoes, parsley leaf, garlic powder, thyme, cilantro, wine, and broth.
4. Let simmer for another 5–10 minutes.
5. Ensure that the excess liquid evaporates for a large part but that there's still enough thick juice for the sauce.

6. Remove the pheasant and sweet potatoes from the pan and set aside.
7. Add the sliced mushrooms, sour cream, and cornstarch.
8. Bring to a slow boil and let simmer until you achieve the desired thickness.
9. Serve on top of the meat and sweet potatoes.

### FACTS AND STATS:

*Pheasant hunting is popular in the United States, particularly in the Midwest and Great Plains regions. Pheasants are not native to North America but were introduced in the late 1800s as a game bird. The USA's top states for pheasant hunting are South Dakota, Kansas, and Iowa. In South Dakota, pheasant hunting is a major industry, with thousands of hunters visiting the state yearly. The annual economic impact of pheasant hunting in South Dakota is estimated to be over $200 million. The pheasant hunting season typically runs from October to January, with the exact dates varying by state.*

# BREADED PTARMIGAN WITH WINE AND BLUEBERRY SAUCE

Sautéing is a terrific method to cook ptarmigan. Start by heating some oil in a pan over medium-high heat. Add the seasoned ptarmigan breasts and cook for 3 to 4 minutes on each side, until browned and cooked. Grilling is an excellent option for cooking ptarmigan, especially during summer. Grilling the ptarmigan on medium-high heat for about 6 to 8 minutes on each side is recommended. Slow-cooking ptarmigan helps to keep the meat moist and tender. You can slow cook the ptarmigan in a crockpot, adding vegetables, herbs, and spices to create a flavorful dish. It is recommended to cook the ptarmigan to an internal temperature of 165°F.

### SERVING SIZE: 4

### INGREDIENTS:

- 1 lb ptarmigan meat, cut into pieces or fillets
- 4–6 eggs
- 1–2 cups flour
- salt and pepper, to your taste
- 1 tsp garlic powder
- 1 tbsp parsley
- 1 tsp oregano
- 1 tbsp dried mint
- 1 cup fresh blueberries
- 1 tbsp wine
- 1 cup vegetable broth
- 1 tbsp cornstarch
- ½ tsp cinnamon
- ½ tsp nutmeg
- ½ tsp basil
- 2 tbsp butter

### DIRECTIONS:

1. Mix the eggs with flour, salt, pepper, garlic powder, parsley, oregano, and dried mint.
2. Dredge the ptarmigan pieces and let them sit while you're making the blueberry sauce.
3. Mix the blueberries with wine and broth in a small pot and bring to a boil.
4. Let simmer for 5–10 minutes and add cornstarch.
5. Simmer for a few more minutes, then add cinnamon, nutmeg, and basil.
6. Grab a frying pan and melt the butter.

7. Take the ptarmigan out of the batter and dredge in bread crumbs.
8. Fry in butter for up to 10 minutes on each side or until ready.
9. Serve on a large plate topped with blueberry sauce.

### FACTS AND STATS:

*Ptarmigans are primarily found in Alaska and are a popular game bird for hunting. Hunting season for ptarmigan in Alaska typically starts in August and runs through February. The bag limit for ptarmigan in Alaska varies depending on the region, but it generally ranges from 10 to 20 birds per day. To hunt ptarmigan in Alaska, you must have a valid hunting license and a game bird stamp. Ptarmigans inhabit high-elevation alpine and tundra environments, often in rocky areas with sparse vegetation.*

# FRIENDLY FRIED PIGEON IN SWEET POTATO APPLESAUCE

While there is no exact count of the total pigeon population in North America, it is estimated to be in the tens of millions. Pigeons are a valuable source of protein and have been used as a food source in many cultures throughout history. Pigeons are considered a symbol of peace and have been used to convey messages of hope and reconciliation.

### SERVING SIZE: 4

### INGREDIENTS:

- 1 lb pigeon meat, cut into pieces
- 4–6 eggs
- 2 cups flour
- salt and pepper, to taste
- 1 tbsp basil
- 1 tbsp dried mint
- 1 tsp thyme
- 3–4 cups sweet potatoes, cubed
- 3–4 apples, cubed
- 2 tbsp butter
- 2 cups bread crumbs
- ½ cup white wine
- ½ tsp cinnamon powder
- ½ tsp nutmeg powder
- 1 tsp basil

### DIRECTIONS:

1. Whisk the eggs with flour, salt, pepper, basil, mint, and thyme.
2. Dredge the pigeon meat pieces and let sit for 10–15 minutes.
3. Start cooking the sweet potatoes and apples for the sauce. Make sure to have as little water as possible, just enough for the food to cook on low-medium heat.
4. Heat a frying pan with the butter.
5. Pour the bread crumbs onto a plate and take the pigeon pieces out of the batter.
6. Dredge the meat in bread crumbs and fry in the butter evenly on each side for approximately 3–5 minutes.
7. Please take out the batter and set it aside.
8. Pour in the sweet potatoes and apples with their cooking water.
9. Mix and mash until you achieve a sauce consistency.

10. Bring to a slow boil and simmer to thicken the sauce further.

11. Add the white wine, cinnamon, nutmeg, and basil for 5–10 minutes before taking off the heat.

12. Serve the sauce over the pigeon meat or on the side.

### FACTS AND STATS:

*The hunting season for rock pigeons varies by state but typically runs from September to March. Rock pigeons can be hunted using various methods, including shotguns, air rifles, and even falcons. Bag limits for rock pigeons also vary by state but are generally quite liberal, with hunters allowed to take dozens of birds per day. Rock pigeon hunting is less popular than hunting other game birds, such as quail or pheasant, but it has a dedicated following of hunters who enjoy hunting these fast and elusive birds.*

# DODGING DOVE RISOTTO ROAST

One of the most popular ways to cook doves is to roast or grill them. This allows the meat to cook slowly and develop a crispy, golden brown skin. You can stuff the doves with herbs, citrus, or other aromatics to add flavor or wrap them in bacon. Doves can be pan-fried in butter or oil until golden brown and cooked through. This method works well for smaller doves and can be a quick and easy way to prepare them. For tougher cuts of dove meat, consider slow-cooking them in a stew or casserole. This can help to tenderize the meat and infuse it with flavor from other ingredients in the dish. Remember to remove the feathers and internal organs before cooking the doves. The internal organs can be saved for making stock or broth.

### SERVING SIZE: 4

### INGREDIENTS:

- 4–6 doves, chopped
- 3–4 tbsp butter
- 1 tbsp parsley, chopped
- 1 cup onions, chopped
- 1 cup carrots, sliced
- 1 cup chicken stock
- 2–3 cups brown rice
- 2 tbsp mustard
- 1 cup of beer

### DIRECTIONS:

1. Preheat your oven to 390 °F.
2. Soak the rice the night before or at least 2 hours before cooking.
3. Cut the doves into larger pieces (separate the legs from the breasts).
4. Fry the onions, parsley, and carrots in butter until the onions turn golden.
5. Pop the rice in and the chicken stock and bring to a boil.
6. Let boil on medium heat for up to 10 minutes and take off the heat.
7. Glaze the bottom of your baking dish with butter.
8. Arrange the doves in the dish and glaze them with butter and mustard.

9. Pour the risotto in and arrange it around the meat.
10. Drizzle with beer.
11. Roast 30 minutes at 390 °F (shorter or longer if needed).

## FACTS AND STATS:

*Doves are one of the most popular game birds in the USA, and dove hunting is a popular outdoor activity. Dove hunting is legal in 42 states, and the season generally runs from September to January. The most commonly hunted dove species in the United States is the mourning dove. According to the U.S. Fish and Wildlife Service, there were over 4.7 million dove hunters in the United States in 2016. The total harvest of mourning doves in the United States in 2016 was around 33 million birds. Texas, California, and Georgia are the top states for dove hunting in the United States.*

# WONDERFUL WILD TURKEY STEW

Wild turkeys are nothing like farmed turkeys. Farm-raised turkeys are much fatter, and their bones are much softer than wild ones. Farm-raised bird meat will cook faster, is less dense, and is less filling than your wild turkey. In the wild, the turkey needs to be strong, which makes its meat grow denser. This is not the same as toughness, although the sinews in a wild turkey get extremely tough. The number#1 difference is the flavor, thanks to the diet. You are sadly mistaken if you expect a frozen game bird from the frozen section at your local grocery store to be the same as your wild game bird that eats natural food like bugs, plants, and insects. Farm turkeys are raised eating grains, which helps them have more flavor and fat. When cooking wild turkey, removing as much fat as possible is best.

## SERVING SIZE: 6

## INGREDIENTS:

- 1 lb wild turkey meat, chopped
- a pinch of salt and pepper
- 2 tbsp butter or olive oil
- 4 cups chicken broth
- 1 cup carrots, chopped
- 1 cup of potatoes, diced
- 1 cup onions, chopped
- 1 cup parsley, chopped
- 1 tbsp red pepper powder
- 1 tbsp celery leaf, chopped
- ½ cup white wine

## DIRECTIONS:

1. Brown the meat and vegetables in butter for 15–20 minutes.
2. Transfer into a pot and add the broth.
3. Let simmer for around an hour.
4. Add the white wine, red pepper powder, celery, parsley, salt, and pepper for 10–15 minutes before taking the stew off the heat.

## FACTS AND STATS:

*Learn to shoot turkeys with both shoulders. It can be challenging to twist your body around far enough to make an accurate shot. One of the most difficult situations in hunting turkeys is having the bird sneak up on you, giving you a heart attack! It's a good idea to practice shooting from your opposite shoulder before the season starts.*

# QUAINT QUAIL VEGETABLE ROAST

Stuffed quail is my favorite dish! You can braise quail by browning it in a Dutch oven, then add liquid and aromatics, such as wine, chicken broth, or beer. Stuff the quail with a flavorful stuffing of your choice, such as wild rice, mushrooms, and herbs, then roast in the oven until the internal temperature reaches 165°F (74°C). This method creates a delicious and impressive presentation.

## SERVING SIZE: 4

## INGREDIENTS:

- 4–6 whole quails
- 1 tbsp beer
- 2–3 tbsp butter
- 1 tbsp honey
- 1 tbsp orange juice
- 1 tbsp mustard
- 1 tbsp parsley leaf
- 1 tsp garlic powder
- 1 tsp cilantro
- 1 tsp dill
- 4 medium-sized potatoes, halved
- 4 cups sweet potatoes, diced
- 1 cup broccoli
- 1 cup cauliflower

## DIRECTIONS:

1. Preheat your oven to 390 °F.
2. Mix a tablespoon of butter, beer, honey, orange juice, mustard, parsley leaf, garlic powder, cilantro, and dill to make the glazing for the quails and vegetables.
3. Glaze the bottom of a baking dish with butter and arrange the quails, potatoes, sweet potatoes, broccoli, and cauliflower.
4. Take a brush and cover the meat and vegetables with the glazing.
5. Roast for 30–45 minutes at 390 °F. You may roast shorter or longer if needed.

## FACTS AND STATS:

*The driving technique involves using several hunters to drive the quail toward other hunters waiting to shoot. This can effectively cover a large area and flush out multiple birds at once. Falconry is a popular method of hunting quail and involves using a trained bird of prey to catch the birds in flight. This is a highly specialized and regulated form of hunting. No matter which hunting technique is used, it is important always to practice safe hunting practices and to obey all hunting regulations and laws.*

# SWEETY POTATO GROUSE STEW

I love planning my meals and try eating as healthy as possible. I like to use various herbs and spices for grouse. Tarragon is a sweet herb and almost has an anise flavor and is absolutely delicious paired with different wild game birds. Pesto is another herb you can experiment with game birds. Wrapping your birds with prosciutto or bacon will have your taste buds exploding with excitement.

## SERVING SIZE: 4

## INGREDIENTS:

- 1 lb grouse meat, diced
- 2 cups onions, diced
- 1 cup carrots, sliced
- 3 cups potatoes, diced
- 1 cup sweet potatoes, diced
- 2 tbsp olive oil
- 1 cup chicken broth
- 1 cup tomato sauce
- 1 cup paprika, chopped
- salt and pepper, to taste
- 1 tbsp sweet pepper powder
- 1 tsp garlic powder
- 1 tbsp parsley, chopped
- 1 tbsp celery leaf, chopped

## DIRECTIONS:

1. Brown the grouse meat, onions, carrots, potatoes, and sweet potatoes in olive oil for 10 minutes.
2. Add the chicken broth and bring it to a boil.
3. Add tomato sauce and paprika.
4. Let simmer for another 40 minutes.
5. Add salt, pepper, sweet pepper powder, garlic powder, parsley, and celery leaf.
6. Let simmer for another 5–10 minutes.

# FACTS AND STATS:

*Good hearing pays off big when you are hunting. When the leaves in the woods are dry and crinkly, you can hear the few steps grouse takes to launch into flight. The sound is a sort of dry, "tick, tick." Once you've listened to it several times, followed by a flushing bird, it won't take long to know what to listen for. Grouse are stay-at-home game birds seldom roaming more than half a mile from where it lives.*

# PARTICULAR PARTRIDGE STEW

The hunting season for partridge in North America can vary depending on the species of partridge and the specific region where you plan to hunt. The hunting season for ruffed grouse typically starts in early fall and lasts until the end of the year. However, the exact start and end dates can vary depending on the state or province where you plan to hunt. The hunting season for spruce grouse usually begins in September and lasts until the end of the year. The hunting season for sharp-tailed grouse can vary depending on the region but generally runs from September to December. It's important to check with the relevant state or provincial wildlife agency to find out the exact hunting season dates and any applicable hunting regulations. Hunting regulations vary by region and include restrictions on bag limits, hunting methods, and weapons used. So, knowing these regulations before going on a hunting trip is essential.

### SERVING SIZE: 4

### INGREDIENTS:

- 1 lb partridge meat, chopped
- 1 cup leeks, chopped
- 1 cup carrots, chopped
- 2 cups sweet potatoes, diced
- 1 tsp garlic powder
- 4 cups chicken stock
- 2 cups sour cream
- ½ cup red wine
- 1 tsp thyme
- 1 tbsp rosemary
- 1 tbsp dill
- salt and pepper, to taste

### DIRECTIONS:

1. Brown the partridge meat with leeks, carrots, garlic powder, and sweet potatoes for 10–15 minutes.
2. Add the chicken stock and bring it to a boil.
3. Pour in the sour cream and wine.
4. Let simmer for another 45 minutes.
5. Add the thyme, rosemary, dill, salt, and pepper for 10 minutes before taking off the heat.

## FACTS AND STATS:

*The ruffed grouse is the state bird of Pennsylvania and the provincial bird of New Brunswick. They are exciting and unique birds that have played an essential role in human culture for centuries. In some cultures, partridges are seen as a symbol of love, fertility, and prosperity. The average lifespan of a partridge is around 1-2 years in the wild. The partridge population can be impacted by habitat loss, disease, and hunting pressure. The partridge's drumming during courtship displays is created by the male beating its wings against the air to make a loud, booming noise. These are just a few fascinating facts and stats about partridge.*

# DIPPING DUCK AND RICE STIR-FRY

There are over 100 different species of ducks worldwide, primarily found in North America, Europe, and Asia. Here are some of the most common species of ducks Mallard, wood duck, American black duck, gadwall, northern pintail, canvasback, redhead, ring-necked duck, lesser scaup, greater scaup, harlequin duck, bufflehead, common eider, barrow's goldeneye, common goldeneye, hooded merganser, common merganser, red-breasted merganser, ruddy duck, and muscovy duck to name a few. Each duck species has unique characteristics, such as plumage coloration, size, and habitat preference. They are an essential part of the world's ecosystem, playing roles as both predator and prey in their respective habitats.

## SERVING SIZE: 4

## INGREDIENTS:

- 1 lb wild duck meat fillets or pieces
- 2 cups brown rice
- 1 cup scallions, chopped
- 1 cup potatoes, chopped
- 1 cup cauliflower, chopped
- 1 cup broccoli, chopped
- 1 cup chicken broth
- 1 tbsp mustard
- salt and pepper, to taste
- 1 tbsp sweet pepper powder
- ½ tbsp cumin powder
- 1 tbsp cilantro
- 1 tbsp dill

## DIRECTIONS:

1. Soak the brown rice the night before.
2. Brown the duck, scallions, potatoes, cauliflower, and broccoli for 10–15 minutes.
3. Drain the rice and pop it into the pan.
4. Add the chicken broth and mustard and bring to a boil.
5. Simmer and stir for another 20–30 minutes.
6. Add salt, pepper, sweet pepper powder, cumin powder, cilantro, and dill.
7. Continue mixing on medium heat until the excess liquid is gone.

## FACTS AND STATS:

*Over 20 species of duck's breed in North America, including the Mallard, Wood Duck, American Black Duck, and Northern Pintail. The Mallard is the most common duck in North America and can be found in almost any freshwater body. The Wood Duck is one of the most colorful ducks in North America and is known for its distinctive green and purple plumage. The Northern Pintail is known for its long, slender neck and pointed tail, giving it a unique flight silhouette. Ducks are strong fliers and can reach up to 60 miles per hour.*

# DOWN DEEP-FRIED GOOSE FILLETS

Before cooking a goose, removing any excess fat is essential, which can make the meat greasy. This can be done by trimming the fat off the bird or using a sharp knife to score the skin and allow the fat to render out during cooking. Geese have a rich, gamey flavor that can be enhanced by seasoning with herbs like thyme, rosemary, and sage. A sprinkle of salt and pepper can also help to bring out the meat's natural flavors. A roasted goose can be served with various side dishes, such as roasted root vegetables, mashed potatoes, or sautéed greens. A rich gravy from the pan drippings can also be delicious. Leftover cooked goose can be used in various dishes, such as soups, stews, and casseroles. The meat can also be sliced thinly and used in sandwiches or salads. With the proper preparation and cooking techniques, a well-roasted goose can be a delicious and impressive addition to any meal.

## SERVING SIZE: 4

## INGREDIENTS:

- 1 lb goose fillets
- 1 cup of wine
- 1 tbsp sweet pepper powder
- 1 tsp garlic powder
- 1 tsp thyme
- 1 tsp cinnamon powder
- 1 tbsp chestnut powder
- 2–3 cups bread crumbs
- 1 cup of potatoes, diced
- 1 cup of carrots, diced
- 1 cup of sweet potatoes, diced
- 6–8 cups vegetable oil

## DIRECTIONS:

1. Mix sweet pepper powder, garlic powder, thyme, cinnamon, chestnut, and bread crumbs in a bowl.
2. Dredge the goose fillets in wine and the mixed seasonings.
3. Do the same with carrots, potatoes, and sweet potatoes.
4. Deep-fry in vegetable oil on medium heat until ready.

## FACTS AND STATS:

*During migration, geese can fly up to 50 mph and cover up to 1,500 miles in a single day. Geese are highly social animals and often mate for life. They form strong bonds with their mates and offspring and are known to mourn the loss of a mate or young. Geese are herbivores and feed mainly on grasses, grains, and other vegetation. They are important grazers and can help to maintain healthy grasslands. Geese can significantly impact the environment, both positively and negatively. While they can help maintain healthy grasslands, their overpopulation in urban areas can cause problems such as fouling parks and golf courses. Hunting of geese is a popular recreational activity in North America, with regulations in place to ensure sustainable populations of geese. The feathers of geese have been used for centuries for various purposes, such as filling pillows and bedding and making quill pens.*

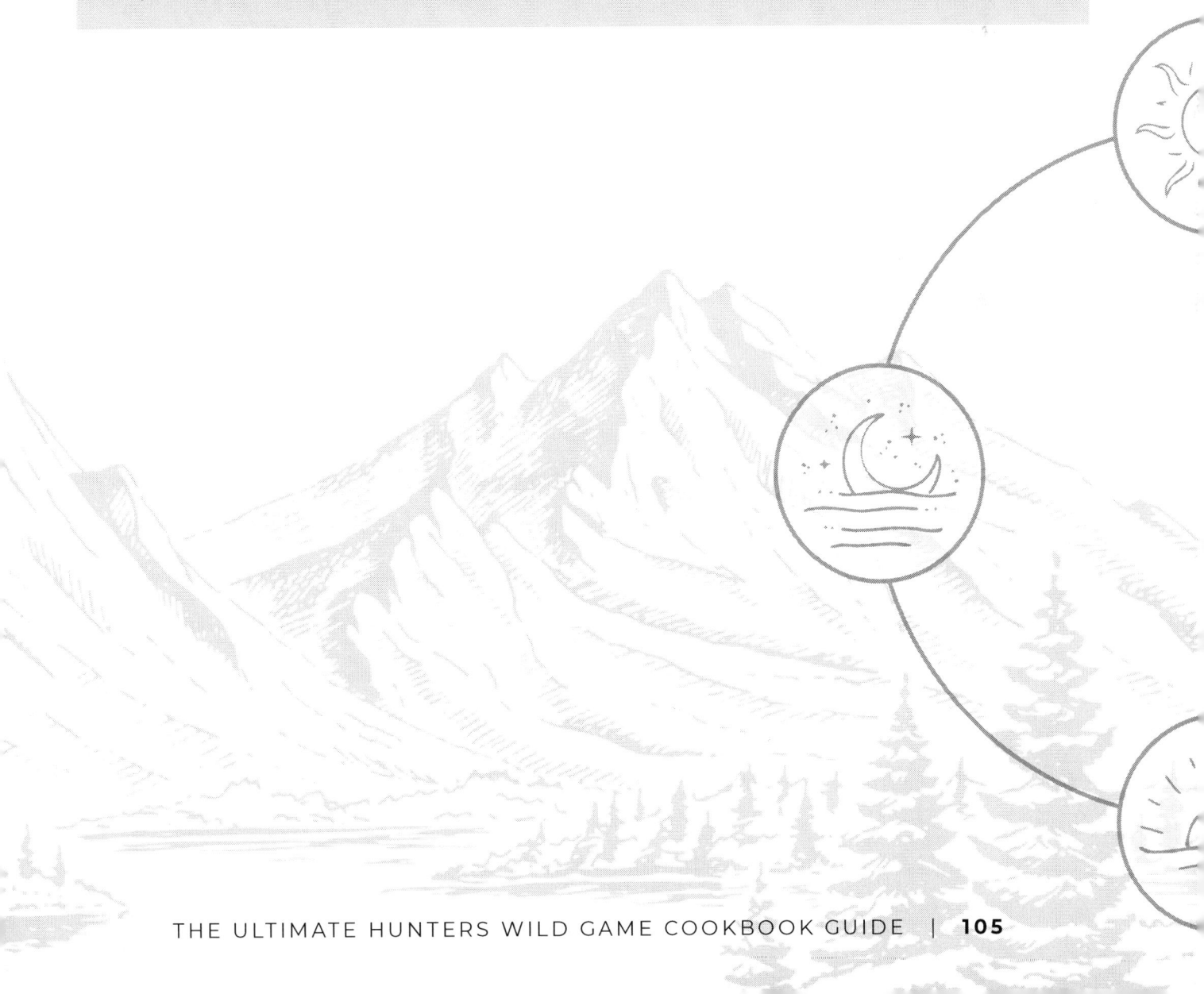

# SPECIAL STUFFED PHEASANTS

Wild pheasant is very lean and, if not cooked with care, will be like chewing on a rubber boot. Pheasant is similar to chicken, with a stronger smell and flavor. The key to cooking fantastic pheasants is to keep it covered, between 250 degrees Fahrenheit to 325 degrees Fahrenheit with moisture. It is the most flavorable when you cook it on the bone and is also beneficial to brine your pheasant. Pheasant meat is a lean source of protein and is considered a delicacy in many cultures.

### SERVING SIZE: 4

### INGREDIENTS:

- 4–6 whole pheasants
- 2–3 cups brown rice, soaked overnight
- 4 leeks, chopped
- 4 carrots, chopped
- 1 tsp garlic powder
- 1 cup chestnut powder
- 1 tsp thyme
- 1 tsp cinnamon powder
- 1 tsp nutmeg powder
- 2 tbsp cooking rum
- 1 tbsp chestnut powder
- 1 cup chicken broth
- salt and pepper, to your taste
- 1 tsp dill
- 1 tsp celery leaf
- 1 cup tomato sauce
- ½ cup sour cream

### DIRECTIONS:

1. Preheat your oven to 390 °F.
2. To make the stuffing, sauté the rice with chicken broth, leeks, carrots, garlic powder, thyme, chestnut, cinnamon, nutmeg, and 1 tbsp rum.
3. Bring to a boil and simmer for another 10–15 minutes. Allow for enough "soup" to remain so as to moisten the meat on the inside.
4. Wipe the pheasant cavities and season well with salt, pepper, dill, and celery leaf.
5. Fill the pheasants with the stuffing and arrange them in a baking dish glazed with butter.
6. Mix a tablespoon of butter with tomato sauce, sour cream, and 1 tbsp of rum.
7. Spread it on the pheasants and roast for up to 45 minutes at 390 °F.

## FACTS AND STATS:

*Pheasants are ground-dwelling birds often found in fields and grasslands, feeding on seeds, grains, and insects. The male pheasant is known for its colorful plumage, which includes an iridescent green head, a coppery-gold body, and a distinctive white ring around its neck. Pheasants have a distinctive crowing call often heard during the breeding season. The male pheasant will also perform a courtship display, where it fans out its tail feathers and makes a series of clucking sounds to attract a mate.*

# WHOLE PTARMIGAN RISOTTO ROAST

Most ptarmigan populations in Canada are found in the Arctic and subarctic regions of the country. The rock ptarmigan is the most common species found in Canada. It is distributed throughout the country's northern parts, including the Yukon, Northwest Territories, Nunavut, and northern regions of Quebec, Labrador, and Newfoundland. The willow ptarmigan is another species found in Canada. It is more common in the country's boreal forests, including parts of Alaska, Yukon, Northwest Territories, and northern British Columbia. The white-tailed ptarmigan is found in the high mountainous regions of western Canada, including the Rocky Mountains in Alberta and British Columbia.

### SERVING SIZE: 4

### INGREDIENTS:

- 4 whole ptarmigans
- ½ cup red wine
- 1 tbsp red pepper powder
- 1 cup tomato sauce
- salt and pepper, to taste
- 1 tbsp cilantro
- 1 tbsp basil
- 1 tsp nutmeg powder
- 2 cups brown rice, soaked for a couple of hours

### DIRECTIONS:

1. Preheat your oven to 390 °F.
2. For the marinade, mix the red wine with red pepper powder, tomato sauce, salt, pepper, cilantro, basil, and nutmeg.
3. Drain the rice and stir-fry in butter with 2–3 tbsp of the marinade for 10 minutes.
4. Arrange the ptarmigans in a large baking dish and glaze them with the marinade.
5. Pour in the risotto and arrange it around the birds.
6. Pour the remaining marinade over the meat and rice.
7. Roast for 30–45 minutes at 390 °F.

## FACTS AND STATS:

*One of the fascinating statistics about ptarmigans in Canada is that they are known for their remarkable adaptation to cold environments. The rock ptarmigan, found in the Arctic and subarctic regions of Canada, can survive in temperatures as low as -40°C (-40°F) due to its specialized feathers and metabolism. Another interesting statistic is that ptarmigans can change the color of their feathers depending on the season to blend in with their surroundings and avoid predators. In the winter, they have white feathers to blend in with the snow, while in the summer, they have brown or gray feathers to blend in with the tundra. Ptarmigans are known for their unique mating behavior. During the breeding season, males compete for females by engaging in elaborate displays such as vocalizations, wing flapping, and fighting. Once a male has successfully attracted a mate, they will remain monogamous for the breeding season.*

# DELIGHT DEEP-FRIED TURKEY

Deep-Fried turkey is my favorite way to cook turkey! If you have yet to try deep-fried turkey, then you have not had the best turkey you are ever going to eat in your life! It doesn't matter how big your turkey is as long as you have a big enough pot, then you are good to go. You will want to deep-fry your turkey outside because you are cooking with large amounts of very hot cooking oil. It takes between 45 - 60 minutes to cook your turkey to perfection. It is crispy on the outside and super juicy on the inside. I guarantee deep-fried turkey will be the most succulent turkey you will ever make. Make sure you don't overcook it because you will have a crunchy turkey nugget!

### SERVING SIZE: 4

### INGREDIENTS:

- 1 whole wild turkey
- 4–5 gallons of vegetable oil
- ½ cup red wine
- 1 cup tomato sauce
- 1 cup Dijon mustard
- 1 tbsp red pepper powder
- salt and pepper, to taste
- 1 tbsp cilantro
- 1 tsp thyme
- 1 tbsp cumin powder
- 1 tbsp basil
- 1 tbsp nutmeg powder
- 1 tbsp cinnamon powder
- a pack of bread crumbs

### DIRECTIONS:

1. Mix the red wine with mustard, tomato sauce, red pepper powder, salt, pepper, cilantro, thyme, cumin, basil, nutmeg, and cinnamon.
2. Dredge the turkey in the marinade.
3. Pour the bread crumbs on a large plate and dredge the whole turkey until fully covered.
4. Heat a pot of vegetable oil to 350 °F. Make sure that the pot is only half full.
5. Lower the whole turkey in the pot and fry for approximately 45 minutes.
6. While the turkey is frying, ensure the oil temperature doesn't exceed 350 °F.

## FACTS AND STATS:

*Removing old chalk makes your box call sound brand new. If your box call starts to sound dull, it could mean that the chalk used to increase friction between the paddle and the sides of the call has become gummed up with foreign material. You can recondition your call by applying a fresh coating, but make sure you remove the old chalk residue using a soft scrubby to avoid damaging your box call.*

# SENSIBLE SNIPE PIE

**Snipes are found throughout much of Canada, particularly in wetland habitats such as marshes, bogs, and the edges of lakes and rivers. They are migratory birds, and their breeding range extends from Alaska to Newfoundland, with some populations wintering in southern parts of the United States and Mexico.**

## SERVING SIZE: 4

## INGREDIENTS:

- 1 lb snipe meat, chopped
- 2 cups mushrooms, sliced
- ½ cup onions, chopped
- 1 cup sour cream
- 1 tsp cooking rum
- 2 tbsp chestnut powder
- 1 tsp cinnamon powder
- 1 tsp nutmeg powder
- 2–3 tbsp Parmesan cheese, ground
- pie crust
- 2 tbsp butter

## DIRECTIONS:

1. Brown the snipe meat and onions in butter for 10–15 minutes.
2. Add mushrooms, sour cream, and cooking rum.
3. Bring to a boil and simmer for another 15 minutes.
4. Add chestnut, cinnamon, nutmeg, and Parmesan.
5. Glaze your baking dish with butter and spread the pie crust across the bottom and sides.
6. Add the filling and top with more pie crust.
7. Bake for 20–30 minutes at 390 °F.

## FACTS AND STATS:

*One of the fascinating statistics about snipe in Canada is their unique aerial courtship display. Male snipes perform a remarkable display during the breeding season, which involves flying in a zigzag pattern high in the air while making a distinctive drumming sound with their wings. This display can last for several minutes and is used to attract females. Another interesting statistic is that snipes are known for their long bills, which they use to probe for insects and other invertebrates in the mud and soil. The bill of a snipe is not only long, but it is also flexible, allowing the bird to probe deeper into the soil to find prey. Snipe are also known for their excellent camouflage, which helps them blend into their surroundings and avoid predators. Their plumage is a mixture of browns, grays, and blacks, which allows them to blend into the vegetation and mudflats where they are typically found.*

# PANFRIED WOODCOCK RISOTTO

Braising is a slow-cooking technique that is great for tough cuts of meat but can also be used for woodcock. Heat a Dutch oven over medium-high heat. Add some oil and brown the woodcock on all sides. Add some vegetables and liquid, such as broth or wine, and bring to a simmer. Cover the Dutch oven and cook in the oven at 325°F (163°C) for about 1 hour or until the woodcock is tender. No matter which technique you choose, let the woodcock rest for a few minutes before serving. This will allow the juices to redistribute and make for a more flavorful and tender bird.

### SERVING SIZE: 4

### INGREDIENTS:

- 1 lb woodcock meat, chopped
- 2 cups brown rice
- 2 tbsp butter
- 1 cup chicken stock
- 1 tsp cumin powder
- 1 tsp garlic powder
- salt and pepper, to taste
- 1 tsp cilantro
- 1 tsp mint

### DIRECTIONS:

1. Soak the brown rice for at least 1–2 hours before cooking.
2. Brown the chopped woodcock meat in butter for 10 minutes with onions and carrots.
3. Add the rice and stir-fry for another 10 minutes. If needed, add more butter.
4. Once the dish is crispy, drizzle with chicken stock to achieve the desired texture and softness.
5. Approximately 10 minutes before the dish is finished, add cumin powder, garlic powder, salt, pepper, cilantro, and mint. You can add any seasoning you like!

## FACTS AND STATS:

*The woodcock is an important species for conservation in Canada. Woodcock are known for their unique courtship displays, which involve the male performing a series of aerial maneuvers, such as spiraling, diving, and zigzagging. These displays are often accompanied by a distinctive "peent" call that can be heard from a distance. Woodcock are primarily nocturnal birds, which means they are most active at night. They feed on various insects, including earthworms, beetles, and moths. Woodcock hunting is a popular pastime in Canada, especially in the eastern provinces. Hunters use specially trained dogs to locate and flush out the birds, then shoot on the wing. The Canadian Wildlife Service has designated the woodcock as a species of special concern, meaning it is at risk of becoming threatened or endangered if its habitat is not managed correctly.*

# PERKY PESTO PIGEON TARTS

Pan-searing is just about building flavor and friends! Use a frying pan over high heat. The best pans to use are cast-iron or stainless steel. Add a tin layer of butter; 1 Tablespoon. Pat the pigeon dry to prevent steaming. Don't put too much in the frying pan. Place it into a skillet, and enjoy a drink! Moving it will interfere with the golden browning. To ensure you have even cooking and avoid steaming, put too much meat in the frying pan. Make a couple of pans if you have to! Friends will be waiting in anticipation waiting for the next one!

### SERVING SIZE: 4-6

### INGREDIENTS:

- 1 lb pigeon meat, deboned and diced
- 1 loaf of bread
- 1 tsp orange zest
- salt and pepper, to taste
- 1 tsp dill
- 1 tsp thyme
- 1 tsp mint
- 4-6 cups pesto sauce

**FOR PESTO SAUCE**

- 4 cups fresh basil leaves, de-stemmed
- 4 tbsp walnuts
- 2 whole garlic cloves
- 1 cup olive oil
- 1 cup Parmesan cheese, ground
- 1 tbsp lemon juice (optional)

### DIRECTIONS:

1. Preheat your oven to 320 °F.
2. Make your pesto by combining fresh basil, walnuts, and garlic.
3. Put through a food processor for a minute, then add the olive oil and Parmesan.
4. Process some more until you have a creamy texture.
5. You can add the lemon juice to the sauce or top the entire dish once finished.
6. Unpack your loaf of bread and remove the crusts from each slice.
7. Roll slices of bread until flat.

8. Cut into circles and mold the bread into the muffin tins.
9. Bake for 10–15 minutes or until crispy.
10. Brown the pigeon meat in butter.
11. Season with orange zest, salt, pepper, mint, dill, and thyme to taste.
12. Fill each tart with pesto sauce and top with pieces of pigeon meat.
13. Serve and enjoy!

### FACTS AND STATS:

*Pigeons have a remarkable sense of hearing and can detect sounds at frequencies beyond the range of human hearing. Pigeons can recognize themselves in mirrors, a trait shared by only a few other animal species, including dolphins and great apes. Pigeons are incredibly adaptable birds and thrive in various environments, from urban cities to rural farmland. Pigeons are monogamous birds and often mate for life, raising multiple broods of offspring together. Pigeons are considered a delicacy in many countries, including France, where they are commonly served in upscale restaurants.*

# WITTY WILD TURKEY AND MUSHROOM RISOTTO

The National Wild Turkey Federation is a non-profit organization conserves wild turkeys and their habitats and promotes responsible turkey hunting practices. According to the National Wild Turkey Federation, there are over 7 million wild turkeys in the United States, a significant increase from less than 30,000 in the early 1900s. Alabama has the longest turkey hunting season in the United States, from March 15th to April 30th and from May 1st to May 10th.

## SERVING SIZE: 4-6

## INGREDIENTS:

- 1-2 lb wild turkey meat, cubed
- 1 cup chicken broth
- ½ cup white wine
- 1 cup mushrooms, sliced
- 1 cup peas
- 1 cup carrots, chopped
- 1 cup onions, chopped
- 1 ½ cups brown rice
- 2 tbsp butter
- 1 tbsp dill
- 1 tbsp celery leaf, chopped
- ½ tsp cumin powder

## DIRECTIONS:

1. Sauté the turkey meat in butter with rice, carrots, and onions over medium heat with drizzles of chicken broth for 15-20 minutes.
2. Add the remaining broth, sliced mushrooms, and wine.
3. Bring to a short boil and let simmer for another 30-45 minutes or as needed.
4. Add dill, celery, and cumin powder for 10 minutes before taking off the heat.

## FACTS AND STATS:

*Turkey hunting can be done with various equipment in Canada, including shotguns, rifles, and archery equipment. According to the Canadian Wildlife Federation, wild turkey populations in Canada have been steadily increasing since their reintroduction to the country in the 1980s. Turkeys are also an important part of Canada's agricultural industry, with over 200 turkey farms. The province of Ontario has the largest population of wild turkeys in Canada, with an estimated 100,000 birds living in the province.*

# CHAPTER 3
# Delicious Deer

Deer is craved for its rich and earthy flavors. These flavors are heightened in those cuts of meat. Deer's main diet consists of acorns, berries, corn, alfalfa, and other herbs. The best cut of meat on the deer is tenderloins & backstrap. The backstrap & tenderloin are lean, tender meat compared to the hind quarters, which are the toughest part. When field-dressing your deer, you want to cut the fat and silverskin off as much as possible. Fat on deer is pungent, and if you get a piece of silver skin, you will be chewing on it for months. The meat from the neck and shoulders is good for grinding into hamburger, and the ribs and brisket are wonderful for braising and stewing.

**Breakfast**
Deer Egg Rolls
Venison Liver Pate
Creamy Venison Salad
Creamy Venison Salad Sandwich
Delicious Venison Wrap
Panfried Venison With Veggies
Venison Morning Hash
Venison Breakfast Fried Egg Toast
Fried Egg and Venison Patties
Venison Breakfast Sausage
Venison Breakfast Pie
Venison Mini Quiche

**Lunch**
Venison Roast Sandwich
Venison Pasta Salad
Venison Kebab
Ground Breaded Venison Kebab
Light Venison Stew
Venison and Wild Mushroom Medley
Venison Pie
Light Dumpling Venison Broth
Venison Bites in Blueberry Sauce
Spaghetti in Venison Sauce
Spaghetti Mushrooms and Venison

**Dinner**
Venison Medallions in Mushroom Sauce
Deer Stew
Deer Pepper Stew
Deer and Broccoli Risotto
Venison Steak Tartare
Venison in Garlic Sauce
Fried Venison With Sweet Potatoes
Breaded Venison With White Mushroom Sauce
Fried Venison Chops With Tomato Sauce
Venison Roast
Easy Venison Wellington With Blueberry Sauce
Baked Venison Pasta
Mouth-Watering Whitetail Axis Bacon Grilled Cheeseburger

# BREAKFAST

# DEER EGG ROLLS

**Aging deer improves flavor, so consider letting your deer hang and age. Hang a whole deer in a refrigerator or walk-in cooler. You don't want to freeze the meat, but keep it cool. Ensure adequate airflow and the temperature is between 34°F to 37°F to prevent bacteria growth. Hanging allows air to circulate evenly through. During this time, a silverskin forms on the meat that must be removed before cooking or freezing. The time you want to let it age is up to you. I like to hang mine for a week. The longer you allow it to age, the less gamey flavor. Aging produces a smoother, firmer texture and desirable flavor of acorns and herbs.**

### SERVING SIZE: 4

### INGREDIENTS:

- 1 lb deer meat, shredded
- 8 whole eggs
- ½ cup mushrooms, chopped
- ½ cup spinach, chopped
- ½ cup bell peppers, chopped
- ½ cup onions, chopped
- ½ tbsp garlic, minced
- 3 oz Parmesan cheese, shredded
- 2 tbsp butter
- salt and pepper, to taste

### DIRECTIONS:

1. Heat a frying pan and fry the deer, mushrooms, peppers, onions, and garlic in butter at medium heat for 15–20 minutes.
2. Take out of the pan and transfer into a bowl.
3. Mix the eggs with the cheese, and pour a small amount (⅙–¼ or less) into the pan.
4. Fry a smaller piece of the omelet in butter for a minute so the top is still raw.
5. Add small filling parts and turn the omelet over, forming a roll.
6. Fry each roll on both sides until you're out of eggs and filling.

# FACTS AND STATS:

*North American whitetail deer is one of North America's most abundant and widespread big game animals, with an estimated population of around 32 million. The range of whitetail deer covers most of the continental United States and southern Canada, although their population density varies widely from region to region. Whitetail deer are adaptable and can be found in various habitats, including forests, grasslands, and agricultural fields.*

# VENISON LIVER PATE

Cooking whitetail deer requires specific techniques and considerations, but it can be a delicious and satisfying meal with the proper preparation and cooking methods. It is important to cook whitetail deer to the appropriate temperature to ensure it is safe. The USDA recommends cooking deer meat to an internal temperature of 160 degrees Fahrenheit for safety. However, some prefer to cook deer meat at a lower temperature for a more tender, juicy result. After cooking, it is essential to let the meat rest for several minutes before slicing or serving. This allows the juices to redistribute throughout the meat, resulting in a more flavorful and tender piece.

### SERVING SIZE: 4

### INGREDIENTS:

- 1 lb venison liver
- 1 cup onions, chopped
- 1 cup shallots, chopped
- 2 whole garlic cloves
- 2 whole carrots
- 1 cup beef stock
- ½ cup brandy
- salt and pepper, to taste
- 1 tsp nutmeg powder
- 1 tbsp celery leaf
- ½ cup chopped parsley
- 1 tbsp dill
- 1 tbsp red pepper powder
- ½ tbsp cumin powder
- buns or toast slices, as needed

### DIRECTIONS:

1. Sauté the venison liver in butter with onions, shallots, garlic cloves, and carrots on low heat for 30–45 minutes.
2. Add beef stock and brandy, and season with salt, pepper, nutmeg, celery leaf, parsley, dill, red pepper powder, and cumin powder.
3. Simmer on low heat for another 15–20 minutes.
4. While simmering, stir and mash the meat with vegetables.
5. Transfer into a food processor and process until creamy, soft, and homogenous.
6. Serve on buns or slices of toast.

## FACTS AND STATS:

*Male whitetail deer, or bucks, typically weigh between 130-300 pounds, while females, or does, typically weigh between 90-200 pounds. Antler size and shape vary widely among individuals and can be used to estimate a deer's age and health. They have distinctive reddish-brown fur in the summer and grayish-brown fur in the winter. They also have a white underbelly and a white tail with a characteristic "flag" that they raise when alarmed. Male whitetail deer grow and shed their antlers annually.*

# CREAMY VENISON SALAD

Whitetail deer has a rich, gamey flavor that pairs well with bold seasonings and spices. Some popular flavorings for deer meat include garlic, rosemary, thyme, and sage. Additionally, using a marinade or dry rub can help add flavor depth and tenderize the meat.

## SERVING SIZE: 4

## INGREDIENTS:

- 1 lb venison meat, chopped
- 2 cups cream cheese
- 2 cups onion, chopped
- 2 tbsp red pepper powder
- Barbecue sauce to taste
- ½ cup red wine
- 2 tbsp butter
- slices of toast or buns, as needed
- salt and pepper, to taste

## DIRECTIONS:

1. Brown the venison in butter for 15–20 minutes.
2. Add red pepper powder, red wine, salt, and pepper.
3. Simmer for another 10–15 minutes.
4. Mix the cream cheese and chopped onions in a bowl.
5. Add the meat and mix.
6. Serve on toast or buns topped with barbecue sauce.

## FACTS AND STATS:

*Whitetail deer are a popular game animal in North America, with millions of hunters pursuing them each year. In the USA, they are hunted with rifles, shotguns, bows, and muzzleloaders during various hunting seasons. The management of whitetail deer populations is an essential aspect of wildlife conservation in North America. State and provincial wildlife agencies use multiple methods to monitor and regulate deer populations to ensure healthy and sustainable populations.*

# CREAMY VENISON SALAD SANDWICH

Cooking whitetail deer can be a unique and enjoyable experience, but it does require some specific techniques to ensure that the meat is tender, juicy, and flavorful. The first step in cooking whitetail deer is to prepare the meat properly. This includes trimming off any fat or connective tissue and removing any silver skin. It is crucial to keep the meat moist while cooking, so marinating the meat for several hours or overnight is recommended.

## SERVING SIZE: 4

## INGREDIENTS:

- 1 lb venison, chopped
- 2 tbsp butter
- ½ cup brandy
- 1 cup chicken stock
- salt and pepper, to taste
- buns or slices of toast, as needed
- tomato slices, as needed
- pickle slices, as needed
- cheese slices, as needed
- lettuce leaf, as needed
- 2–4 tbsp cream cheese

## DIRECTIONS:

1. Sauté the venison in butter and brandy for 10–15 minutes.
2. Add chicken stock, salt, and pepper.
3. Top the buns with cream cheese, slices of tomatoes, pickles, cheese, and lettuce.
4. Put the venison between the buns and enjoy!

## FACTS AND STATS:

*Whitetail deer hunting is a significant economic driver in many rural areas of North America, generating billions of dollars in revenue each year through license sales, equipment purchases, and tourism. Whitetail Deer are typically solitary or live in small family groups consisting of a mother and her offspring. During the breeding season, males compete to mate with females, often engaging in fierce battles with their antlers. Whitetail deer are also known for their keen senses, including exceptional hearing and sense of smell, which they use to detect predators and avoid danger.*

# DELICIOUS VENISON WRAP

**Several cooking techniques work well for whitetail deer. One popular method is to slow-cook the meat in a crockpot, using a flavorful liquid such as beef broth or red wine to add moisture and depth of flavor. Another option is to grill or sear the meat quickly over high heat, which can help retain the meat's natural juices and flavors.**

## SERVING SIZE: 4

## INGREDIENTS:

- 1 lb venison, ground
- 2 tbsp butter
- 1 cup tomato sauce
- ½ cup red wine
- salt and pepper, to taste
- 1 tbsp celery leaf
- 1 cayenne pepper, chopped
- 1 tsp oregano
- 1 tsp thyme
- 4–6 tortillas
- 4–6 tbsp cream cheese
- 3–4 tbsp Parmesan cheese, grated
- 2 onions, sliced
- 2–3 paprikas, sliced
- 2 tomatoes, sliced

## DIRECTIONS:

1. Brown the ground venison in butter with tomato sauce and red wine for 10–15 minutes.
2. Add salt, pepper, celery leaf, cayenne pepper, oregano, and thyme.
3. Continue simmering until there's no excess fluid.
4. Heat tortillas as instructed by the manufacturer.
5. Top the tortillas with cream cheese, Parmesan, onion, paprika, and tomato slices.
6. Add the desired amount of ground venison, wrap, and enjoy! Remember, you can replace all the vegetables with those you like better! Optionally, you can also add olives, mushrooms, cabbage, or anything else that comes to mind. You can also add your favorite salsa.

## FACTS AND STATS:

*The North American whitetail deer (Odocoileus virginianus) is a Deer species native to the United States, Canada, Mexico, Central America, and South America. The whitetail deer's coat is reddish-brown in the summer and grayish-brown in the winter. They have a white belly and throat and their namesake white tail. The average weight of a male whitetail deer is around 150-300 pounds, while females weigh about 90-200 pounds.*

# PANFRIED VENISON WITH VEGGIES

Field dressing a whitetail deer is an important step in how your deer will taste! If not done properly, the meat will not be good. Here are the steps to field dress a deer in the easiest way:

1. Use a knife to cut around the rectum and anus of the deer. (There is a nifty tool I use now that speeds up the process and makes life easier called" Butt Out!")

2. Place the Deer on its back with its legs spread apart.

3. Use a sharp knife to make a shallow cut from the base of the breastbone to the anus, taking care not to puncture any organs.

4. Be careful around the genitals, and be aware some states/provinces require you to leave the genitals attached.

5. Reach inside the body cavity and carefully cut the diaphragm away from the ribcage, then gently pull out the intestines, not puncturing them. Field-dressing Deer continues the next recipe…

### SERVING SIZE: 4

### INGREDIENTS:

- 1 lb venison, ground
- 1 cup peas
- 1 cup onions, chopped
- 1 cup carrots, chopped
- 4–5 eggs
- 1 cup flour
- 1 cup sour cream
- salt and pepper, to taste
- 1 tsp garlic powder
- 1 tsp ginger powder
- 1 tsp thyme
- 1 cup cheddar cheese, grated

## DIRECTIONS:

1. Mix the eggs with flour, sour cream, salt, pepper, garlic powder, ginger powder, and thyme.
2. Sauté ground venison with peas, onions, and carrots in butter for 10–15 minutes.
3. Drain any excess liquid and mix with the batter in a bowl.
4. Add grated cheddar cheese.
5. Fry in butter until crispy.

## FACTS AND STATS:

*Whitetail deer are herbivores and eat various plants, including grasses, leaves, fruits, and nuts. Whitetail deer have a lifespan of 6-14 years in the wild but can live up to 20 years in captivity. Whitetail deer are typically found in forested areas, but they can also be found in grasslands, swamps, and agricultural fields.*

# VENISON MORNING HASH

Field-dressing Deer continues…

6. Reach inside the body cavity and carefully remove the heart, lungs, and liver, careful not to puncture them.

7. Clean the inside of the body cavity, removing any remaining blood, tissue, or debris.

8. Rinse the body cavity with clean water, removing debris or blood.

9. After the Deer has been field dressed, it can be transported to your preferred location for further processing and preparation.

It is important to note that proper field dressing techniques are important to ensure the quality and safety of the meat. It is very crucial to use clean tools to prevent contamination. If you need help with how to field dress a deer, it is recommended to seek assistance from an experienced hunter or professional. If you are in Wildlife Management Unit (WMU 28) in Ontario, Canada, give me, Pat Gatz, a call, and you can field-dress in Hunting for Greatness shop!

## SERVING SIZE: 4

## INGREDIENTS:

- 1 lb venison meat, ground
- 1 cup leeks, chopped
- 1 tsp garlic powder
- 1 cup carrots, chopped
- 1 cup mushrooms, sliced
- 2–3 tbsp butter
- ½ cup red wine
- 4–5 eggs
- 1 cup sour cream
- 1 tsp ginger powder
- 1 tsp orange zest
- 1 cup Parmesan or cheddar cheese, shredded

## DIRECTIONS:

1. Sauté ground venison with leeks, garlic, carrots, and mushrooms for 10–15 minutes in butter, adding drizzles of wine to avoid sticking.
2. Allow simmering until the excess liquid has evaporated.
3. Whisk the eggs and mix with sour cream, ginger powder, and orange zest.
4. Pour over the meat and veggies and stir so the dish has a more scramble-like consistency.
5. Serve sprinkled with Parmesan or cheddar cheese to taste.

## FACTS AND STATS:

The largest whitetail deer ever recorded was shot in Saskatchewan, Canada, in 1993 by Milo Hanson. It weighed 402 pounds and had a typical antler score of 213 5/8 inches. The most fascinating fact was that it was 3 ½ to 4 ½ years old. There is no question that Buck wasn't even at its prime yet! The Boone and Crockett Club, a conservation organization that keeps records of big game animals, lists the top ten biggest typical whitetail deer ever harvested in North America. All of them were harvested in either the United States or Canada.

# VENISON BREAKFAST FRIED EGG TOAST

Here are the different cuts of a whitetail deer for the freezer. Use a saw or sharp knife to remove the legs of the deer at the joints. Start by making a cut around the leg bone and then separate the joint. This will give you four leg quarters. The backstraps are long, tender cuts of meat that run along the spine on either side. To remove them, make a cut along the spine from the neck to the hindquarters, careful not to damage the meat. Use a knife to remove the backstraps from the spine carefully. The tenderloins are small, tender cuts of meat that run along the inside of the deer's ribcage. To remove them, use a knife to cut along the ribcage and remove the tenderloins carefully.

### SERVING SIZE: 4

### INGREDIENTS:

- 1 lb venison fillets
- 2–3 tbsp butter
- 4 eggs
- 1 cup beef broth
- salt and pepper, to taste
- 1 tsp garlic powder
- 1 tbsp celery leaf, chopped
- 3–4 paprikas, sliced
- 1 onion, sliced
- 1 tomato, sliced
- slices of toast or buns, as needed
- 1–2 tbsp sour cream
- 1–2 tbsp mayonnaise
- 1 cup of your favorite salsa
- cheese, grated to taste

### DIRECTIONS:

1. Melt the butter in a frying pan and fry the eggs.
2. Set eggs aside and pop in venison fillets.
3. Brown the fillets on each side for a couple of minutes and drizzle with beef broth as needed to prevent sticking.
4. Season with salt, pepper, garlic powder, and celery leaf.
5. Let the fillets simmer for 10–15 more minutes, and add slices of paprika, onions, and tomatoes.
6. The dish is finished with cooking once the vegetables have softened and the meat is tender and cooked.

7. Grab your toast slices and top them with sour cream, mayo, and your favorite salsa.
8. Place one fillet on each slice of toast and layer a fried egg over it.
9. Sprinkle with the seasoning you like and the grated cheese to taste.

### FACTS AND STATS:

*In the United States, whitetail deer are found in every state except for Hawaii. However, their population is most dense in the Midwest and Southeast regions. In Canada, whitetail deer are found in every province except Newfoundland and Labrador. Their population is most dense in the southern regions of the country. Whitetail deer have a mating season in the fall, known as the rut. During this time, males compete for females by fighting and displaying their antlers.*

# FRIED EGG AND VENISON PATTIES

The shoulder meat is a flavorful, tough cut of meat that can be used for stews, roasts, or ground meat. To remove the shoulder meat, make a cut along the shoulder blade and use a saw or sharp knife to separate it from the bone. The neck meat is a flavorful, tough cut of meat that can be used for stews, roasts, or ground meat. To remove the neck meat, make a cut at the base of the skull and use a saw or sharp knife to separate it from the spine.

## SERVING SIZE: 4

## INGREDIENTS:

- 1 lb venison, ground
- salt and pepper, to taste
- ½ tbsp red pepper powder
- 1 tbsp celery leaf, chopped
- 1 tsp garlic powder
- 1 tsp ginger powder
- ½ cup onions, chopped
- ½ cup cheddar cheese, grated
- 2–3 tbsp butter
- 4 eggs

## DIRECTIONS:

1. Season the raw ground venison with salt, pepper, red pepper powder, celery leaf, garlic powder, and ginger powder. Mix in a bowl so that the seasoning is distributed evenly.
2. Add chopped onions and cheddar cheese and mix thoroughly once again.
3. Shape the mix into patties.
4. Melt the butter in a frying pan and fry the patties on each side for a couple of minutes.
5. Once the patties are fried, continue by frying eggs and serve them next to the patties.

## FACTS AND STATS:

*In the wild, whitetail deer have several predators, including wolves, coyotes, mountain lions, and bears. Whitetail deer are an important part of many ecosystems and play a role in maintaining plant diversity and controlling populations of smaller animals.*

# VENISON BREAKFAST SAUSAGE

**Suggestions for what you can do with each cut of deer. The neck you can use for stews, soups, braises, and ground hamburger. Shoulders, you can use stews, soups, jerky, sausages, hamburger, and roasts. Ribs you can braise or use in ground meat. Shanks are good for stews, soups, osso buco, roasts, hamburgers, and sausages. Osso buco is the deer's hard-working muscle starts tough, but the proper method will yield a tender and decadent dish.**

## SERVING SIZE: 4

## INGREDIENTS:

- 1 lb venison, ground
- 1 tbsp red pepper flakes
- 1 tsp garlic powder
- 1 tsp cumin powder
- ½ tsp ginger powder
- 2–3 tbsp butter
- 4 eggs
- 8–10 bacon slices
- salt and pepper, to taste

## DIRECTIONS:

1. Start by making your sausage meat. Mix the ground venison with red pepper flakes, garlic powder, cumin powder, and ginger powder.
2. Shape the meat into sausages and brown in butter for 10–15 minutes, turning the sausages to be fried evenly.
3. Next, make your omelet by frying the bacon, pouring the eggs over, and seasoning with salt and pepper.
4. Serve next to the venison sausages, and enjoy!

## FACTS AND STATS:

*Before you head out to hunt, scout the area where you plan to hunt. Knowing where the deer are likely to be will increase your chances of success. Look for signs of deer activity, such as tracks, droppings, and bedding areas. Deers have a keen sense of smell, so using scent control measures such as scent-blocking clothing, scent eliminator sprays, and avoiding strong-smelling foods and soaps is important.*

# VENISON BREAKFAST PIE

Before you observe whitetail deer, take some time to learn about their behavior, habits, and natural history. This will help you understand what to look for and how to approach them without causing undue stress. When observing whitetail deer, it's important to dress in appropriate clothing that is comfortable and non-restrictive. Neutral colors such as greens, browns, and grays can help you blend in with your surroundings.

## SERVING SIZE: 4

## INGREDIENTS:

- 1 lb venison, ground
- salt and pepper, to taste
- 1 tsp red pepper powder
- 1 tbsp celery leaf, chopped
- 6 eggs
- 2 cups flour
- 1 cup of milk
- 1 cup cheese, shredded
- 8–10 bacon slices
- ½ cup paprika, chopped
- 1 cup mushrooms, sliced
- 3 tbsp butter

## DIRECTIONS:

1. Preheat your oven to 390 °F.
2. Brown the ground venison in 2 tbsp butter and season with salt, pepper, red pepper powder, and celery leaf.
3. Mix 5 eggs in a bowl, add milk, shredded cheese, bacon, paprikas, mushrooms, and ground venison, and stir well.
4. Transfer into a baking dish glazed with 1 tbsp butter at the bottom and sides.
5. Mix one more egg with flour and salt to create the pie crust.
6. Flatten the pie crust to the size of the baking dish.
7. Glaze the baking dish with butter and line it with the pie crust.
8. Add the meat filling and sprinkle with cheddar cheese.
9. Bake for 20–30 minutes at 390 °F.

## FACTS AND STATS:

*Whether you're using a rifle, bow, or crossbow, make sure you choose a weapon you're comfortable with and proficient in using. Be patient because hunting whitetail deer will require all the patience you have. You may have to wait for several hours or even days before you have an opportunity to take a shot. Whitetail deer are the second most challenging animal to hunt in North America.*

# VENISON MINI QUICHE

Whitetail deer are often shy and skittish, so using binoculars can help you observe them from a distance without causing them stress. Look for movement and listen for sounds such as rustling leaves or twigs breaking. When observing whitetail deer, respecting their personal space and not getting too close is important. Approaching too closely can cause them to become stressed and dangerous for you. Male deer in the rut has been known to attack hunters. Be careful, friends, at all times!

## SERVING SIZE: 4

## INGREDIENTS:

- 1 lb venison, ground
- ½ cup wine
- salt and pepper, to taste
- 1 tsp cilantro
- 1 tsp dill
- 1 tsp thyme
- 5–6 eggs
- 1 cup flour
- 1 cup sour cream
- 1 cup cheese, shredded
- 8–10 bacon slices
- 1 cup mushrooms, sliced
- ½ cup pickles, sliced
- ½ cup paprika, sliced
- 1 tsp garlic powder
- 2 tbsp butter

## DIRECTIONS:

1. Brown the venison in butter with drizzles of wine and season with salt, pepper, cilantro, dill, and thyme.
2. Mix the eggs with the flour, sour cream, shredded cheese, bacon, mushrooms, pickles, and paprikas in a larger bowl. Add more salt, pepper, and garlic powder.
3. Mix the fried venison with the batter and distribute it in quiche molds.
4. Bake for 20–30 minutes at 390 °F.
5. If you feel like baking outside of your oven, you can also take out a spoonful of the batter and fry in butter in a regular frying pan. Ensure that all of the quiches are fried evenly and that each side gets to cook for a few minutes.

## FACTS AND STATS:

*Using decoys and calls can be an effective way to attract deer. Decoys can simulate a deer, and calls can mimic vocalizations such as grunts, bleats, and snorts. The rut is the breeding season for deer, and it typically occurs in November. During this time, bucks are more active and are more likely to respond to calls and decoys.*

# LUNCH

# VENISON ROAST SANDWICH

**Practice Good Shot Placement:** When you can take a shot, it's important to practice good shot placement. Try to position yourself upwind from where you expect the deer to be. Aim for the deer's vitals, which are located in the chest cavity. Deer rely heavily on their sense of smell, so it's important to hunt with the wind in your favor.

### SERVING SIZE: 4

### INGREDIENTS:

- 1 lb venison meat, sliced
- 1 onion, minced
- 2–3 tbsp butter
- 1–2 tbsp vegetable oil
- 2 cups bread crumbs
- salt and pepper, to taste
- 1 tbsp celery leaf, chopped
- 1 tsp garlic powder
- 1 tsp cumin powder
- ½ tsp ginger powder
- 4–5 potatoes, halved
- 1 cup sweet potatoes, diced
- 1 cup mushrooms, whole
- 2–3 paprikas, sliced
- 2–3 tomatoes, sliced
- 1 cup beef broth
- buns or slices of toast, as needed
- 2–3 tbsp sour cream

### DIRECTIONS:

1. Glaze a baking dish with butter.
2. Preheat your oven to 390 °F.
3. Dredge the venison slices first in vegetable oil and then in the mix of bread crumbs, salt, pepper, celery leaf, garlic powder, cumin powder, and ginger powder.
4. Do the same with potatoes, sweet potatoes, paprikas, and tomatoes.
5. Pour the beef broth over the dish before roasting.
6. Roast for about 20 minutes at 390 °F and pop in the buns. You can soak the cut-up sides at the bottom of the dish to let the outer parts of the buns roast and get crispy.
7. Roast for another 10 minutes and take out of the oven.
8. Remove the buns first and serve them on plates. Top with some sour cream.

9. Use a regular spoon to pick up the residue broth from the bottom of the dish, and then use it to glaze the buns, meat, and vegetables.
10. Top the buns with onions, potatoes, mushrooms, tomatoes, and paprikas first. Then, you can add slices of meat between two buns or on top of each bun.

### FACTS AND STATS:

*When observing whitetail deer, it's important to watch them from a distance and avoid disturbing their natural behavior. Avoid making loud noises, sudden movements, or shining bright lights on them. Observing whitetail deer in the wild will take time. Be prepared to spend days waiting for the right opportunity to observe them.*

# VENISON PASTA SALAD

**Whitetail deer hunting often requires sitting in a stand or blind for long periods of time, so make sure you dress appropriately for the weather conditions. Hunting can be dangerous, so take all necessary safety precautions, such as wearing a harness when hunting from a tree stand and identifying your target before taking a shot.**

## SERVING SIZE: 4

## INGREDIENTS:

- 1 lb venison meat, diced
- 2–3 tbsp butter
- salt and pepper, to taste
- 1 cup tomato sauce
- ½ cup red wine
- 1 tsp oregano
- 1 tsp basil
- 1 tsp thyme
- 1 tsp dill
- 1 pack of dry pasta
- 1 tbsp orange juice
- 1 tbsp vinegar
- 1 cup Parmesan or cheddar cheese, shredded
- 1 cup tomatoes, diced
- 1 cup paprikas, sliced
- 1 cup cucumber, diced

## DIRECTIONS:

1. Brown the venison in butter and season with salt and pepper for 10–15 minutes.
2. Add the tomato sauce, red wine, oregano, basil, thyme, and dill, and let simmer for 15 more minutes.
3. Cook the pasta per package instructions and mix it with fresh paprikas, tomatoes, and cucumbers.
4. Season with a bit of salt and pepper.
5. Mix in venison and tomato sauce.
6. Drizzle with orange juice and vinegar, and top with generous cheese.

## FACTS AND STATS:

*Deers communicate with body language, so learning to read their signals can help you better understand their behavior. For example, a deer with its ears laid back may feel threatened or nervous. The rut is the breeding season for whitetail deer and can be an exciting time to observe them. Bucks are more active and vocal during this time, and you may be able to witness courtship behavior such as chasing and vocalizing.*

# VENISON KEBAB

Don't shoot bucks that look insecure because dominant bucks hold their heads high and walk like a champ with their tails held straight out. A subordinate buck walks with its head low, stiff legs, hunched back, and keeps its tail between its legs. If you see a nice buck in a subordinate posture, consider waiting a moment because there could be a giant buck in the area.

## SERVING SIZE: 4

## INGREDIENTS:

- 1 lb venison, sliced
- ½ cup red wine
- 1 tsp garlic
- 1 tbsp olive oil
- 1 tbsp celery leaf
- 1 tsp dill
- 3–4 potatoes, quartered
- 1 onion, quartered
- 1 cup sweet potatoes, cut into thicker slices
- 4 carrots, quartered widthwise
- 4 paprikas, quartered
- 6–8 kebab sticks

## DIRECTIONS:

1. Marinade the venison meat the night before or at least a few hours before cooking.
2. Make the marinade by mixing the wine with garlic, olive oil, celery leaf, and dill. Dredge the meat in it and let it sit in the fridge.
3. Run the kebab sticks through the slices of meat, potatoes, onion, sweet potatoes, carrots, and paprika.
4. Fry in butter for 10 minutes on each side.
5. Serve with your favorite salsa or sauce.

## FACTS AND STATS:

*Whitetail deer are most active at dawn and dusk, so these times can be the best for observing them. Be sure to arrive early and stay until after sunset to maximize your chances of seeing them. When watching whitetail deer, it's important to respect their natural environment and leave it as you found it. Do not litter, damage vegetation, or disturb other wildlife.*

# GROUND BREADED VENISON KEBAB

**Whitetail deer have a long and fascinating history that dates back thousands of years. They are native to North America and are believed to have evolved from a group of deer living in Europe and Asia around 5 million years ago during the Pliocene epoch.**

### SERVING SIZE: 4

### INGREDIENTS:

- 1 lb venison, ground
- 1 cup onion, chopped
- 1 cup paprika, finely chopped
- 1 tbsp parsley, finely chopped
- 2–3 garlic cloves, minced
- salt and pepper, to taste
- 2 tsp red pepper flakes
- 1 tsp ground cumin
- 1 tsp cayenne pepper
- 1 tsp ginger powder
- 3–4 eggs
- 2 tbsp sour cream
- 3 cups bread crumbs
- 2–3 tbsp butter

### DIRECTIONS:

1. Mix the ground venison with chopped onions, paprikas, parsley, and minced garlic.
2. Season with salt and pepper, then add red pepper flakes, ground cumin, cayenne pepper, and ginger powder.
3. Mix the seasoning with the meat thoroughly and shape it into kebabs. Run a stick through each kebab.
4. Break the eggs and whisk them. Mix in the sour cream.
5. Dredge each kebab in the egg and then in bread crumbs.
6. Fry the kebabs on each side for 5–6 minutes, or deep-fry them if you prefer.

## FACTS AND STATS:

*As the climate changed and forests expanded, deer populations thrived and diversified. By the time humans arrived in North America around 15,000 years ago, whitetail deer were widespread and adapted to various habitats. Native American tribes hunted whitetail deer for food, clothing, and tools and developed a deep respect for these animals. European settlers later arrived in North America and began hunting deer for their meat and hides.*

# LIGHT VENISON STEW

In the 20th century, whitetail deer populations declined due to habitat loss and over-hunting. Conservation efforts were put in place to protect the species, and populations began to recover. Today, whitetail deer are one of North America's most common and widespread deer species and are an important game animal for hunters. They also play an essential role in their ecosystems as herbivores and prey for predators such as wolves and coyotes.

### SERVING SIZE: 4

### INGREDIENTS:

- 1 lb venison meat, diced
- 1 cup onions, chopped
- 1 cup carrots, chopped
- 1 cup parsley, chopped
- 2 cups potatoes, diced
- 1 cup sweet potatoes, diced
- 1 paprika, chopped
- 1 tbsp red pepper powder
- ½ cup tomato sauce
- a pinch of salt and pepper
- 1 tbsp celery leaf
- 2 tbsp butter or vegetable oil
- 4 cups beef broth

### DIRECTIONS:

1. Sauté the venison with onions, carrots, and parsley in butter or vegetable oil for 10–15 minutes on medium heat.
2. Add the potatoes, sweet potatoes, paprika, and broth.
3. Bring to a boil and let simmer for 30–45 minutes.
4. Add red pepper powder, tomato sauce, salt, and celery leaf.
5. Simmer for another 10–15 minutes and take off the heat.

## FACTS AND STATS:

*The first whitetail deer fossils in North America date back to the Pleistocene epoch, around 1.75 million years ago. During this time, the continent was covered in glaciers, and the deer adapted to the harsh conditions by evolving longer legs and larger hooves for traveling over snow and ice. When the glaciers receded around 10,000 years ago, whitetail deer populations expanded and spread throughout North America. They thrived in a variety of habitats, including forests, grasslands, and wetlands.*

# VENISON AND WILD MUSHROOM MEDLEY

Native American tribes hunted whitetail deer for food, clothing, and other resources for thousands of years. They developed a deep understanding of the deer's behavior and habits and used various hunting techniques, including hunting with dogs, stalking, and using traps.

## SERVING SIZE: 4

### INGREDIENTS:

- 1 lb venison, chopped
- 2–3 tbsp butter
- 1 cup onions, chopped
- 1 cup beef broth
- 2 cups mushrooms, sliced
- 1 cup sour cream
- 1 egg
- salt and pepper, to taste
- 1 tbsp celery leaf, chopped
- 1 tsp cilantro
- 1 tbsp basil

### DIRECTIONS:

1. Melt the butter in a frying pan and sauté the venison with onions and broth on medium heat for 15–20 minutes.
2. Add the mushrooms, sour cream, egg, salt, pepper, celery leaf, cilantro, and basil.
3. Stir and simmer for another 15–20 minutes.

## FACTS AND STATS:

*With the arrival of European settlers, the whitetail deer population declined due to overhunting, habitat destruction, and disease. However, conservation efforts in the 20th century helped restore the deer population to health. Today, whitetail deer are one of North America's most common and widespread big game animals, and they continue to be an important part of North America's natural heritage.*

# VENISON PIE

The antlers of a whitetail deer can grow up to an inch per day during the summer months, making them one of the fastest-growing structures in the animal kingdom. Bucks (male deer) use their antlers to fight for dominance during the breeding season or rut. Whitetail deer shed their antlers annually.

## SERVING SIZE: 4

## INGREDIENTS:

- 1 lb venison, ground
- 2–3 tbsp butter
- 1 cup onions, chopped
- 1 cup peas
- 1 cup carrots, chopped
- Salt and pepper, to taste
- 1 tbsp sweet pepper powder
- 1 tsp cumin powder
- 1 tbsp celery leaf, chopped
- ½ cup sour cream
- 1 tbsp fresh mint, chopped

## DIRECTIONS:

1. Preheat your oven to 390 °F.
2. Melt the butter in a frying pan and sauté the meat with chopped onions, peas, and carrots.
3. After 10–15 minutes, add salt and pepper. Season with sweet pepper powder, cumin powder, celery leaf, and mint.
4. Bring to a soft boil, add sour cream, and stir.
5. Simmer for 15–20 more minutes.
6. Spread the pie crust across the bottom and sides of a baking dish glazed with butter.
7. Add the filling and top with another layer of pie crust.

## FACTS AND STATS:

*Whitetail deer can run up to 40 miles per hour and jump up to 10 feet vertically and 30 feet horizontally. Whitetail deer are excellent swimmers and can swim up to 13 miles per hour. During the winter, whitetail deer can survive on woody browse (such as twigs and buds) when other food sources are scarce.*

# LIGHT DUMPLING VENISON BROTH

The scientific name for whitetail deer is Odocoileus virginianus, which means "toothed grazer from Virginia" in Latin. In some Native American cultures, the whitetail deer symbolizes grace, agility, and spiritual strength.

## SERVING SIZE: 4

## INGREDIENTS:

- 10 cups beef broth
- 1 lb venison, chopped
- 1 whole onion
- 3–4 whole potatoes
- 1 whole parsley root
- 1 egg
- 4–5 tbsp cornstarch
- 1 tsp baking powder
- salt, to taste

## DIRECTIONS:

1. Pour the broth into a stockpot and add the meat, onion, potatoes, and parsley.
2. Bring to a boil and simmer on low-medium heat for another 45 minutes to an hour.
3. Break and whisk the egg. Add the cornstarch and baking powder. Season with salt and mix to create the dumpling batter.
4. Use a teaspoon to drop balls of batter into the boiling soup.
5. Simmer for 10–15 more minutes and take off the heat.

## FACTS AND STATS:

*Whitetail deer have a special adaptation called a Jacobson's organ, which allows them to detect pheromones (chemical signals) used for communication between individuals. Whitetail deer have a keen sense of smell, which they use to detect predators and other potential threats. Fawns (baby deer) are born with white spots on their fur, which help to camouflage them in the dappled light of the forest.*

# VENISON BITES IN BLUEBERRY SAUCE

Whitetail deer have a layer of reflective cells in their eyes called the tapetum lucidum, which allows them to see well in low-light conditions. Whitetail deer have a strong sense of direction and can navigate long distances using landmarks and other cues.

## SERVING SIZE: 4

## INGREDIENTS:

- 1 lb venison meat, diced
- 1 cup brandy
- 1 tsp cinnamon powder
- 1 tbsp orange zest
- 1 tsp nutmeg powder
- 1 tbsp honey
- 3 cups blueberries
- 2 tbsp butter

## DIRECTIONS:

1. Brown the venison in butter with brandy for 10–15 minutes.
2. Add cinnamon, orange zest, nutmeg, and honey.
3. Simmer for another 10–15 minutes, and take the meat out. Leave the sauce in the pan.
4. Add blueberries and bring to a soft boil.
5. Simmer for another 10–15 minutes or until the blueberries completely break down.
6. Serve venison bites covered in sauce.

## FACTS AND STATS:

*There are a few ways to hunt deer. It all depends on your preference. Still-hunting involves moving slowly and quietly through the woods, looking for signs of deer and waiting for them to come into range. This method requires patience and a good understanding of the deer's behavior. A deer drive involves a group of hunters moving through an area, making noise, and trying to push deer toward other hunters waiting in ambush. This method is typically used in areas with dense cover and can be dangerous if not done correctly. Ensure if you are hunting this method that, it is carefully planned out!*

# SPAGHETTI IN VENISON SAUCE

There are many ways to hunt whitetail deer, and the best method depends on the hunter's personal preferences, experience, and the environment they are hunting in. This is a popular method where hunters set up a tree stand, a platform that is elevated in a tree, and wait for deer to pass by. The advantage of this technique is that it provides a good vantage point and can help hunters stay concealed. Spot-and-stalk hunting involves locating deer from a distance and then stalking them on foot until the hunter is within range. This method requires good tracking skills and knowledge of the deer's behavior and habitat.

### SERVING SIZE: 4

### INGREDIENTS:

- 2–3 tbsp butter
- 1 lb venison, ground
- 1 cup brandy
- 2–3 cups cherries
- 1 tsp cinnamon powder
- 1 tsp nutmeg powder
- 1 tsp ginger powder
- 1 box of spaghetti

### DIRECTIONS:

1. Brown the ground venison in butter with brandy for 15–20 minutes.
2. Add cherries, cinnamon, nutmeg, and ginger powder.
3. Bring to a slow boil and let simmer for 15 more minutes.
4. Cook the spaghetti, drain, and mix with the sauce.

## FACTS AND STATS:

*No matter which technique a hunter chooses, it is important to follow local hunting regulations, practice ethical hunting practices, and prioritize safety at all times! Calling involves using deer calls, such as grunts, bleats, or rattling antlers, to lure deer into range. This technique requires skill and knowledge of the different calls and when to use them. Bow hunting involves using a bow and arrow to take down a deer. This method requires high skill, patience, and knowledge of the deer's behavior and habits.*

# SPAGHETTI MUSHROOMS AND VENISON

Whitetail deer are herbivores and have a diverse diet, which depends on the season and food availability. Browse refers to woody vegetation, such as leaves and twigs from shrubs and small trees. When other food sources are scarce in the winter, whitetail deer rely heavily on browse. Examples of plants that whitetail deer browse include dogwood, sumac, and maple. Forbs are herbaceous plants that grow in open areas like fields and meadows. Examples of forbs that whitetail deer eat include clover, alfalfa, and goldenrod. Acorns are a favorite food of whitetail deer, and they can eat large quantities in the fall when they are abundant. Acorns are high in fat and protein, which makes them an important source of nutrition for deer.

## SERVING SIZE: 4

## INGREDIENTS:

- 1 lb venison, chopped
- 1 cup tomato sauce
- ½ cup red wine
- 2 tbsp butter
- 2 cups mushrooms, sliced
- salt and pepper, to taste
- 1 cup heavy cream
- 1 tsp dill
- 1 tsp basil
- 1 box of spaghetti

## DIRECTIONS:

1. Sauté chopped venison in butter, tomato sauce, and red wine. Bring to a boil and let simmer gently for 15–20 minutes.
2. Add mushrooms, heavy cream, dill, basil, salt, and pepper. Simmer for another 10–15 minutes.
3. Cook the spaghetti as instructed, drain, and mix with the sauce.

## FACTS AND STATS:

*To ensure that whitetail deer have access to a healthy and balanced diet, conservationists and wildlife managers often plant food plots and manage habitats to promote the growth of nutritious plants. Additionally, hunters are encouraged to practice selective harvesting, which involves targeting mature bucks and leaving younger animals to help maintain a healthy population and ensure enough food to go around.*

# DINNER

# VENISON MEDALLIONS IN MUSHROOM SAUCE

Deer eat whatever is readily available, and here is some more food the Whitetail consume. Whitetail deer eat fruits and berries, including apples, blackberries, and raspberries. These foods are rich in vitamins and minerals and can help keep deer healthy. Whitetail deer feed on crops such as corn, soybeans, and wheat. While this can be a nuisance for farmers, it provides a reliable food source for deer.

## SERVING SIZE: 4

## INGREDIENTS:

- 1 lb venison meat, cut into medallions
- ½ cup red wine
- 1 tsp garlic powder
- 2 tsp dill, finely chopped
- 1 tsp basil, finely chopped
- 1 tbsp lemon juice
- 2–3 tbsp butter
- 1 cup brandy
- salt and pepper, to taste
- 1 cup beef broth
- 1 cup sour cream
- 4 cups mushrooms, sliced

## DIRECTIONS:

1. Cut up the venison meat into medallions and marinate them the night before.
2. Mix the red wine, garlic powder, 1 tsp dill, and lemon juice for the marinade. Soak the meat in it and leave it in the fridge for at least a couple of hours before cooking.
3. Sear the venison in butter and drizzle with ½ cup of brandy every couple of minutes to soften the meat and prevent it from sticking. Add salt and pepper.
4. Let the meat simmer on each side for 10–15 minutes, then take them out of the pan.
5. Add the rest of the brandy, beef broth, sour cream, mushrooms, dill, and basil.
6. Simmer for 10–15 minutes or until you achieve the desired thickness.
7. Serve the venison topped with mushroom sauce.

## FACTS AND STATS:

*It is important to note that not all food sources are equal in terms of nutrition. Whitetail deer need a balanced diet that provides all the necessary nutrients, including protein, fiber, and vitamins. A diet deficient in any of these nutrients can lead to health problems, such as poor body condition, weakened immune system, and reproductive issues.*

# DEER STEW

Keep going on a hunting spot when a big buck is taken in your area because a host of suitors will be coming through to fill the vacated territory. If you can hunt where another hunter has bagged a big buck, do it!

### SERVING SIZE: 6

### INGREDIENTS:

- 1 lb deer meat, diced
- 2–3 tbsp of unsalted butter
- 3 cups beef broth
- 1 cup of malty beer
- 1 cup onions, chopped
- 1 tbsp garlic, minced
- 1 cup carrots, chopped
- 1 tbsp celery leaf, chopped
- 1 tbsp red pepper powder
- 1 cup tomato sauce
- salt and pepper, to taste

### DIRECTIONS:

1. Brown the meat with onion, garlic, and carrots for 15–20 minutes.
2. Pour in a cup of beef broth and simmer for another 15 minutes.
3. Transfer into a stockpot and add the remaining broth, tomato sauce, and beer.
4. Bring to a boil and simmer for another 30–45 minutes.
5. Add the remaining ingredients and simmer for another 15–20 minutes.

## FACTS AND STATS:

*There are many great places to hunt whitetail deer in the United States, as they are found in nearly every state. However, one of the most popular places is Texas, which is home to some of the largest whitetail deer populations in the country and offers a variety of hunting opportunities. Texas has one of the largest populations of whitetail deer in the United States, with an estimated population of around 5.3 million as of 2021. The state's whitetail population is spread throughout its diverse landscape, which includes everything from dense forests to open grasslands. Due to its large size and variety of habitats, Texas offers many opportunities for resident and non-resident hunters to pursue whitetail deer. The state has a long hunting season, usually from early November to mid-January, allowing plenty of opportunities to hunt these animals. It is important to research and understand Texas's specific hunting regulations, seasons, and licensing requirements before planning a hunting trip.*

# DEER PEPPER STEW

You will see more deer by scanning an area twice. When you arrive in an area, allow your eyes to relax and move them slowly back and forth over the surrounding terrain. Relaxed eyes automatically focus on any movement within your vision. Focus on shadows that look out of place and parts of deer like antlers sticking out, ears flicking, or the back of a whitetail. Only move on when you did a nice and slow look a couple of times.

## SERVING SIZE: 6

## INGREDIENTS:

- 1 lb deer meat, cubed
- 4 cups beef broth or water
- 1 cup potatoes cubed
- 1 cup onions, chopped
- 1 cup carrots, chopped
- 1 tbsp garlic, minced
- 1 tbsp red pepper powder
- 1 tbsp dill, chopped
- 1 tbsp mustard seeds
- ½ cup white wine
- 2 tbsp butter

## DIRECTIONS:

1. Brown, the deer meat in butter at medium heat, adding drizzles of beef broth as needed.
2. Transfer into a stockpot and add the remaining ingredients except for the herbs.
3. Simmer for another 45 minutes, and add seasoning and wine.
4. Bring to a short boil and simmer for another 10–15 minutes.

## FACTS AND STATS:

*Midwest states such as Illinois, Iowa, Kansas, and Missouri are known for producing trophy-class whitetails, with many outfitters and private landowners offering prime hunting opportunities. Southeastern states such as Georgia, Alabama, and Mississippi provide excellent hunting opportunities, with large deer populations and mild climates.*

# DEER AND BROCCOLI RISOTTO

**Blood trail 101. When a blood trail begins to spread out, mark the locations of the blood drops. Eventually, the tape will point to the wounded deer's general direction, giving you useful information when the blood stops. If you plan to use scent from the glands of a freshly-killed deer, make sure to use less of it than the store-bought stuff. The fresh gland scent is way more potent.**

### SERVING SIZE: 4–6

### INGREDIENTS:

- 1–2 lb marinated deer meat

**FOR MARINADE**

- ½ cup olive oil
- ½ cup beer
- 3 garlic cloves, minced
- 1 tsp mustard
- 1 tsp pepper powder

**FOR COOKING**

- 1 cup vegetable broth
- 1 ½–2 cups brown rice
- 1 cup broccoli, chopped
- 1 cup onions, chopped
- 1 cup carrots, chopped
- ½ tbsp turmeric powder
- ½ tbsp pepper powder
- ½ tsp salt
- ½ tsp pepper
- 2 tbsp butter

### DIRECTIONS:

1. Mix all the ingredients for the marinade and soak the deer meat in it. Let it marinate in your fridge overnight.
2. Drain and pat dry before cooking.
3. Sauté the deer meat with rice and vegetables at low-medium heat for 15–20 minutes.
4. Drizzle with vegetable broth as needed.
5. Add spices and pour the rest of the broth.
6. Bring to a short boil and let simmer for 30 more minutes.

## FACTS AND STATS:

*Western states such as Montana and Wyoming offer unique hunting experiences and the chance to harvest a trophy whitetail in a beautiful mountainous setting. Northeastern states such as Pennsylvania, New York, and Ohio provide excellent hunting opportunities and large deer populations. It is important to research and understand each state's specific hunting regulations, seasons, and licensing requirements before planning a hunting trip. Hiring a knowledgeable guide or outfitter who can help ensure a safe and successful hunting experience is also recommended.*

# VENISON STEAK TARTARE

**When you are sitting in your Deer stand, don't be fooled by loud noises coming your way because deer don't always sneak through the woods. Avoid startling animals with loud calls, like squirrels, birds, and other animals. A smart hunter doesn't worry about how nearby deer may hear but goes to great lengths to make sure he does not spook other creatures that will sound a warning signal to the deer. I swear they all work together! LOL!**

### SERVING SIZE: 4

### INGREDIENTS:

- 2–3 tbsp butter
- 1 lb venison steaks
- ½ cup red wine
- salt and pepper, to taste
- 1 cup of potatoes, diced
- 1 cup sweet potatoes, diced
- 1 cup carrots, diced
- 1 cup broccoli, chopped
- 1 cup cauliflower, chopped
- 1 cup pickle relish
- 1 cup mayonnaise
- 1 cup sour cream
- 1 tbsp dill
- 1 tbsp basil

### DIRECTIONS:

1. Sear the venison steaks in butter for 5–10 minutes on each side, depending on how well done you want them to be. Add drizzles of red wine every couple of minutes until you've used up the entire cup.
2. Add salt and pepper to taste.
3. To create a delicious crust, turn the steaks every minute or so once the butter and wine have evaporated.
4. Take the steaks out of the pan and add more butter and wine. Bring to a boil and pop in the potatoes, sweet potatoes, carrots, broccoli, and cauliflower.
5. Let simmer for 15–20 minutes and take off the heat. Serve the vegetables next to the steaks on a large plate, covered in butter and wine sauce (see previous step).

6. Now, start making your tartar sauce. Mix the pickle relish with the mayonnaise and sour cream. Add dill and basil and stir until the sauce is fully mixed.

7. Serve the sauce next to the steak and vegetable plate.

## FACTS AND STATS:

*Canada is also home to some great places to hunt whitetail deer. Here are some of the best locations to hunt. Saskatchewan is known for producing some of the largest whitetail deer in the world. Saskatchewan's vast wilderness and farmland provide excellent habitats for these majestic animals. The western Canadian province of Alberta is home to some of the largest whitetail deer in North America. Alberta has a healthy Deer population and offers various hunting opportunities.*

# VENISON IN GARLIC SAUCE

There are three steps to proper still-hunting. Proper still-hunting has a three-step process. Step one is to stand behind an object that will break up your body outline while searching the surrounding area for deer activity. Step two is to remain still and look for the quietest path forward, trying to make the less noise as possible. Step three is to scan the woods for Deer one more time, then slowly & silently proceed through the route you've picked out. Repeat steps one through three until you find your buck. Do not rush! A proper still-hunt could take an hour to travel 100 yards in heavy cover. Animals have way better hearing and sight than humans, so time and quiet are all we have.

## SERVING SIZE: 4

## INGREDIENTS:

- 2–3 tbsp butter
- 1 cup scallions, chopped
- 1 cup carrots, chopped
- 2 ½ cups beef broth
- 1 lb venison steaks
- 1 cup white wine
- 1 tsp garlic powder
- 1 tsp mustard powder
- 1 tbsp celery leaf
- 1 cup sour cream
- 1 tbsp flour or cornstarch (optional)

## DIRECTIONS:

1. Brown the scallions and carrots in butter on low heat for 15–20 minutes while stirring frequently.
2. Add the 2 cups of beef broth and the meat.
3. Simmer on low heat for up to an hour until the excess liquid evaporates.
4. Take the steaks off the heat after 30–45 minutes and begin making the sauce.
5. Add the white wine, ½ cup of beef broth, garlic powder, mustard powder, and celery leaf. Bring to a boil and mix in the sour cream.
6. If needed, add a tablespoon of flour or cornstarch.
7. Simmer until the sauce thickens.
8. Serve the steaks covered in sauce.

## FACTS AND STATS:

*Manitoba is another province that is well known for its large whitetail deer. The province has a lot of forests and farmland, which provide ideal habitat for these animals. Ontario is home to many large whitetail deer, particularly in the southern part of the province. The area has a mix of farmland and forest, making it a great place to hunt. Quebec has a healthy population of whitetail deer, particularly in the southern part of the province. The area has a lot of farmland, which provides great habitat for deer. It is important to research and understand each province's specific hunting regulations, seasons, and licensing requirements before planning a hunting trip.*

# FRIED VENISON WITH SWEET POTATOES

**Catch a smart monster buck off guard during lunch hour. Increased pressure during the rut will often change the smart buck's pattern to avoid hunter activity. Many become nocturnal, but some will spend more time searching for does during the middle of the day, when most hunters are having lunch at the camp. Try sitting in your stand all day because that's where you will catch those monster bucks sneaking through. Having a monster buck slip up takes time and patience, but the rut season is when it happens!**

## SERVING SIZE: 4

## INGREDIENTS:

- 1 lb venison, ground
- 2–3 tbsp butter
- 1 cup shallots, chopped
- 1 cup carrots, chopped
- salt and pepper, to taste
- 1 tsp cumin powder
- 1 tsp ginger powder
- 2 eggs
- 2 cups flour
- 1 tsp baking powder
- 1 tbsp orange zest
- 1 cup sour cream
- 1 cup cherry brandy
- cream cheese, as needed

## DIRECTIONS:

1. Brown the ground venison in butter with shallots and carrots for 10–15 minutes.
2. Add salt, pepper, cumin powder, and ginger powder.
3. Mix the eggs in flour, baking powder, orange zest, sour cream, and cherry brandy. Add the cooked venison and vegetables and mix well.
4. Melt more butter in the frying pan.
5. Take the meat from the batter with a spoon and fry on each side for a couple of minutes.
6. Serve with cream cheese. This dish also goes well with your favorite salad and relishes. You can also enjoy it with a cup of plain yogurt or milk.

## FACTS AND STATS:

Ontario is home to a healthy population of whitetail deer, with an estimated population of around 500,000 to 1 million as of 2021. The province's whitetail population is primarily concentrated in the southern part of the province, where a mix of farmland and forested areas provides ideal habitat for these animals. Ontario offers a variety of hunting opportunities for whitetail deer, including archery, rifle, and muzzleloader seasons. The hunting season typically runs from mid-September to mid-December, depending on the specific hunting zone. It is important to research and understand Ontario's specific hunting regulations, seasons, and licensing requirements before planning a hunting trip.

# BREADED VENISON WITH WHITE MUSHROOM SAUCE

**You will want to use different routes to your deer stand at sunrise and sunset. Never walk through a field in the early morning because deer are likely feeding under cover of darkness. You want to have a back route to your stand. Be aware of the wind direction on the route you will take to the deer stand. The opposite is true when approaching your same stand in the evening. Deer are likely bedded in cover that you used to hide going in the morning. The deer are usually waiting for the sun to go down to feed. It would be best to approach your stand through the field at this time of day, depending on wind direction.**

### SERVING SIZE: 4

### INGREDIENTS:

- 2 eggs
- 1 lb venison meat, sliced
- 1 tsp garlic powder
- 2 tsp dill, chopped
- 1 tsp basil, chopped
- 1 tbsp celery leaf, chopped
- 1 tsp cumin powder
- 1 tsp ginger powder
- 2 cups bread crumbs
- 1 cup of potatoes, diced
- 1 cup sweet potatoes, diced
- 4 cups mushrooms, sliced
- 1 cup sour cream

### DIRECTIONS:

1. Break the eggs and whisk them. Dredge the venison slices in garlic powder, dill, celery leaf, cumin powder, and ginger powder.
2. Then, soak the slices in eggs while not removing the spices.
3. Cover the slices in bread crumbs until a crust-like layer has formed.
4. Fry the venison slices in butter on each side for 5–10 minutes.
5. Take the venison from the frying pan and pop the diced potatoes, sweet potatoes, and mushrooms in. Mix with the sour cream and bring to a boil.
6. Simmer for 10–15 minutes, and add the rest of the dill and basil during the last couple of minutes of cooking.
7. Serve the sauce next to the fried venison.

## FACTS AND STATS:

*Saskatchewan is known for its large population of whitetail deer, with an estimated population of around 250,000 to 300,000 as of 2021. The province's vast wilderness and farmland provide great habitats for these animals, and the lack of human disturbance in many areas has allowed the population to thrive. Saskatchewan offers a variety of hunting opportunities for whitetail deer, including archery, rifle, and muzzleloader seasons. The hunting season typically runs from mid-September to mid-December, depending on the specific hunting zone.*

# FRIED VENISON CHOPS WITH TOMATO SAUCE

**Before giving up finding a wounded deer, the last thing to do is look at where they were first hit. Deer and other big game animals, for whatever reason, often go back to the area where they were first shot to find their companions. Whatever the reason is, it has happened on too many occasions, so if you are having trouble locating the deer, go back and search the area where it was shot.**

### SERVING SIZE: 4

### INGREDIENTS:

- 1 lb venison chops
- salt and pepper, to taste
- 1 tbsp sweet pepper powder
- 1 tsp ginger powder
- 1 tsp thyme
- 1 cup soy sauce
- 4 whole tomatoes, crushed
- 6–8 whole potatoes

### DIRECTIONS:

1. Dredge raw venison chops in a seasoning mix (salt, pepper, sweet pepper powder, ginger powder, and thyme), and fry them in butter mixed with soy sauce for 5–6 minutes on each side.
2. Once the chops are done, take them out of the pan and leave the sauce to simmer for a couple more minutes.
3. Add the crushed tomatoes and simmer lightly until the sauce thickens. Stir frequently.
4. In a separate pot, boil whole potatoes with skin on. Season with salt. Remove the skins once the potatoes are tender and cooled down.
5. Serve the chops and boiled potatoes topped with tomato sauce.

## FACTS AND STATS:

*Alberta is home to a healthy population of whitetail deer, with an estimated population of around 150,000 to 200,000 as of 2021. The province's diverse landscape, including forests, grasslands, and agricultural areas, provides ideal animal habitat. Alberta offers a variety of hunting opportunities for whitetail deer, including archery, rifle, and muzzleloader seasons. The hunting season typically runs from mid-September to mid-December.*

# VENISON ROAST

Rattling is a technique hunters use to imitate the sound of two bucks fighting, which can attract nearby whitetail bucks during the rut. The best time to rattle for whitetail bucks is during the rut, typically in most areas in November. However, the timing may vary depending on the location, so it's essential to research and understand the specific rut timing in the area you plan to hunt. Here are some tips for effective rattling. To effectively imitate two bucks fighting, use a realistic rattling sequence. Start with a few light rattles to imitate bucks sizing each other up, followed by a series of aggressive rattles to imitate two bucks clashing antlers. After this, follow up with lighter rattles to imitate the bucks separating and moving away.

## SERVING SIZE: 4

## INGREDIENTS:

- 1 lb venison, sliced
- 1 cup soy sauce
- 1 cup brandy
- 1 tsp garlic powder
- 1 tsp thyme
- 1 tbsp orange juice
- 1 tbsp orange zest
- 6–8 potatoes, halved
- 2 cups sweet potatoes, sliced
- 1 tbsp Dijon mustard
- 1 tbsp honey

## DIRECTIONS:

1. Marinate the venison in soy sauce, brandy, garlic powder, thyme, orange juice, and orange zest. Leave to sit in the fridge for a minimum of 2 hours.
2. Preserve the leftover marinade.
3. Preheat your oven to 400 °F.
4. Glaze a baking dish with butter, add the potatoes and sweet potatoes first, then place the meat over them.
5. Mix the mustard and honey with the marinade and pour in the meat and vegetables.
6. Roast for 30–45 minutes at 400 °F.

## FACTS AND STATS:

*Don't rattle too loud or too soft. Start with a moderate volume and increase the intensity gradually. Vary the duration and intensity of the rattling sequences, as this will help to make the sound more realistic. Rattling can take time to work, so be patient and wait for at least 20-30 minutes after rattling before moving to a new location. Remember that bucks may approach silently, so be vigilant and watchful. Position yourself near cover, such as a brush pile or thicket, so that any approaching bucks will have to move through the cover, giving you a better chance for a shot.*

# EASY VENISON WELLINGTON WITH BLUEBERRY SAUCE

**A doe will tell you when a buck is nearby by a couple of different actions. One thing to watch for is her ears. If she is walking, unalarmed, and has one ear cupped backward, and the other is pointed forward, chances are she's keeping tabs on a buck following her trail. A second thing to look out for is the doe will keep stopping and looking back toward where she came from. Get ready because there could be a buck coming your way!**

### SERVING SIZE: 4

### INGREDIENTS:

- 1 lb venison (whole piece)
- 2 tbsp olive oil
- 1 tsp garlic powder
- 1 tbsp celery leaf
- 1 tbsp sweet pepper powder
- 1 tsp cumin powder
- 2–3 tbsp butter
- 4 cups mushrooms, sliced
- 1 cup brandy
- 1 cup sour cream
- 1 cup Parmesan or cheddar cheese, shredded
- 1 store-bought pastry dough or pie crust
- 1 egg
- 4 cups blueberries
- 1 cup beef broth

### DIRECTIONS:

1. Preheat your oven to 400 °F.
2. Rub the venison with olive oil, garlic powder, celery leaf, sweet pepper powder, and cumin powder.
3. Melt the butter in a frying pan and fry the large piece of meat for 2–3 minutes on each side.
4. Take the meat out of the pan and set aside.
5. Add mushrooms and ½ cup brandy to the pan and bring to a boil. Let simmer until the sauce thickens, take off the heat, and add sour cream and Parmesan or cheddar cheese.
6. Sprinkle your countertop with flour and spread the pastry dough.
7. First, distribute the mushroom sauce evenly across the dough.
8. In a bowl, break and whisk the egg and glaze an inch of the dough edges so that they can stick together.

9. Place the meat an inch away from the edge. Gently fold the dough over toward the other side. Please pay attention that the sauce doesn't leak, and it stays evenly distributed around the meat. Use a fork to seal the edges.
10. Bake in the oven for 30–45 minutes, depending on how you want the meat done.
11. While the meat is baking, make the blueberry sauce.
12. Melt the butter in a frying pan (you can use the same one you used for the meat and mushrooms).
13. Mix in the blueberries, ½ cup brandy, and the beef broth.
14. Bring to a boil and simmer until the sauce thickens.
15. Once the Wellington steak is done, slice it up and serve it covered with the sauce.

### FACTS AND STATS:

*As of 2021, the estimated population of Deer in Quebec is around 750,000 to 1 million. The province has a diverse landscape, which includes forests, agricultural lands, and wetlands, that provides excellent habitats for different species of deer, including white-tailed deer and moose. Quebec offers a variety of hunting opportunities for deer, including archery, rifle, and muzzleloader seasons. The hunting season typically runs from early September to late December.*

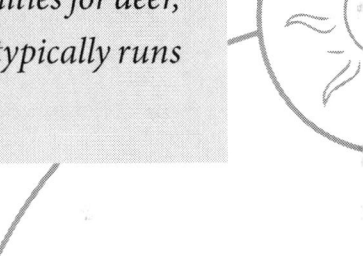

# BAKED VENISON PASTA

Several sub-species of whitetail deer differ in appearance, size, and habitat. Here are some of the main sub-species of whitetail deer found in North America and their distinguishing characteristics. Eastern Whitetails are the most widespread and abundant, from the East Coast to the Great Plains. They have a reddish-brown coat with a white belly and a distinctive tail with a white underside that they raise when alarmed. Western Whitetail is a sub-species found in the western United States and Mexico. They are smaller than eastern whitetails and have a grayish-brown coat with a white belly. Their tails are shorter and more brown than the eastern Whitetail.

### SERVING SIZE: 4

### INGREDIENTS:

- 1 lb ground venison
- 2–3 tbsp butter
- 1 cup brandy
- 1 tsp thyme
- salt and pepper, to taste
- 1 cup heavy cream or sour cream
- 2 cups mushrooms, sliced
- 1 pack of dry macaroni
- 1 cup cheddar cheese, shredded
- 2 eggs
- 2 cups sour cream
- 1 cup Parmesan cheese, grated
- 1 tbsp lemon zest

### DIRECTIONS:

1. Fry the ground venison in butter and brandy and season with thyme, salt, and pepper for 10–15 minutes.
2. Preheat your oven to 400 °F.
3. Add the heavy cream or sour cream and mushrooms and stir.
4. Let simmer for another 10 minutes.
5. Cook the macaroni as instructed. Drain and mix the sauce with the pasta.
6. Add shredded cheddar cheese.
7. Glaze a baking dish with butter at the bottom and the sides and transfer the dish.

8. Mix two eggs with sour cream, Parmesan, and lemon zest.
9. Pour the toppings over the pasta, making sure that it's distributed evenly.
10. Bake for 20–30 minutes at 400 degrees Fahrenheit.

### FACTS AND STATS:

*Key deer are found only in the Florida Keys and are much smaller than other whitetail deer, with males (bucks) weighing only 80 to 100 pounds. They have a reddish-brown coat and a white belly, and their tails are dark brown on top and white on the underside. Coues Deer are found in the southwestern United States and Mexico. They are smaller than eastern whitetails and have a grayish-brown coat with a white belly. Their tails are shorter and have a more pronounced black tip. Sitka Deer are found in the Pacific Northwest region of North America. They have a dark brown coat, a white rump patch, and a small tail. Males (bucks) have relatively short antlers and a distinctive "palmate" shape. Each sub-species of whitetail deer has adapted to the specific environment and habitat in which it lives, resulting in distinct physical and behavioral differences.*

# MOUTH-WATERING WHITETAIL AXIS BACON GRILLED CHEESEBURGER

You can use any wild game hamburger. Wild game hamburger is so lean you can add bacon to add fat and delicious flavor. You can add various ingredients to satisfy your taste buds in this recipe.

## SERVING SIZE: 6 BURGERS

## INGREDIENTS:

- 1 lb of whitetail axis hamburger or wild game meat of your choice
- 1 lb of bacon
- 1 loaf of bread
- 1 Mozzarella cheese block

## DIRECTIONS:

1. Preheat the frying pan at medium heat.
2. Mix hamburger in a bowl and press into thick hamburger patties.
3. Cook bacon in a frying pan.
4. Make two thin grilled cheese sandwiches for the buns in another frying pan.
5. Cook hamburger patties in the bacon frying pan and melt mozzarella cheese.
6. When everything is cooked, put grilled cheese, cheeseburger, bacon, and other grilled cheese for the most amazing cheeseburger you will ever eat!

## FACTS AND STATS:

*Native to India, where it is known as chital and was introduced into Texas in about 1932 and is in a number of counties in the central and southern part of the state. There are more than 15,000 free-living individuals. Axis deer are the most abundant exotic ungulate in Texas.*

# CHAPTER 4
# ELECTRIFYING ELK

Elk meat is a rich and almost beefy flavor. It has a similar texture to its cousin Whitetail. Elk tends to be much leaner and carries a much less gamey flavor, making it a favorite of mine. The best thing to preserve elegant flavor is to bleed every last drop out of the carcass the best you can. This will keep your meat the most flavorful. Since elk is extremely lean, cooking with fat like butter or bacon is always best.

**Breakfast**
Spinach and Mushrooms Elk Omelet
Panfried Elk Pate
Elk Breakfast Casserole
Delicious Elk Pie Wraps
Elk Breakfast Quiche
Simple Elk and Spinach Scramble
Elk Breakfast Tart
Elk Bacon Breakfast Wraps
Oven-Baked Grilled Elk and Cheese Sandwich
Elk and Bacon With Fried Eggs

## Lunch

Apple and Elk Salad
Roasted Elk and Leek Risotto
Oven-Roasted Elk Sandwich
Elk Macaroni Salad
Tortilla Elk Salad (Gyros)
Cool Elk Spaghetti Salad
Fried Elk Mini Kebabs
Elk Burger With Fries

## Dinner

Elk Wellington Steak
Elk Fillet in Blackberry Brandy Sauce
Fried Elk With Veggie Mash
Elk Cheese and Veggie Soup
White Elk and Mushroom Macaroni
Elk Meatballs
Sweet Elk Shepherd's Pie
Elk Meat Loaf in Cherry Sauce

# BREAKFAST

# SPINACH AND MUSHROOMS ELK OMELET

**Elk meat is considered a healthy food option due to its high protein and low-fat content. Elk meat is an excellent source of high-quality protein essential for building and repairing muscle tissues. Elk meat is low in fat compared to other red meats like beef or pork. This makes it a good option for those watching their fat intake. Do I have to say it's frigging delicious!**

### SERVING SIZE: 4-6

### INGREDIENTS:

- 1 lb elk meat, cubed
- 6–8 whole eggs
- ½ cup bell peppers, chopped
- 1 cup spinach, chopped
- 1 cup mushrooms, sliced
- ½ cup cheddar cheese, shredded
- 2 tbsp olive oil
- salt and pepper, to taste

### DIRECTIONS:

1. Brown the elk meat with spinach, bell peppers, and mushrooms in olive oil for 15–20 minutes. Add a bit of water as needed.
2. Whisk the eggs and pour it over, and top with cheese.
3. Fry the omelet on each side.

## FACTS AND STATS:

*Elk, also known as wapiti, are a type of large deer that are native to North America. According to the Rocky Mountain Elk Foundation, there are over 1 million elk in North America, with the largest populations found in Colorado, Wyoming, Montana, and Idaho. Elk are one of the largest species of deer, with adult males (known as bulls) weighing up to 1,000 pounds and standing up to 5 feet tall at the shoulder.*

# PANFRIED ELK PATE

**Elk meat is low in cholesterol, which is important for maintaining good heart health. Elk meat is a good source of essential vitamins and minerals, including zinc, iron, and vitamin B12. Elk meat is low in calories, making it a good option for those trying to maintain a healthy weight. Overall, elk meat is one of the best big game out there!**

### SERVING SIZE: 4

### INGREDIENTS:

- 1 lb elk liver, diced
- 1 cup onions, chopped
- 1 cup carrots, chopped
- 1 cup parsley, chopped
- salt and pepper, to taste
- 2 cups beef broth
- 2 tbsp butter
- 2 tbsp heavy cream
- 2 tbsp thyme
- 1 tbsp basil
- 1 tsp garlic powder

### DIRECTIONS:

1. Prepare one cooking pot and one frying pan.
2. Mix the onions, carrots, parsley, and elk liver in a cooking pot with salt and pepper to taste.
3. Fill the cooking pot with just enough beef broth to cover the food.
4. Bring to a boil, turn off the heat, and let simmer briefly (5–10 minutes). If your burner cools down too quickly, simmer on low heat.
5. Heat a frying pan with butter, then transfer the meat, veggies, and broth into it.
6. Sauté on low heat (if needed, boil first) until the meat is well done. Most likely, it will be 10–15 minutes.
7. Allow the broth to evaporate almost completely while keeping enough moisture in the food to be processed into a creamy consistency.
8. Transfer the contents to a food processor and add heavy cream, thyme, basil, and garlic powder.
9. Process in a food processor as needed to create a creamy pate texture with no lumps.
10. Transfer in a bowl and serve on toast, buns, or any other way you like.

## FACTS AND STATS:

*Elk are social animals that live in herds. Elk bulls have impressive antlers that can grow up to 4 feet long and weigh up to 40 pounds. They shed and regrow their antlers each year. Bulls often gather harems of females (known as cows) during mating season and defend their territory against other bulls. Elk can be found in various habitats, including forests, grasslands, and mountainous regions. They are well-adapted to cold weather and can survive in snowy conditions.*

# ELK BREAKFAST CASSEROLE

It's worth noting that the specific health benefits of elk meat may vary depending on how it's prepared and cooked. For example, if elk meat is heavily processed or cooked in unhealthy oils, it may not be as healthy as if grilled or baked with minimal added fats. Additionally, as with any meat, it's important to consume elk meat in moderation and as part of a balanced diet.

## SERVING SIZE: 4

## INGREDIENTS:

- 1 lb elk meat, diced
- 2 tbsp flour
- 1 cup bacon (or elk shoulder bacon), chopped
- 2 cups mushrooms, sliced
- 1 cup cheddar cheese, grated
- 1 cup heavy cream or sour cream (or Greek yogurt will do)
- ½ tbsp dill
- ½ tbsp oregano
- ½ tbsp parsley leaf
- 2 tbsp butter
- 1 cup green beans, chopped
- 4–6 eggs

## DIRECTIONS:

1. Preheat your oven to 400 °F.
2. Cook the elk meat in a stockpot with as little beef stock as needed. You don't want excess liquid!
3. Bring to a boil and simmer for 10–15 minutes, drain and set aside.
4. Mix the eggs with flour, bacon, mushrooms, cheddar cheese, dill, oregano, parsley leaf, heavy cream, sour cream, or Greek yogurt.
5. Grab a baking dish and glaze it with butter at the bottom and sides.
6. Spread the meat across the bottom of the dish and mix in chopped green beans.
7. Pour the egg mixture over the meat and beans.
8. You can top it with more cheddar cheese and leftover ingredients that didn't go into the casserole.
9. Bake for up to an hour at 350 °F. However, this might take away from the casserole's flavor and texture. If you wish to speed up the baking, turn the heat to 400 °F and bake for 30–40 minutes.

## FACTS AND STATS:

*Elk are herbivores that primarily eat grasses, shrubs, and leaves. They have four-chambered stomachs that allow them to digest tough vegetation. Elk were nearly hunted to extinction in the United States in the late 1800s, but conservation efforts have helped their populations recover. Today, elk hunting is carefully managed through hunting permits and regulations to ensure sustainable populations.*

# DELICIOUS ELK PIE WRAPS

**Some studies suggest that moderation of lean red meat, like elk, can lower the risk of certain diseases, such as heart disease and diabetes. Elk is considered a sustainable meat option as it is generally raised and hunted in a more environmentally friendly way compared to traditional livestock farming.**

## SERVING SIZE: 4

## INGREDIENTS:

- 2–3 tbsp salted butter
- 1 lb elk meat, ground
- ½ tsp cinnamon, ground
- salt and pepper, to taste
- ½ tsp ginger powder
- 2 cups sweet potatoes, grated
- 1 cup beef broth
- 1 store-bought pie crust
- 1 egg
- 1 cup sour cream
- 1 cup Parmesan cheese, grated

## DIRECTIONS:

1. Brown your ground elk in salted butter for 10–15 minutes.
2. Add salt, pepper, cinnamon, ginger powder, and grated sweet potatoes.
3. If needed, drizzle with beef broth to prevent it from burning and sticking.
4. Sauté for 10–15 minutes or less if you feel like the meat and potatoes are well done.
5. Spread the pie crust and top it with a thin layer of the whisked egg.
6. Cut up to as many pieces as you want.
7. Once the filling has cooled down, mix in the sour cream and Parmesan. Stir well for an even consistency.
8. Add as much filling as you want at the center of your pie crust pieces and wrap in rolls.
9. Glaze your baking dish with butter at the bottom, line your mini pies, and bake for 30–40 minutes at 400 °F.

## FACTS AND STATS:

*Elk have played an essential role in Native American cultures, where they were revered for their strength and beauty. Elk hunting also has a long history in North American culture and is popular among many hunters. Elk are a popular attraction for wildlife viewing and photography. Many national parks and wildlife reserves in North America offer elk viewing opportunities, particularly during the fall mating season when the bulls display their impressive antlers.*

# ELK BREAKFAST QUICHE

Elk is considered a sustainable meat option as it is generally raised and hunted in a more environmentally friendly way compared to traditional livestock farming. Elk meat can be cooked using various methods, and the best one depends on the meat cut and personal preference. Grilling is one of the most popular methods for cooking elk meat. It's a great way to get a delicious smoky flavor while keeping the meat tender and juicy. To grill elk meat, preheat your grill to medium-high heat, brush the meat with oil, and grill for 5-7 minutes per side for medium-rare.

## SERVING SIZE: 4

## INGREDIENTS:

- 1 lb elk meat, ground
- salt and pepper, to taste
- 2 tbsp butter
- ½ tsp cinnamon powder
- ½ tsp ginger powder
- ½ tsp orange zest
- bread slices, as needed
- 2–3 eggs
- ½ cup sour cream
- 1 tbsp flour
- 1 cup mushrooms, sliced

## DIRECTIONS:

1. Sauté your ground elk in butter for 10–15 minutes and season with salt, pepper, cinnamon powder, ginger powder, and orange zest.
2. While the elk is cooking, make your quiche cups. Roll and flatten slices of bread and cut up circular shapes (you can do so with a regular cup or mug of the desired shape and size).
3. Shape the pieces into cups and bake for 5 minutes at 400 °F.
4. Take the elk meat off the heat and transfer it into a bowl.
5. Mix with the eggs, sour cream, flour, and mushrooms.
6. Fill your quiche cups and bake for 10–15 minutes at 400 °F.

## FACTS AND STATS:

*Elk are a fascinating and important species in North America, with a rich cultural history and significant ecological and economic value. Elk hunting is a popular activity in the United States and Canada. In the United States, elk hunting is regulated by state wildlife agencies and is typically only allowed during specific seasons and with a limited number of permits. In Canada, elk hunting is regulated by provincial wildlife agencies. Elk hunting and watching contribute significantly to the economies of many rural communities in North America. According to a study by the Rocky Mountain Elk Foundation, elk hunting alone generates over $1 billion in economic activity each year in the United States.*

# SIMPLE ELK AND SPINACH SCRAMBLE

**Roasting is a great way to cook larger cuts of elk meat, such as roasts or tenderloins. Preheat the oven to 375°F, and place the seasoned elk meat on a roasting rack in a roasting pan. Roast the meat until it reaches an internal temperature of 135°F (for medium-rare), which can take around 20-30 minutes per pound. Let the meat rest for 10-15 minutes before carving. Elk meat is well-suited to slow cooking methods such as braising or stewing. To make elk stew, for example, sear cubed elk meat in a hot skillet and then transfer it to a slow cooker with vegetables, herbs, and broth. Cook on low heat for 6-8 hours or until the meat is tender.**

### SERVING SIZE: 4

### INGREDIENTS:

- 2–3 tbsp butter
- 1 lb elk meat, diced
- 1 cup beef broth
- 1 cup spinach, chopped
- ½ cup brandy
- 4–5 eggs
- 1 tbsp flour
- 1 cup sour cream
- ½ cup Parmesan cheese, grated
- salt and pepper, to taste
- 1 tsp orange zest
- 1 tsp garlic powder
- 1 tsp thyme

### DIRECTIONS:

1. Melt butter in a frying pan and pop in your elk meat to fry. Drizzle with some beef broth and brandy, and let simmer for 5–10 minutes.
2. In a separate bowl, break the eggs and mix with flour, Parmesan, sour cream, salt, pepper, spinach, orange zest, garlic powder, and thyme.
3. Pour it over the meat and stir until the scramble is done.

## FACTS AND STATS:

*Hunting elk in the United States or Canada can be a challenging and rewarding experience. Here are some tips and tricks to help you have a successful hunt. Before hunting, scout the area to find where the elk are most active. Look for signs such as tracks, droppings, and rubs on trees. You can also use trail cameras to monitor elk activity. Ensure you have the right hunting gear, including a high-quality rifle or bow, a reliable GPS device, and appropriate clothing and footwear for the terrain and weather conditions. You should also invest in a good set of binoculars or a spotting scope to help you locate elk from a distance.*

# ELK BREAKFAST TART

Elk meat is well-suited to slow-cooking methods such as braising or stewing. To make elk stew, for example, sear cubed elk meat in a hot skillet and then transfer it to a slow cooker with vegetables, herbs, and broth. Cook on low heat for 6-8 hours or until the meat is tender.

## SERVING SIZE: 4

## INGREDIENTS:

- 1 lb elk meat, ground
- 2 eggs
- 2 tbsp milk
- ½ cup flour
- 1 tbsp butter
- 1 tsp baking powder
- 1 tsp orange zest
- Salt and pepper, to taste
- 2 tbsp butter
- ½ cup cream cheese
- 1 tsp garlic powder
- 1 tsp red pepper powder
- 2 tsp celery leaf, chopped

## DIRECTIONS:

1. Fry your ground elk in butter for 10–15 minutes.
2. Start making your tarts by mixing the eggs, milk, flour, baking powder, orange zest, and a little salt.
3. You can panfry your tarts by pouring them into molds or take a spoonful of the batter and fry them into a simpler, more pancake-like shape.
4. Fry your tarts for up to 5 minutes.
5. Top the tarts with cream cheese mixed with garlic powder, red pepper powder, and celery leaf.
6. Top with as much ground elk as you like and serve.

## FACTS AND STATS:

*Be familiar with the hunting regulations in the area where you plan to hunt, including any restrictions on hunting methods, tags, and seasons. Try to approach the area from downwind and use the cover to stay hidden. Elk have a keen sense of smell and are easily spooked, so plan your approach carefully to avoid alerting them to your presence.*

# ELK BACON BREAKFAST WRAPS

**Smoking elk meat is another popular method, which can infuse it with delicious smoky flavors. Start by seasoning the meat with your favorite spices, then smoke it at a low temperature (around 200°F) for several hours until it reaches an internal temperature of 145°F.**

## SERVING SIZE: 4

## INGREDIENTS:

- ½ lb free-range elk meat, chopped
- ½ lb elk bacon
- 2 tbsp butter
- salt and pepper, to taste
- ½ tsp cinnamon
- ½ tsp orange zest
- 2–3 tbsp sour cream
- 1 cup cheddar cheese, grated

## DIRECTIONS:

1. Fry the elk meat briefly in butter for 10–15 minutes. Leave the butter in the pan. Season with salt, pepper, cinnamon, and orange zest, and set aside to cool down.
2. Spread your bacon slices to a desired width and length. Top them with sour cream and cheddar cheese.
3. Add 1 tbsp of the elk meat to the center of the bacon slices and wrap in a roll. Seal tightly with toothpicks.
4. Repeat the process of making bacon rolls until all of the meat is used up.
5. Fry for a couple of minutes in butter and serve.

## FACTS AND STATS:

*Elk calls can be an effective way to attract elk during the mating season. Various calls are available, including bugles, cow, and calf calls. Practice using the calls before your hunt to ensure you are comfortable and proficient. Elk hunting requires patience and persistence. It can take time to locate elk and to get into a good position for a shot. Be prepared to spend long hours in the field and make multiple trips if necessary.*

# OVEN-BAKED GRILLED ELK AND CHEESE SANDWICH

**Sous vide is a precise and gentle cooking method that involves vacuum-sealing elk meat and cooking it in a temperature-controlled water bath. Cook the meat in a water bath at 132°F for 1-2 hours, and then sear it in a hot skillet or on the grill to add flavor and texture. Sous vide is great for cooking elk tenderloin, as it controls precise temperature and prevents overcooking.**

### SERVING SIZE: 4

### INGREDIENTS:

- 1 lb elk bacon slices, chopped
- bread slices, as needed
- 2–3 eggs
- 2 tbsp butter
- 2–3 tbsp sour cream
- 1 cup mushrooms, sliced
- 1 cup cheddar cheese slices
- 2–3 tomatoes, sliced
- 1–2 paprikas, sliced

### DIRECTIONS:

1. Soak your bread slices in the egg and spread at the bottom of a baking dish glazed with butter.
2. Top with sour cream, mushrooms, and bacon.
3. Add cheddar cheese and top with tomatoes and paprikas.
4. Dredge the second half of your bread slices in the egg mixture and top the sandwiches.
5. Bake for 15–20 minutes at 400 °F.

## FACTS AND STATS:

*Hunting can be a dangerous activity, especially in remote or rugged terrain. Always carry a first-aid kit and be aware of your surroundings. Tell someone where you are hunting and when you expect to return. Successful elk hunting requires preparation, skill, and patience. With the right gear, knowledge, and approach, you can increase your chances of having a safe and successful hunt.*

# ELK AND BACON WITH FRIED EGGS

**Remember, the key to cooking elk meat is not overcooking it, as it can become tough and dry. Always use a meat thermometer to ensure the elk meat is cooked to the proper internal temperature, and let it rest for a few minutes before cutting to allow the juices to redistribute.**

### SERVING SIZE: 4

### INGREDIENTS:

- 1 lb elk bacon slices
- 2–3 tbsp butter
- 4–6 eggs
- salt and pepper, to taste
- 1 cup cheddar or Parmesan cheese, grated
- bread or bun slices, as needed
- 2 tbsp sour cream

### DIRECTIONS:

1. Fry the elk bacon slices in butter for a couple of minutes on each side and take them out of the pan.
2. Fry the eggs to your liking and season with salt and pepper.
3. Serve with the elk bacon sprinkled with cheddar or Parmesan cheese and slices of bread or buns. Or, if you prefer, you can top the bread or buns with sour cream and add bacon slices and fried eggs to make a sandwich.

## FACTS AND STATS:

*Elk hunting is typically best during the rut, which occurs in the fall. Bulls will be actively bugling and seeking out cows, making locating them easier. If you are new to elk hunting or unfamiliar with the area, consider hiring a reputable guide to help increase your chances of success. Elk are also important ecologically, as they help to maintain healthy ecosystems by grazing on vegetation and creating open areas that benefit other wildlife species.*

# LUNCH

# APPLE AND ELK SALAD

**Field dressing an elk can be challenging, but here are some general steps to make it easier. First, position the elk on its back and spread its legs apart to make it easier to access the internal organs. Use my favorite field dressing tool, "The Butt Out!" Tie off the anus. Use a sharp knife to make a vertical incision from the base of the breastbone to the pelvic bone. Be careful not to puncture the intestines or bladder, as this could contaminate the meat. Continues next recipe…**

## SERVING SIZE: 4

## INGREDIENTS:

- 1 lb elk meat, ground
- ½ cup white wine
- 1 tbsp lemon juice
- 1 cup sour apple salsa
- 1 cup Greek yogurt
- 3 oz mozzarella cheese, chopped
- salt and pepper, to taste
- 2 tbsp butter
- 1 tsp garlic, minced

## DIRECTIONS:

1. Brown the elk meat in butter for 10 minutes. Add wine and seasoning. Then stir-fry for another 10 minutes.
2. Mix the Greek yogurt with garlic, lemon juice, salt, pepper, and mozzarella for the dressing in a bowl.
3. Mix the fried elk meat with the sour apple salsa.
4. Top with the mozzarella dressing.

# FACTS AND STATS:

*Elk (Cervus canadensis) is native to North America and have a long history in the United States. Here is a brief history of elk in the U.S. Elk were widespread throughout the continent and were an important food source for Native American tribes, who hunted them for meat, hides, and bones. Elk also played a significant cultural and spiritual role in many Native American societies.*

# ROASTED ELK AND LEEK RISOTTO

**Reach inside the body cavity and carefully remove the internal organs, including the heart, lungs, liver, and kidneys. You may need to cut through connective tissue or bone to remove the organs. Cut the diaphragm away from the body cavity and remove it. This will allow you to access the tenderloins and other cuts of meat located along the spine.**

### SERVING SIZE: 4-6

### INGREDIENTS:

- 1–2 lb of elk meat, marinated overnight
- 1 cup vegetable broth
- 1 cup leeks
- 1 cup carrots, chopped
- 1 cup brown rice

- 1 cup onions, chopped
- 1 tsp thyme
- ½ tbsp turmeric powder
- ½ tbsp pepper powder
- 2 tbsp butter

**FOR MARINADE**

- ½ cup red wine
- ½ cup olive oil
- ½ cup lemon juice

- 3 garlic cloves, minced
- 1 tbsp red pepper powder

### DIRECTIONS:

1. Mix the ingredients for the marinade in a large bowl and dredge the pieces of elk meat.
2. Preheat your oven to 350 °F.
3. Sauté the butter, broth, elk meat, leeks, rice, and vegetables over medium heat for 15–20 minutes.
4. Bring spices to a boil, and let simmer for another 20 minutes.
5. Roast at 350 °F for 15–20 minutes.

## FACTS AND STATS:

*In the 1800s, European settlers began moving westward. They encountered large elk populations in the Great Plains, Rocky Mountains, and Pacific Northwest. Elk hunting became popular among settlers and was largely unregulated, leading to population declines in many areas. In the early 1900s, concerns over declining elk populations led to the establishment of the first elk preserves and refuges in the U.S. in the early 1900s. These efforts were successful in some areas, and elk populations began to recover.*

# OVEN-ROASTED ELK SANDWICH

**If you plan to transport the elk on foot or horseback, you may need to remove the pelvis to make it easier to pack. Use a saw or knife to cut through the pelvic bone and remove it. Rinse the body cavity with cool water to remove blood or debris, and pack the cavity with ice to cool the meat. Be sure to transport the elk to a cooler as soon as possible to prevent spoilage.**

## SERVING SIZE: 4

## INGREDIENTS:

- 1 lb elk meat, chopped
- ½ cup white wine
- 1 tbsp Dijon mustard
- ¼ tsp salt
- ¼ tsp pepper
- 2–3 tbsp butter
- bread slices or halved buns, as needed
- 1 paprika, sliced
- 1 onion, sliced
- 2–3 tomatoes, sliced
- 2 tbsp sour cream
- salsa, relish, or any of your favorite sauce, to taste

## DIRECTIONS:

1. Glaze a baking dish with butter and bake your buns or slices of bread for 5 minutes at 400 °F or until crispy. Take the dish out of the oven and set it aside.
2. Add more butter to the dish and add the elk meat, paprikas, onions, and tomatoes so that the meat covers the veggies.
3. Mix the wine, Dijon mustard, salt, pepper, and sour cream and pour over evenly.
4. Roast for 15 minutes at 400 °F.
5. Top your toasted buns or bread slices with butter, sour cream, mayonnaise, or any other toppings you like. Add pieces of elk meat and vegetables and top with another slice of bread or bun to make a sandwich.

## FACTS AND STATS:

*In the mid-1900s, elk hunting became more regulated, with states establishing hunting seasons and bag limits to ensure sustainable populations. Many states also began translocating elk to areas where populations had been extirpated. In the modern day, elk are found in various habitats throughout the western U.S., with populations ranging from several thousand in some states to less than 100 in others. Elk hunting remains popular and is an important part of many state economies. However, there are also concerns about the impact of hunting, habitat loss, and climate change on elk populations.*

# ELK MACARONI SALAD

**It's important to note that field dressing an elk can be a complex and physically demanding task. If you need to become more experienced with field dressing large game animals, it's a good idea to seek guidance from a more experienced hunter or take a hunter education course to learn proper techniques.**

### SERVING SIZE: 4

### INGREDIENTS:

- 1 lb elk meat, chopped
- 1 cup beef broth
- ½ cup red wine
- ½ cup flour
- ½ cup sour cream
- salt and pepper, to taste
- 1 tsp ginger powder
- 1 tsp oregano
- 1 tsp cinnamon powder
- 1 box of macaroni
- 1–2 paprikas, chopped
- 1–2 tomatoes, chopped
- 1–2 cucumbers, chopped
- Parmesan cheese, grated to taste

### DIRECTIONS:

1. Fry the elk meat in butter, drizzled with beef broth and a bit of red wine, on low-medium heat for 10–15 minutes.
2. Add the rest of the broth and wine, turn up the heat, and bring to a boil.
3. Add the flour and sour cream and stir.
4. Simmer for 10–15 more minutes and season with salt and pepper, ginger powder, cinnamon powder, and oregano.
5. Cook the macaroni and drain. Transfer into a salad bowl.
6. Mix in the elk sauce, chopped paprikas, tomatoes, and cucumbers.
7. Top with a generous amount of grated Parmesan.

## FACTS AND STATS:

*Elk (Cervus canadensis) is native to Canada and has a long history there. Elk were an important food source for Indigenous peoples across Canada, who hunted them for their meat, hides, and bones. Elk also played a significant cultural and spiritual role in many Indigenous societies. In the 1800s, European settlers began moving westward and encountered large elk populations in the western provinces. Elk hunting became popular among settlers and was largely unregulated, leading to population declines in many areas.*

# TORTILLA ELK SALAD (GYROS)

There are many great places to hunt elk in the United States, as elk are found in a variety of habitats throughout the western part of the country. Colorado is home to the largest elk population in North America and is a popular destination for resident and non-resident hunters. The state offers a variety of hunting opportunities, from high-elevation wilderness hunts to private land hunts.

### SERVING SIZE: 4

### INGREDIENTS:

- 1 lb elk meat, ground
- 2–3 tbsp butter
- 1 tsp oregano
- 1 tsp garlic powder
- 1 tsp ginger powder
- Salt and pepper, to taste
- ½ cup red wine
- ½ cup sour cream
- 1 tsp dill
- 1–2 potatoes, thinly cut
- 1 sweet potato, thinly cut
- tortillas, as needed
- barbecue sauce to taste
- 1 onion, sliced
- 1 paprika, sliced
- 1 tomato, sliced

### DIRECTIONS:

1. Brown the ground elk in butter and season with oregano, garlic powder, ginger powder, salt, and pepper.
2. Toward the end of the frying, drizzle with red wine.
3. Mix in the sour cream and dill and stir.
4. In a separate pan, fry your potato and sweet potato slices.
5. Heat the tortillas as instructed on the packaging.
6. Top each tortilla with barbecue sauce and sliced onions, paprikas, and tomatoes.
7. Add a desired amount of the meat topping and potato chips to each tortilla and wrap.

## FACTS AND STATS:

*Elk are found in various habitats throughout the western provinces of Canada, with populations ranging from several thousand in some areas to less than 100 in others. Elk have played an important role in the history and culture of Canada and continue to be an important part of the country's wildlife heritage. In the mid-1900s, elk hunting became more regulated, with provinces establishing hunting seasons and bag limits to ensure sustainable populations. Many provinces also began translocating elk to areas where populations had been extirpated. Elk hunting remains popular and is an important part of many provincial economies. However, there are also concerns about the impact of hunting, habitat loss, and climate change on elk populations.*

# COOL ELK SPAGHETTI SALAD

Hunting elk requires various techniques, depending on the hunting method you choose. Here are some techniques commonly used for hunting elk. Spot and stalk is a popular technique for hunting elk, especially in open terrain. It involves locating elk from a distance using binoculars or a spotting scope, then making a stalk to get within range for a shot. Still-hunting involves moving slowly and quietly through elk habitat, looking for signs of elk activity, and listening for bugling or other vocalizations. This technique requires patience and stealth, as elk are easily spooked.

## SERVING SIZE: 4

## INGREDIENTS:

- 1 lb elk meat, ground
- 2 tbsp olive oil
- 1 tbsp Dijon mustard
- ½ cup beer
- 1 tsp garlic powder
- 1 tbsp celery leaf, chopped
- 1 cup beef broth
- 1 cup heavy cream
- ½ tbsp dill
- 1 cup Parmesan cheese, grated
- 1 box of dry spaghetti
- 1 cup beets, grated
- 1 cup carrots, grated
- 1 cup sweet potatoes, grated

## DIRECTIONS:

1. Marinate the elk meat in olive oil, Dijon mustard, beer, garlic powder, and celery leaf.
2. Fry the marinated elk in butter for 10–15 minutes. You may also include the marinade if you like.
3. Add beef broth, bring to a boil, and simmer for another 10–15 minutes.
4. Take off the burner and mix in the heavy cream, Parmesan, and dill.
5. Cook the spaghetti as instructed on the packaging, drain, and transfer it into a salad bowl.
6. Mix in the elk sauce and add grated beets, carrots, and sweet potatoes.

## FACTS AND STATS:

*New Mexico is home to some of the largest elk in North America, with many record-breaking bulls taken in recent years. The state offers public and private land hunts, with rifle, archery, and muzzleloader hunting opportunities. Idaho is home to a large population of Rocky Mountain elk and offers both general and controlled hunts. The state is known for its high success rates and beautiful mountain landscapes.*

# FRIED ELK MINI KEBABS

**Elk are vocal animals and respond well to calls, especially during the rut when bulls actively seek out cows. Using a variety of elk calls, such as bugles, cow calls, and grunts, can help bring elk within range for a shot. Some hunters use dogs to track and locate elk, especially in thick cover or difficult terrain. Hunting with dogs requires specialized training and equipment and may be prohibited in some areas.**

## SERVING SIZE: 4

## INGREDIENTS:

- 1 lb elk meat, ground
- 2 eggs
- 1 tbsp flour
- 1 cup cheddar cheese, grated
- 1 cup onions, chopped
- 1 tbsp garlic powder
- 1 cup paprika, chopped
- bread slices or buns, as needed
- sour cream, to taste
- mayonnaise to taste
- ketchup, to taste
- salsa of your choice to taste
- ¼ tsp salt
- ¼ tsp pepper
- ½ tsp cumin powder
- ½ tsp cinnamon powder
- 2 tbsp butter
- ½ cup paprika, chopped
- ½ cup tomatoes, chopped

## DIRECTIONS:

1. Mix the ground elk meat with the eggs, flour, cheddar cheese, onions, garlic, and paprikas. Season with salt, pepper, cumin powder, and cinnamon powder.
2. Shape into kebab or sausage-like pieces.
3. Fry in butter for 10–15 minutes or until done.
4. Halve your buns and top them with sour cream, mayonnaise, ketchup, your favorite salsa, and other toppings you like.
5. Put the kebabs between bun slices and top with chopped paprikas and tomatoes to your taste.

## FACTS AND STATS:

*Canada offers some of the best elk hunting opportunities in North America. Alberta is home to a large population of Rocky Mountain elk and is known for producing some of the largest bulls in North America. The province offers both guided and unguided hunts on public and private land.*

# ELK BURGER WITH FRIES

**Hunting from a blind or tree stand can be an effective way to ambush elk, especially during the early morning or late afternoon when they are most active. It's important to choose a location that offers good visibility and cover and to remain still and quiet while waiting for elk to approach. These are just a few examples of the many techniques used for hunting elk. It's essential to choose a method that fits your hunting style and experience level and to follow all hunting regulations and safety guidelines.**

### SERVING SIZE: 4

### INGREDIENTS:

- 1 lb elk meat, ground
- salt and pepper, to taste
- 1 tbsp red pepper flakes
- 1 tsp garlic powder
- 1 tbsp celery leaf, chopped
- 2 tbsp butter
- 1 cup potatoes, sliced into fries
- 1 cup sweet potatoes, sliced into fries
- 1 tbsp olive oil
- 1 tbsp sweet pepper powder
- 1 tsp ginger powder
- 1 tsp cumin powder
- 4 buns

### DIRECTIONS:

1. Mix the ground elk meat in a bowl with salt, pepper, red pepper flakes, garlic powder, and celery leaf.
2. Shape into patties to your preference.
3. Fry in butter on each side for a couple of minutes and set aside when done.
4. Pour the potatoes and sweet potatoes into a bowl and drizzle with oil. Stir with a wooden spoon so that the oil distributes evenly. Sprinkle with sweet pepper, ginger, and cumin powder, and stir again to cover the pieces.
5. Melt some more butter in the pan if needed and heat.
6. Pop the fries into the pan and stir-fry for 10–15 minutes or until done.
7. Fill the buns with patties and serve with fries.

## FACTS AND STATS:

*British Columbia is another popular destination for elk hunting, with a mix of Rocky Mountain and Roosevelt elk found throughout the province. The province offers both guided and unguided hunts on public and private land. Saskatchewan is home to a growing elk population, with opportunities for guided and unguided hunts on public and private land. The province is known for producing high-quality bulls with impressive antlers.*

# DINNER

# ELK WELLINGTON STEAK

Elk were once native to Ontario but were extirpated from the province in the 19th century due to overhunting and habitat loss. However, in recent years, elk have been reintroduced to several areas in Ontario as part of a conservation and management program. As of 2021, the estimated elk population in Ontario is around 500 animals, most of which are located in the Bancroft and Timmins areas.

### SERVING SIZE: 4

### INGREDIENTS:

- 1 lb elk tenderloin meat
- 2–3 tbsp butter
- 1 cup of beer
- 1 tsp garlic powder
- ½ tsp ginger powder
- ½ tsp orange zest
- 1 tsp honey
- 2 cups mushrooms, sliced
- 1 cup carrots, sliced
- 1 cup sweet potatoes, diced
- 1 tbsp brandy
- 1 cup sour cream
- 1 store-bought pastry dough or pie crust
- 1–2 eggs

### DIRECTIONS:

1. Preheat your oven to 400 °F.
2. Marinate the steak in beer, garlic powder, ginger powder, orange zest, and honey for a couple of hours before cooking or the night before.
3. Melt butter in a frying pan, fry the meat on each side for a couple of minutes, and take it out of the pan.
4. Add the remaining marinade and mushrooms, carrots, and sweet potatoes. Bring to a boil and simmer for 10 minutes.
5. Add the brandy and let simmer for 5 more minutes. Pour in the sour cream and let simmer until the sauce reaches jam-like thickness.
6. Spread the dough on your kitchen counter and glaze the edges with whisked eggs.
7. Spread the mushroom sauce evenly across the dough, leaving the edges clean.

8. Wrap the steak in the dough while ensuring the sauce doesn't spill, and the steak is evenly covered. Press the edges using a fork to seal the crust.
9. Glaze a baking dish with butter and transfer the wrapped steak.
10. Brush the dough's top and sides again with egg and bake at 400 °F (20 minutes, rare; 30 minutes, medium; 40 minutes, well done).

### FACTS AND STATS:

*Manitoba offers limited-entry and open-season elk hunts, with rifle and archery hunting opportunities. The province is known for its remote wilderness hunting areas. The Yukon Territory offers some of North America's most remote and rugged elk hunting. The territory is home to a population of Rocky Mountain elk and offers limited-entry hunts on public land.*

# ELK FILLET IN BLACKBERRY BRANDY SAUCE

In the summer, elk feed on herbaceous plants like sedges, grasses, and forbs, providing them the nutrients they need to grow and gain weight. In the fall and winter, they may also eat woody shrubs, such as willow, aspen, dogwood, and coniferous trees, such as pine and fir. During winter, when food is scarce, elk may eat tree bark and twigs.

## SERVING SIZE: 4

## INGREDIENTS:

- 1 lb elk fillets
- ½ cup brandy
- 1 tsp orange zest
- 1 tsp orange juice
- 1 tbsp olive oil
- ½ tsp ginger powder
- 1 tsp garlic powder
- 3 tbsp butter
- ½ lb blackberries

## DIRECTIONS:

1. Marinate the elk fillets in brandy, orange zest, orange juice, olive oil, ginger powder, and garlic powder for at least 4 hours before cooking.
2. Take the steaks out of the marinade and preserve the marinade for later cooking.
3. Melt butter in a frying pan and fry the fillets for a couple of minutes on each side or until done.
4. Take the fillets out of the pan and set them aside.
5. Add the blackberries and the marinade to the pan.
6. Bring to a boil and simmer for up to 20 minutes with frequent stirring. The sauce is done once you've achieved the desired thickness and the blackberries have fully broken down.

## FACTS AND STATS:

*Elk have played an essential role in the history and culture of many indigenous peoples throughout North America. In many indigenous cultures, elk were regarded as a symbol of strength, power, and resilience. Elk were also an important source of food, clothing, and other resources for many indigenous communities.*

# FRIED ELK WITH VEGGIE MASH

Elk are known to be opportunistic feeders, meaning they will eat whatever food is available to them at the time, including agricultural crops such as alfalfa, corn, and oats. However, it is important to note that elk can cause significant crop damage and may need to be managed to prevent conflicts with farmers and landowners.

### SERVING SIZE: 4

### INGREDIENTS:

- 1 lb elk meat, chopped
- 1 tbsp Dijon mustard
- 1 tbsp honey
- 1 tsp cinnamon powder
- 1 tsp lemon zest
- 1 tbsp lemon juice
- ½ tsp ginger powder
- 2 cups bread crumbs
- 2 tbsp butter
- 1 cup of potatoes, diced
- 1 cup sweet potatoes, diced
- 1 cup carrots, diced
- 1 cup vegetable stock
- 1 cup heavy cream
- 1 cup Parmesan cheese, grated
- 1 tsp mint
- 1 tsp thyme
- Salt, to taste

### DIRECTIONS:

1. Marinade the chopped elk meat in Dijon mustard, honey, cinnamon powder, lemon zest, lemon juice, and ginger powder for a couple of hours before cooking.
2. Take out the marinade and save it for later cooking.
3. Dredge the fillets in bread crumbs.
4. Heat the butter in a frying pan and fry the fillets for up to 5 minutes or until done.
5. Take the fillets out of the pan and set them aside.
6. Add the diced potatoes, sweet potatoes, and carrots to the pan and drizzle with vegetable stock.
7. Bring to a boil and simmer for 10–15 minutes.
8. Reduce the heat and begin mashing the vegetables. After mashing, add the heavy cream, Parmesan, mint, thyme, and salt. Stir on low heat until creamy.
9. Serve next to the breaded fillets.

## FACTS AND STATS:

*The Blackfoot Confederacy of Montana, Alberta, and Saskatchewan relied heavily on elk for their subsistence. Elk was also a central figure in their spiritual and ceremonial practices. The Blackfoot believed that elk were responsible for bringing the sun back to the earth each day, and they used elk hides and antlers to make clothing, tools, and ceremonial items.*

# ELK CHEESE AND VEGGIE SOUP

**Elk have been present on the continent for thousands of years. The exact date of their discovery is unknown, as they have been a part of the natural landscape for so long. Elk was an important part of the diet and culture of many Native American tribes, who hunted them for food, clothing, and other resources. Early European explorers and settlers also encountered elk as they moved across the continent, and they quickly recognized the value of elk meat as a food source. Elk remain an essential part of North America's natural heritage and are widely hunted for sport, food, and conservation purposes. While their populations have fluctuated over time due to hunting, habitat loss, and other factors, elk remains a beloved and iconic species in the United States and Canada.**

### SERVING SIZE: 4

### INGREDIENTS:

- 2–3 cups heavy cream
- 4 cups vegetable stock
- 1 cup cauliflower, chopped
- 1 cup peas
- 2 cups cheddar cheese, shredded
- 1 lb elk meat, ground
- 1 onion, chopped
- 2 carrots, chopped
- 1 cup potatoes, diced
- 1 parsley root, chopped
- 2 tbsp butter
- salt and pepper, to taste
- 2 tsp basil
- 1 tsp dill
- 1 tsp celery leaf, chopped
- ½ cup white wine
- 2 tbsp apple cider vinegar

### DIRECTIONS:

1. Melt the butter in a stockpot and heat it on medium heat.
2. Brown the elk meat with chopped onions, carrots, peas, and cauliflower in butter for 10–15 minutes.
3. Add the vegetable stock and heavy cream. Bring to a short boil and reduce the heat. Let simmer for 10 minutes and add wine.

4. Simmer for 10 more minutes and reduce the heat to the lowest.
5. Add the shredded cheddar cheese and seasoning.
6. Stir until the cheese melts evenly.
7. Wait for 15–20 minutes for the soup to cool down, and add vinegar.

## FACTS AND STATS:

*The Nez Perce Tribe of Idaho and Oregon had a strong connection to elk. They relied on elk for food and other resources, and elk were a common subject in their traditional stories and art. The Nez Perce also believed that elk had spiritual power, and they used elk hides and antlers in their ceremonies and rituals. Many other indigenous cultures throughout North America also have strong historical and cultural ties to elk and continue to value and respect these animals to this day.*

# WHITE ELK AND MUSHROOM MACARONI

**Compound bows are popular for hunters and archery enthusiasts because of their accuracy and power. Choosing a compound bow that is the right size and weight for your body and shooting style is important. Ensure you get properly fitted for your bow, and consider factors like your draw length and weight when selecting a bow. Here are some tips to help you use a compound bow effectively.**

## SERVING SIZE: 4

## INGREDIENTS:

- 1 lb elk meat, ground
- 1 cup onions, chopped
- 1 cup vegetable broth
- 1 cup heavy cream
- 1 cup mushrooms, sliced
- 1 box of macaroni
- 1 tbsp celery leaf
- 1 tsp dill
- 1 tsp mint
- 2 eggs
- ½ cup cheddar cheese, shredded
- ½ cup bacon, chopped
- 2–3 tbsp butter

## DIRECTIONS:

1. Preheat your oven to 400 °F.
2. Melt the butter in a frying pan.
3. Brown the elk meat and onions for 10–15 minutes.
4. Add the vegetable broth, ½ cup of heavy cream, mushrooms, and macaroni.
5. Stir and add celery, dill, and mint.
6. In a separate bowl, break the eggs and mix them with cheddar cheese and bacon.
7. Pour the second half of the heavy cream.
8. Glaze your baking dish with butter and pour in the pasta and meat.
9. Top with the bacon mixture and roast for 20–30 minutes at 400 °F.

## FACTS AND STATS:

*The hunting dates for elk in the United States vary by state and hunting season. Generally, elk hunting seasons take place in the fall, typically from September to November. However, specific dates can vary depending on the state, the hunting unit, and the type of elk tag or permit a hunter has. It's important to check with the appropriate state wildlife agency or department to determine the exact hunting dates and regulations for the area where you plan to hunt. Each state has its own set of rules and regulations for elk hunting, and it's essential to follow these guidelines to ensure a safe and legal hunting experience.*

# ELK MEATBALLS

**Good bow etiquette is to practice at least a few times a week and focus on developing good form and technique. Consider taking lessons or working with a coach to help you improve your skills. The arrows you use can significantly impact your accuracy and effectiveness with a compound bow. Make sure you choose arrows that are the right length and weight for your bow, and consider factors like the type of arrowhead you are using and the conditions you will be shooting in.**

## SERVING SIZE: 4

## INGREDIENTS:

- 1 lb elk, ground
- 2 eggs
- 1 tbsp celery leaf, chopped
- Salt and pepper, to taste
- 1 tsp garlic powder
- 1–2 tsp cumin powder
- 1 cup onion, chopped
- 1 tbsp flour
- 1 cup heavy cream
- 2 cups tomato sauce
- 1 lb whole potatoes
- 1–2 cups of white wine
- 2 tbsp butter

## DIRECTIONS:

1. Cook the potatoes with skins on in a stockpot until done.
2. Peel the skins once the potatoes have cooled down.
3. Mix the elk, onions, garlic powder, celery, salt, pepper, and cumin powder in a medium-sized bowl.
4. Mix well with your hand or a wooden spoon and shape into meatballs your desired size.
5. Cool in your fridge for 15–20 minutes. Cooling will tighten the meat and help maintain its shape.
6. Melt the butter in a frying pan. Fry the meatballs for 10–15 minutes. Turn the meatballs as needed to cook them evenly.
7. Add the tomato sauce, flour, heavy cream, and wine.

8. Bring to a soft boil and simmer for 10–15 minutes. You may simmer as much as you want for the sauce to have the desired consistency. However, you should take off the heat if you notice that the meatballs are getting too soft.

9. Season to taste and serve with boiled potatoes.

### FACTS AND STATS:

*The hunting dates for elk in Canada vary by province and territory, and they can depend on the type of elk and the hunting method being used. Generally, elk hunting seasons in Canada occur in the fall, typically from September to December. However, specific dates can vary depending on the province or territory you plan to hunt. Each province and territory has its own set of rules and regulations for elk hunting, and it's important to follow these guidelines to ensure a safe and legal hunting experience.*

# SWEET ELK SHEPHERD'S PIE

**Good form is essential for accurate and consistent shooting with a compound bow. Focus on keeping your form consistent from shot to shot. Ensure you have a stable stance, keep your bow arm straight, and use your back muscles to draw the bowstring smoothly and evenly.**

## SERVING SIZE: 4

## INGREDIENTS:

- 1 lb elk meat, ground
- 2 eggs
- 4 tbsp butter
- 1 tbsp flour
- 1 cup green peas
- 1 cup mushrooms, sliced
- 1 cup onions, chopped
- 2 cups cheddar cheese, grated
- 1 tsp lemon or orange zest (optional, to emphasize sweetness)
- 1 large sweet potato
- 2 tbsp milk
- a pinch of basil, ground
- a pinch of sage, ground
- salt and pepper, to taste
- 1 cup heavy cream

## DIRECTIONS:

1. Preheat your oven to 400 °F.
2. Brown the ground elk meat, onions, green beans, and mushrooms on 2 tbsp butter for 5–10 minutes.
3. Mix the eggs, heavy cream, flour, 1 cup of cheddar cheese, and orange or lemon zest (optional) in a separate bowl and add to the pan.
4. Bring to a soft boil and simmer for another 5–10 minutes with frequent stirring.
5. Cook the sweet potato whole, mash it, and mix it with butter, milk, cheddar cheese, sage, and basil.
6. Add salt and pepper to taste.
7. Glaze a baking dish with butter and pour the filling. Distribute the filling evenly and flatten it with a spoon.
8. Top with the mashed sweet potato and bake for 20–30 minutes at 350 °F.

## FACTS AND STATS:

*Hunting has been a part of human history for thousands of years, dating back to pre-historic times when early humans relied on hunting for survival. Here are some facts and stats about the history of hunting. The first recorded evidence of hunting dates back to around 2 million years ago, when early humans used crude stone tools for hunting large animals like mammoths and bison. Hunting is how we humans exist today!*

# ELK MEAT LOAF IN CHERRY SAUCE

**To be an effective hunter or archer, practicing shooting in different conditions, such as windy or low-light conditions, is important. You can become a skilled and effective compound bow user by following these tips and practicing regularly. This will help you develop the skills to make accurate shots in real-world hunting or competition situations.**

### SERVING SIZE: 4

### INGREDIENTS:

- 1 lb elk meat, ground
- 1 cup onions, chopped
- 2 tbsp flour
- 2 eggs
- 2 tbsp Parmesan cheese, grated
- Salt and pepper, to taste
- 1 lb fresh cherries, pitted
- ½ cup scallions
- ¼ cup brown sugar
- 2 tbsp brandy or wine vinegar
- ½ tsp cayenne pepper
- ¼ tsp garlic powder
- ½ tbsp butter
- 1 cup heavy cream

### DIRECTIONS:

1. Preheat your oven to 350 °F.
2. To make your cherry sauce, in a food processor, process the cherries, scallions, brown sugar, brandy or wine vinegar, garlic powder, and cayenne pepper until there are no lumps.
3. Sauté on medium-low heat for 25 minutes.
4. Add butter to prevent sticking.
5. Add heavy cream and Parmesan cheese.
6. Leave the pot partially open to allow the steam to escape and speed up cooking.
7. If the sauce is still too runny after 20 minutes, you can thicken it by adding 1 tbsp flour.
8. Grab a bowl and mix your elk meat, 1/2 of the sauce, 1 tbsp flour, eggs, onions, salt, and pepper.
9. Shape into a meatloaf, place on a baking sheet, and bake for 1 hour and 15 minutes at 350 °F.
10. Serve topped with the sauce.

# FACTS AND STATS:

*Hunting was an important part of human culture in ancient civilizations like the Egyptians, Greeks, and Romans. Hunting was often associated with royalty and nobility, and elaborate hunting expeditions were staged as entertainment. In the Middle Ages, hunting became even more popular among the aristocracy, who often hunted with trained falcons or hounds. Hunting was also an important part of feudal society, with hunting rights usually granted to lords as a form of political power. Hunting played an important role in the exploration and settlement of the New World. Early settlers relied on hunting to supplement their diets and to trade with Native American tribes for furs and other goods. In the late 19th and early 20th centuries, hunting began to be seen as a threat to wildlife populations. Unregulated hunting led to the near-extinction of species like the bison and the passenger pigeon. This led to the rise of conservation movements and the establishment of national parks and wildlife refuges to protect wildlife populations. Hunting continues to be a popular pastime and an important part of wildlife management in many parts of the world.*

# HEY, THERE FOODIES!

**Have you ever read a cookbook that made you feel like a true master of the kitchen?**

**The kind that inspired you to step out of your culinary comfort zone and try new and exciting recipes?**

If not, let me introduce you to "The Hunters Wild Game Cookbook Guide" - a cookbook that will take your taste buds on a wild ride!

But this isn't just any cookbook! It's a guide to mastering the art of cooking popular North American animals with over 200 mouth-watering recipes! This cookbook has everything from deer to elk, moose to boar. And not only that but it's packed full of fascinating facts and stats about each animal, making it both an educational and delicious read!

Now, you may be wondering, "Why should I leave a review?" Well, let me ask you this - how does it feel when someone recommends a product or service to you that turns out to be amazing? Pretty good, right? You feel grateful for the recommendation and glad that you tried it out. Well, leaving a review is your chance to provide that same feeling of gratitude and happiness to others who are considering purchasing this cookbook.

Leaving a review is easy and only takes a few minutes. Simply go to the (website: www.patgatz.com) where you purchased the book, find "The Hunters Wild Game Cookbook Guide," and leave an honest review. Tell us what you loved about the book, what recipes you tried, and how they turned out. Your review will help others decide whether or not to purchase the book, and it will also provide valuable feedback to the author.

**So why is leaving a review important?** Well, imagine you were trying to decide between two similar cookbooks, but one had dozens of glowing reviews while the other had none. **Which one would you choose?** Most likely, you'd choose the one with the positive reviews. Your review can be the deciding factor for someone who is on the fence about purchasing this cookbook.

**So what are you waiting for?** Grab your copy of "The Hunters Wild Game Cookbook Guide," try out some of the delicious recipes, and leave an honest review. Your review will not only help others make an informed decision, but it will also show support for the author and their work.

**Let's spread the word about this amazing cookbook and inspire others to step back and reconnect with mother nature!**

https://www.amazon.com/Simple-Hunting-Guide-Beginners-Tracking/dp/B09BGM1TB5/ref=sr_1_2?crid=29BWQ87TWEGEP&keywords=Pat+gatz&qid=1681428763&sprefix=pat+gatz%2Caps%2C136&sr=8-2

# CHAPTER 5
# Marvelous Moose

The word moose comes from the Algonquin Indians, meaning "twig-eater" or "the animal that strips bark off of trees." Through the years, it eventually changed into "moose." Mi'kmaq people saw the moose as an important animal. It supplies them with food and other things for their survival. Moose meat is a source of nourishment during the long winters. It is very healthy for you. The hide was used to make clothing and provide shelter, and moose bones and antlers were shaped into useful tools. The moose is the world's largest deer.

**Breakfast**
Scrumptious Moose Scramble
Cheesy Moose Breakfast Casserole
Moose Spring Salad
Cesar Moose Salad
Easy Moose Scramble
Moose Morning Toast With Cherry Sauce

**Lunch**
Moose Sandwich
Cool Moose Bacon Salad Toast
Breaded and Stuffed Moose Fillet
Moose Omelet
Munching Moose Taco Salad
Moose Burritos

**Dinner**
Moose Kebab
Moose Carbonara
Veggie Moose Soup
Moose Moussaka
Moose Ragu–Goulash
Algonquin Moose Stew
Moose Meat One Dish
Moose Whispers Marvel Fast Fry
Gammy's Crazy Lasagna
Mandy's Moose Death Row Soup

# BREAKFAST

# SCRUMPTIOUS MOOSE SCRAMBLE

**You can substitute any wild meat with this recipe. You can use turkey, bear, deer, elk, and wild boar. It depends on what you have sitting around the freezer. This dish will give you fuel for the whole day!**

### SERVING SIZE: 4

### INGREDIENTS:

- 1 lb moose meat, cubed
- 8 whole eggs
- ½ cup bell peppers, chopped
- ½ cup onions, chopped
- ½ cup carrots, chopped
- ½ tbsp garlic, minced
- 2 tbsp olive oil
- salt and pepper, to taste

### DIRECTIONS:

1. Heat a frying pan and add the olive oil.
2. Pop the meat and vegetables in and stir-fry until ready.
3. In a bowl, break the eggs and whisk.
4. Pour the eggs over the meat and veggies to make a scramble.

## FACTS AND STATS:

*Moose can live up to 20 years in the wild. Female moose, also named cow, can gain 1.5 kg per day. Moose pregnancy periods can last for 243 days. The plural of moose is moose.*

# CHEESY MOOSE BREAKFAST CASSEROLE

**Moose meat can be a healthy protein, iron, and other nutrient sources. Moose are not farmed, so their meat is free from the hormones and antibiotics often used in industrial animal agriculture. Moose meat can be high in cholesterol, so people with high cholesterol levels may want to limit their consumption. Additionally, as with all wild game, there is a risk of exposure to diseases such as chronic wasting disease, so it's important to handle and cook moose meat properly to reduce the risk of illness.**

### SERVING SIZE: 4-6

### INGREDIENTS:

- 1 lb wild moose meat, chopped
- 8 whole eggs
- ½ cup fresh scallions, chopped
- ½ cup bell peppers, chopped
- 1-2 zucchinis, sliced
- ½ tbsp garlic, minced
- ½ cup Parmesan cheese, shredded
- 1 cup cheddar cheese, shredded
- 2 cups sweet potatoes, diced
- salt and pepper, to taste
- 2 tbsp butter

### DIRECTIONS:

1. Heat your oven to 350 °F.
2. Brown the moose meat, peppers, garlic, sweet potatoes, zucchini, and scallions in butter over medium heat for 10 minutes.
3. Glaze your baking dish with some butter.
4. In a bowl, break the eggs, whisk, and mix the Parmesan and cheddar cheese.
5. Pour the eggs over the moose and vegetables.
6. Bake for 40 minutes at 400 °F.

## FACTS AND STATS:

*Moose are the largest member of the deer family and can stand over 6 feet tall at the shoulder and weigh up to 1,500 pounds. Moose can be found in several states across the US, including Alaska, Maine, Montana, New Hampshire, Vermont, and Wyoming. Moose are herbivores and feed on various plants, including willow, birch, and aspen.*

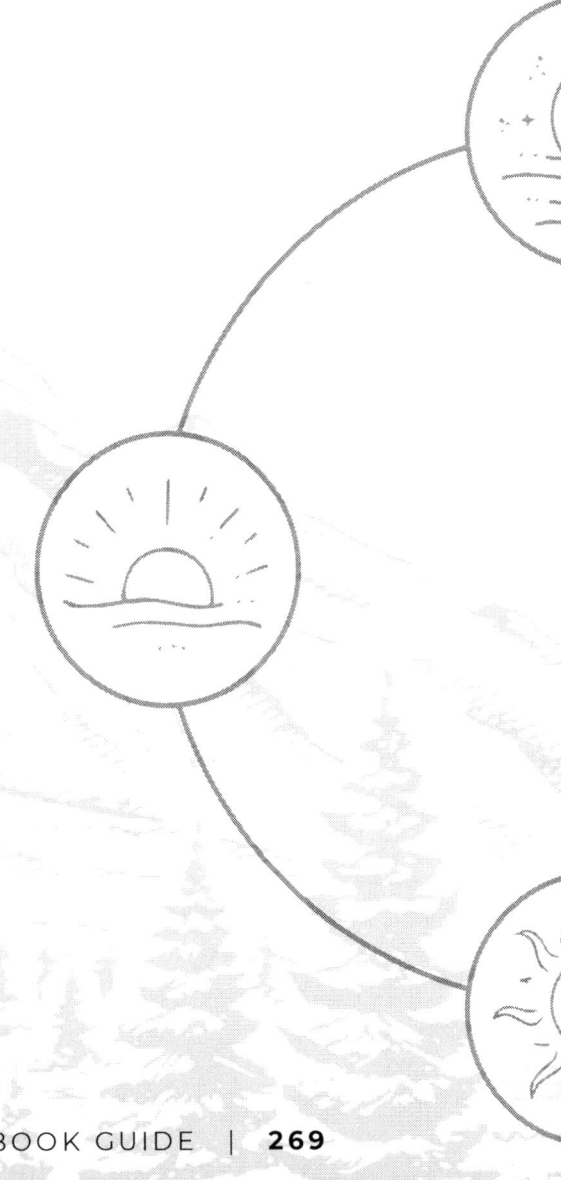

# MOOSE SPRING SALAD

Some potential health benefits of eating moose meat is a good source of lean protein, which is essential for building and repairing tissues and maintaining muscle mass. Moose meat is typically low in fat, particularly saturated fat, which can benefit heart health.

## SERVING SIZE: 4

## INGREDIENTS:

- 1 lb moose meat, ground
- 1 cup tomatoes, chopped
- 1 cup cucumber, chopped
- 1 cup paprika, chopped
- 3 tbsp Parmesan cheese, ground
- 1 cup feta cheese, crushed
- 1 tbsp lemon juice or vinegar
- 1 cup sour cream
- salt and pepper, to taste
- 1 tbsp celery leaf, chopped
- 1 tsp oregano
- 1 tsp dill
- 2 tbsp butter

## DIRECTIONS:

1. Brown the moose meat in butter for 10–15 minutes.
2. Season and add a drizzle of water.
3. Fry for 10 more minutes.
4. Grab a salad bowl and mix the meat with the chopped vegetables.
5. Grab a small bowl and mix vinegar or lemon juice with sour cream, Parmesan cheese, feta cheese, oregano, dill, and celery to make a dressing.
6. Top the salad with the dressing, mix, and enjoy!

## FACTS AND STATS:

*Male moose have antlers, which they shed and regrow each year. The size and shape of the antlers can vary depending on the age and health of the moose. Moose are excellent swimmers and can swim up to 6 miles per hour. They swim across lakes and rivers to find food or escape predators.*

# CESAR MOOSE SALAD

**Moose meat is my favorite big game meat next to elk. Your body gets all the nutrients that it needs from wild game. Moose meat is a rich source of vitamins and minerals, including iron, zinc, and vitamin B12. Moose meat is a good source of omega-3 fatty acids, which can help reduce inflammation and promote heart health.**

### SERVING SIZE: 4

### INGREDIENTS:

- 1 lb moose meat, chopped
- 2 tbsp butter
- 4 tbsp sour cream
- 1 tbsp mayonnaise
- 1 tbsp balsamic vinegar
- 1 tsp brown sugar
- 1 tsp celery leaf, chopped
- 1 tsp dill
- ½ tsp garlic powder
- 1 hard-boiled egg
- 3–4 (moose) bacon slices
- 4–6 bread slices, cubed and toasted
- olives, sliced, as needed
- bacon slices, as needed

### DIRECTIONS:

1. Melt the butter in a frying pan and brown the moose meat for 15–20 minutes.
2. Mix the meat, sour cream, mayo, balsamic vinegar, sugar, celery, dill, and garlic powder in a salad bowl.
3. Add the toasted bread cubes and stir.
4. Chop the boiled egg and mix it in the salad.
5. Fry the bacon slices for 1–2 minutes, chop, and mix into the salad bowl.
6. Enrich the salad with olives as needed.

## FACTS AND STATS:

*Although moose may appear docile, they can be dangerous when threatened or provoked. They have been known to charge people and vehicles, causing serious injury or death. In some states, moose populations have declined due to hunting and habitat loss. As a result, conservation efforts are underway to protect and manage moose populations.*

# EASY MOOSE SCRAMBLE

**Moose is fabulous game meat if you ask me! It has a similar taste to beef, but it has its own taste. Moose meat is tremendously lean, and I recommend cooking it with butter. It is a bit sweeter than elk, pairing great with red wine and berries. The best cuts of meat are tenderloins. Moose being how big they are, the tenderloins are about the same size as beef tenderloins. Tenderloins are easily removed by hand by pulling them free from where the ribs meet the spine.**

### SERVING SIZE: 4

### INGREDIENTS:

- 1 lb moose meat, chopped
- 6–8 eggs
- 2 tbsp flour
- 1 tbsp mushrooms, chopped
- 1 tbsp shallots, chopped
- lemon zest, to taste
- 1 tsp garlic, minced
- ½ cup heavy cream
- 2–3 tbsp Parmesan cheese, ground
- 2–3 tbsp butter
- Salt and pepper, to taste

### DIRECTIONS:

1. Brown the moose meat with garlic in butter until ready.
2. Add the mushrooms, shallots, salt, pepper, and lemon zest after 10–15 minutes.
3. Mix the eggs with flour, heavy cream, and Parmesan.
4. Pour the egg mixture over the fried meat. You can fry it into an omelet or a scramble.

## FACTS AND STATS:

*Alaska is known for having the largest moose population in the United States, and the state offers resident and non-resident hunting opportunities. The exact moose population in Alaska is difficult to determine, as it fluctuates depending on hunting regulations, predation, and habitat availability. According to the Alaska Department of Fish and Game, there are estimated to be between 175,000 and 200,000 moose in Alaska. Moose are an important part of the Alaskan ecosystem and provide a valuable food source for both humans and predators such as wolves and bears. The state manages moose populations through hunting regulations and surveys to ensure that the population remains healthy and sustainable.*

# MOOSE MORNING TOAST WITH CHERRY SAUCE

Moose have existed for thousands of years and were known to indigenous peoples long before written records. Moose are native to the northern regions of North America, Europe, and Asia. They have been essential to these regions' ecosystems and cultural traditions for centuries. The scientific name for moose is Alces alces, and they are also known by various other names depending on the region, such as elk (in Europe), Eurasian elk (in Asia), or simply "the moose" in North America.

### SERVING SIZE: 4

### INGREDIENTS:

- 1 lb moose meat, ground
- 1 lb cherries, pitted
- 2 tbsp butter
- salt and pepper, to taste
- ½ cup white wine
- 1 tbsp white wine vinegar
- 1 tbsp brown sugar
- ½ cup heavy cream
- 1 cup shallots, chopped
- 1 tbsp cinnamon powder
- 1 tbsp nutmeg powder
- slices of toast, as needed
- 1 tbsp flour

### DIRECTIONS:

1. Sauté the moose meat in butter, wine, and the seasoning on low-medium heat until ready.
2. Make your cherry sauce by processing cherries, shallots, white wine vinegar, brown sugar, nutmeg, cinnamon, flour, and heavy cream.
3. Simmer in a metal pot or pan for 20–25 minutes or until the sauce has thickened to your liking.
4. Top your toast slices with a little bit of moose meat and sauce.

## FACTS AND STATS:

*Individual states in the United States regulate moose hunting, and availability and regulations vary depending on the location. Moose hunting is popular in Maine, and the state has a lottery system for hunters to obtain a permit. Montana has a limited moose hunting season, and the state offers a lottery system for hunting permits. New Hampshire offers a lottery system for hunting permits, and the state has a healthy moose population.*

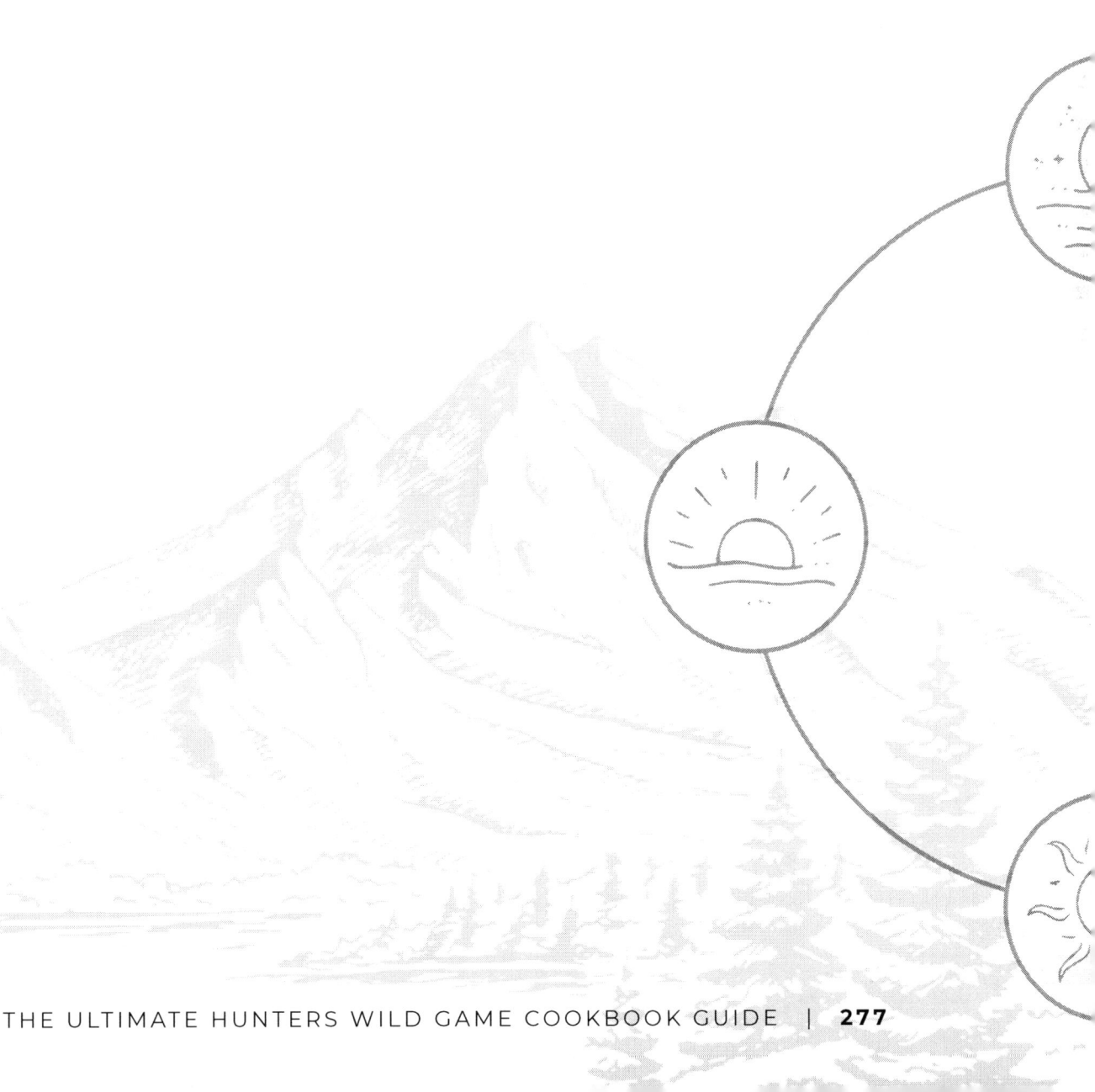

# LUNCH

# MOOSE SANDWICH

**Vermont has a limited moose hunting season, and the state offers a lottery system for permits. It's important to note that hunting regulations and seasons can change, and hunters should always check with the state's wildlife agency for current regulations and restrictions before planning a hunting trip. Additionally, it's important to hunt responsibly and ethically, following all safety guidelines and regulations.**

## SERVING SIZE: 4-6

## INGREDIENTS:

- 1 lb moose meat, ground
- 1 cup onions, chopped
- salt and pepper, to taste
- sour cream, as needed
- 1 tsp cayenne pepper
- slices of cheddar cheese, as needed
- 3-4 tbsp butter
- buns, as needed

## DIRECTIONS:

1. Mix the moose meat in butter with onions, salt, pepper, and cayenne pepper.
2. Shape into patties and brown in butter on medium heat for 6-10 minutes or until ready.
3. Top the buns with sour cream or any other condiments like mayonnaise.
4. Add the meat and cheddar cheese to the sandwich, and enjoy!

## FACTS AND STATS:

*Moose have played an essential role in Canada's history and culture for thousands of years. Indigenous peoples have hunted moose for food, clothing, and other resources for generations and continue to do so today. In the early 1600s, French fur traders began trading with Indigenous peoples for furs, including moose hides. Moose hides were prized for their durability and were used to make clothing, shoes, and other goods.*

# COOL MOOSE BACON SALAD TOAST

Moose are native to North America and have a long history in the United States. Moose were historically found across much of the northern United States, but populations declined due to habitat loss and overhunting. In the late 1800s and early 1900s, moose populations in the United States were severely depleted due to overhunting and habitat loss. However, conservation efforts began in the mid-1900s, and moose populations have started to recover in some areas.

## SERVING SIZE: 4

## INGREDIENTS:

- ½ lb smoked moose meat, sliced
- 4–6 moose or bacon slices
- 1 tbsp butter
- 4–5 eggs, hard-boiled
- 2 tsp garlic, minced
- sour cream, as needed
- mayonnaise, as needed
- salt and pepper, to taste
- 2 tbsp Parmesan cheese, ground
- 1 pack of bread, toasted
- 7 oz cheddar cheese, sliced
- salt and pepper, to taste

## DIRECTIONS:

1. Peel the hard-boiled eggs and grate them into a bowl.
2. Mix the eggs with sour cream, mayonnaise, garlic, Parmesan cheese, salt, and pepper.
3. Chop the bacon slices and fry them briefly in butter. Once done, take out of the pan and set aside.
4. Grab a larger plate and line it with baking paper.
5. Layer four slices of bread against each other to form a larger rectangular shape.
6. Top with a layer of egg–sour cream mixture, and then top with a layer of chopped bacon.
7. Top with another layer of bread, this time first laying down slices over the line between the slices of the bottom layer (similar to laying down bricks). Start in the middle and work toward the end. Cut out the excess bread from the edges with a sharp knife.
8. Add two more layers of bread and repeat the process with the egg mixture and bacon.

9. Once you've completed all four layers, glaze the "sandwich cake" outside with the remaining mixture, the same way you'd ice a cake.
10. Cool down in the fridge for 20–30 minutes.
11. When serving, cut into slices in the same fashion you'd cut a loaf of bread.

### FACTS AND STATS:

*Moose are excellent swimmers and can dive up to 20 feet deep to reach underwater plants. Moose have a unique appendage on their necks called a "bell," a flap of skin under their chin that can communicate with other moose. Moose are solitary animals, except during the breeding season when males compete for females' attention. Moose are an important part of many Native American cultures and are often depicted in art and storytelling.*

# BREADED AND STUFFED MOOSE FILLET

**Hunting moose requires skill, experience, and careful planning to ensure a safe and successful hunt. Before hunting moose, you must obtain the necessary permits and licenses from the state or provincial wildlife agency where you plan to hunt. It's important to scout where you plan to hunt, looking for signs of moose activity, such as tracks, droppings, and browsing patterns.**

### SERVING SIZE: 4

### INGREDIENTS:

- 1 lb moose meat, sliced into thin fillets
- 3 eggs
- ½ cup heavy cream
- 2 cups bread crumbs
- salt and pepper, to taste
- 1 cup cream cheese
- 1 tbsp celery leaf, chopped
- 1 tbsp basil, chopped
- 1 tsp garlic powder
- 1 tbsp red wine
- 3–4 tbsp butter

### DIRECTIONS:

1. Make your batter by mixing the egg, heavy cream, and seasoning.
2. Spread the fillets on a larger plate.
3. Top each fillet with cream cheese and roll.
4. Fix the rolls with toothpicks at the side and on the ends.
5. Dredge the fillet rolls in the egg mixture and let sit for 10–20 minutes.
6. Dredge in bread crumbs and fry in butter for 3–4 minutes on each side or until ready.

## FACTS AND STATS:

*There are several methods for hunting moose, each with advantages and challenges. Stalking is a method of quietly moving through the woods to locate and get within range of a moose. This requires patience, careful observation, and the ability to move silently through the bush. Calling is a technique that involves imitating the sounds that moose make to attract them closer. This can be done using various tools, including grunt tubes, cow calls, and bull calls, which are the most effective in the fall.*

# MOOSE OMELET

**Moose are wary animals and can be difficult to approach. Consider using a combination of stalking and calling techniques to lure the moose within range. When you have a clear shot, aim for the vital organs, including the lungs and heart, to ensure a quick and humane kill. The vital organs are located just behind the front shoulders. After the moose is down, it's important to field dress it as soon as possible to ensure the meat stays fresh.**

## SERVING SIZE: 4-6

## INGREDIENTS:

- ½ lb wild moose meat, ground
- 2 tbsp butter
- 1 tbsp basil, chopped
- 1 tbsp celery leaf, chopped
- 1 tsp ginger powder
- 1 tsp garlic powder or minced garlic
- 4-6 eggs
- 1 cup sour cream
- 1 cup of milk
- 1 tsp baking soda
- 2-3 tbsp flour
- 2-3 tbsp Parmesan cheese, grated

## DIRECTIONS:

1. Brown the moose meat in butter with the seasoning.
2. Whisk the eggs and mix with milk, sour cream, baking soda, and flour, mix in the fried meat and stir.
3. Melt more butter and fry in the pan, several spoonfuls at a time.
4. Sprinkle your mini omelets with Parmesan cheese and serve.

## FACTS AND STATS:

*Spot and stalk is a method that involves scanning for moose from a distance and then approaching them on foot. This can be effective in open terrain where moose are visible from a distance. Still hunting involves moving slowly and quietly through the woods, frequently stopping to listen and observe. This method requires patience and a keen eye for spotting moose.*

# MUNCHING MOOSE TACO SALAD

I know what you are thinking, but we all still need greens with our wild meats. I came up with this salad style that you get your daily fill of meat protein, too! You can use other wild game hamburger.

### SERVING SIZE: 4

### INGREDIENTS:

- 1 lb moose meat, ground
- 2 tomatoes, sliced
- 1 head of romaine lettuce
- 3 oz cheddar cheese (or any cheese), shredded
- 1 cup salsa of your choice
- 1 cup sour cream
- Salt and pepper, to taste
- Seasoning of your choice to taste
- 2 tbsp butter

### DIRECTIONS:

1. Brown the ground moose meat with seasoning in butter until ready.
2. Cut up the romaine lettuce and mix it with shredded cheese in a separate bowl.
3. Mix the fried meat with the lettuce and cheese.
4. Top with sour cream, and enjoy!

# FACTS AND STATS:

*Hunting from a stand involves sitting in a stationary position and waiting for moose to come within range. This method can be effective in areas with a lot of moose activity. Some hunters use trained hunting dogs to track and locate moose. This method can be particularly effective in areas with dense vegetation or deep snow. It's important to note that different hunting methods may be more appropriate for different regions and terrain types.*

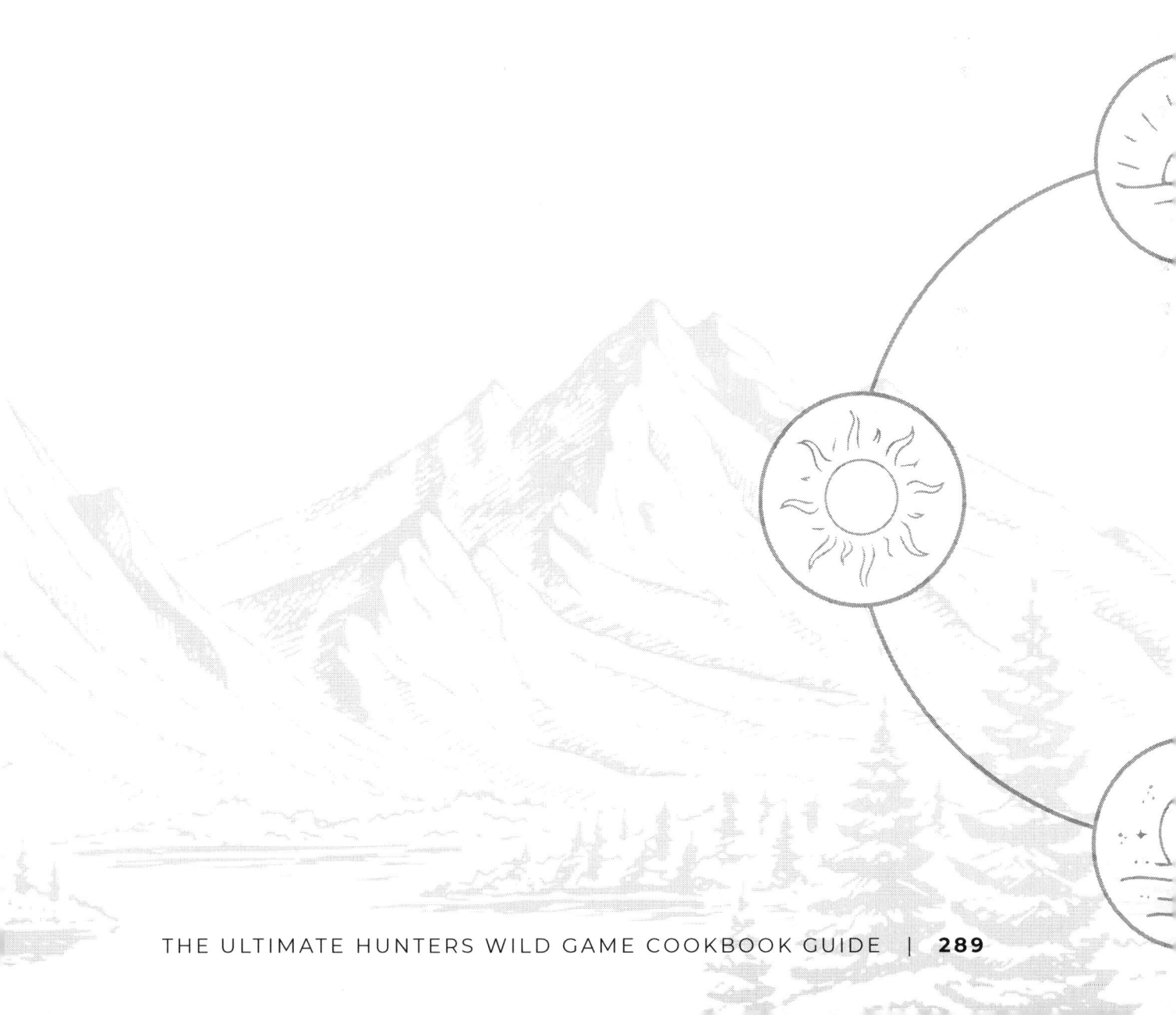

# MOOSE BURRITOS

**Moose meat can be pretty heavy, so it's important to have a plan for transporting it out of the field. Once the meat is back at camp or home, it can be processed into steaks, roasts, and other cuts. It's important to note that hunting regulations and techniques can vary by region and season, so it's important to consult with local wildlife agencies and experienced hunters before planning a moose hunt.**

### SERVING SIZE: 4–6

### INGREDIENTS:

- 1 lb moose meat, ground
- 2–3 tbsp butter
- ½ cup heavy cream
- ½ cup cheese, shredded
- 1 tbsp garlic, minced
- 8–12 eggs
- ½ tbsp salt
- ½ tbsp pepper
- ½ tbsp celery leaf
- ½ tbsp thyme
- ½ tbsp red pepper powder
- ½ tbsp cumin powder
- 6 burrito tortillas
- ½ cup sour cream

### DIRECTIONS:

1. Melt the butter in a saucepan and add the moose, seasoning, and heavy cream.
2. Bring to a boil and simmer for 15–20 minutes or until done.
3. Prepare the tortillas as instructed by the packaging and add the filling.
4. Top the tortillas with the heavy cream, shredded cheese, and other toppings you like. You can also serve it with your favorite salsa, relish, and salad.

## FACTS AND STATS:

*The moose has been an important symbol and source of sustenance for many Native American tribes, including the Algonquin people. In Algonquin culture, the moose is considered a powerful and respected animal, often associated with strength, agility, and endurance. The Algonquin people traditionally hunted moose for their meat and hides and used various parts of the animal for tools, clothing, and other items. Moose antlers were prized for their strength and durability and were often used to make tools such as shovels and scrapers.*

# DINNER

# MOOSE KEBAB

Field dressing a moose is an important step in preparing the animal for processing and consumption. Here are some steps to field dress a moose as easily as possible. Move the moose to a flat, stable area. Moving the moose to a flat, stable area is important before beginning the field dressing process. This will make it easier to access the various parts of the animal. It's easier to have a partner to help hold the legs apart. It definitely makes life easier with more hands. Using a sharp knife, make a small incision near the anus of the moose. Be careful not to cut too deeply, as you don't want to puncture any organs. I have mentioned it before with other game animals. My favorite tool for the anus is called "Butt Out." It is quick and easy, and you don't need to worry about puncturing anything. (You insert "Butt Out "into the anus to the base. Turn until you feel it catches the membrane, do another 1 ½ turn, pull out 10 to 12 inches, tie off, and cut the access membrane.) That's it, off you go to the next step. Using the knife, cut up from the breastbone to the anus to avoid cutting any organs. You may need to use your hands to help pull the skin and fat away from the body. I always use my other hand to keep me from cutting any organs. To be continued on the next recipe…

### SERVING SIZE: 4

### INGREDIENTS:

- 1 lb moose meat, ground
- 1 cup mushrooms, sliced
- 1 tsp ground turmeric
- 1 tbsp celery leaf, chopped
- 1 tsp dill
- 1 tbsp parsley
- 1 tbsp red pepper powder
- 1 tsp ginger powder
- 2 tbsp honey
- 2 tbsp balsamic vinegar
- 2 tbsp butter
- salsa, sauce, or relish of your choice
- kebab skewers, as needed

### DIRECTIONS:

1. Heat the butter in a large saucepan.
2. Grab a large bowl and mix all ingredients together except for the salsa and skewers.
3. Shape the meat mixture into kebabs of the desired size.
4. Brown the kebabs in butter on medium heat for around 15–20 minutes or until done.
5. Turn the sides frequently so that the kebabs fry evenly.
6. You can serve it on a plate or on kebab skewers.
7. You can top it with any sauce, relish, or salsa.

### FACTS AND STATS:

*Hunting seasons for moose in the United States vary by state and are subject to change. So, checking with the relevant state wildlife agency for up-to-date information on hunting regulations and seasons is important. The moose hunting The season in Alaska typically runs from August to September, although the dates may vary by region. The moose hunting season in Maine typically runs from late September to mid-November. The moose hunting season in New Hampshire typically runs from late September to mid-November.*

THE ULTIMATE HUNTERS WILD GAME COOKBOOK GUIDE | **295**

# MOOSE CARBONARA

Once you cut up the belly, you can remove the organs. Start by cutting the diaphragm and separating the chest and abdominal cavities. Then, remove the organs in the abdominal cavity, careful not to puncture the bladder or intestines. After removing the abdominal organs, you can remove the heart and lungs from the chest cavity. These are important organs to remove quickly, as they can spoil the meat if left inside the animal. The next recipe is the last step on field dressing moose!

## SERVING SIZE: 4

## INGREDIENTS:

- 1 lb moose meat, chopped or ground
- 2 tbsp butter
- 1 cup moose bacon, chopped
- 1 cup mushrooms, sliced
- 1 tbsp garlic powder
- 4 eggs
- ½ cup sour cream
- 2 tsp olive oil
- 2–3 tbsp Parmesan cheese, grated
- 1 tsp thyme
- 1 tsp dill
- 1 box of spaghetti
- 1 1/2 cup water or beef stock, if needed

## DIRECTIONS:

1. Brown your ground or chopped moose in butter with bacon and mushrooms for 10–15 minutes.
2. Add the remaining ingredients (except for the Parmesan and spaghetti) and stir. If more liquid is needed, you can add water or beef stock. Beef stock will make the sauce more satiating and increase its "meaty" flavor, while water will slightly dilute the sauce and prevent sticking without altering the taste.
3. Bring to a soft boil and simmer until the desired consistency is achieved.
4. Cook the pasta, transfer it into a larger serving bowl, and mix it with the sauce.
5. Sprinkle with Parmesan.

## FACTS AND STATS:

*The moose hunting season in Vermont typically runs from mid-October to late October. Moose hunting season in Wyoming typically runs from mid-September to mid-October. It's important to note that moose hunting seasons can change based on factors such as population size and other conservation concerns.*

# VEGGIE MOOSE SOUP

Once you have removed all the organs, rinse the inside of the moose cavity with clean water to remove any blood or debris. After field dressing the moose, it's vital to cool the meat as quickly as possible. This can be done by hanging the moose in a cool, dry place or placing the meat in a cooler with ice. It's important to know that field dressing a moose can be a messy and physically demanding process, and it's important to prioritize safety and hygiene throughout the process.

### SERVING SIZE: 4-6

### INGREDIENTS:

- 1 lb moose meat, chopped
- 8–10 cups beef stock
- 1 zucchini, chopped
- 1 cup pumpkin flesh, chopped
- 2 medium-sized potatoes, diced
- 2 carrots, chopped
- 1 onion, chopped
- Salt and pepper, to taste
- 1 tbsp celery leaf, chopped
- 1 egg
- ½ cup heavy cream

### DIRECTIONS:

1. Brown the moose with carrots and onions in butter until half done.
2. Add the stock and vegetables, bring to a boil, and simmer for 15–20 minutes.
3. Reduce the heat and add the celery leaf and heavy cream.
4. Break the egg into a bowl and whisk it.
5. Pour it into the pot, stir, and remove it from the stove.

## FACTS AND STATS:

*Moose hunting season in Ontario typically runs from mid-September to mid-December. The moose hunting season in Quebec typically runs from late September to early November. The moose hunting season in Yukon typically runs from late August to mid-September. Different weapons are also allowed at different times of the season, like bow or rifle.*

# MOOSE MOUSSAKA

Moose are known for their distinctive vocalizations, which range from grunts and snorts to high-pitched whines and moans. They use these vocalizations to communicate with other moose and to establish dominance. Moose have a keen sense of smell. Their sense of smell is so sensitive that they can detect scents up to a mile away. Moose have a highly developed sense of smell, which they use to locate food, mates, and predators.

## SERVING SIZE: 4

## INGREDIENTS:

- 1 lb moose meat, ground
- ½ cup beef stock
- salt and pepper, to taste
- 1 egg
- 1 cup heavy cream
- ½ cup cheddar cheese, grated
- 4–8 moose bacon slices, chopped
- 2–3 tbsp Parmesan cheese, grated
- 2–3 large sweet potatoes, thinly sliced
- 2 large zucchinis, thinly sliced
- 1 eggplant, thinly sliced
- 1 cup mushrooms, finely chopped
- 1 tsp basil, chopped

## DIRECTIONS:

1. Brown the ground moose in butter and season with salt and pepper for 5–10 minutes.
2. Add beef stock, stir, and simmer until the excess liquid evaporates.
3. Preheat your oven to 400 °F.
4. Break and beat the egg in a bowl.
5. Mix it with the heavy cream, basil, and mushrooms.
6. Glaze a baking dish with butter.
7. Spread one layer of sweet potato slices and top with the moose filling.
8. Top with half of the zucchini and eggplant slices, and pour half of the egg and the mushroom sauce over it.
9. Top with the second half of the filling and again top with sweet potato slices.

10. Pour half of the remaining topping over and finish with the layer of zucchini and eggplant.
11. Pour the rest of the topping and sprinkle with cheddar cheese, Parmesan, and bacon.
12. Bake for 40–50 minutes at 400 °F.

> **FACTS AND STATS:**
>
> *Moose have a specialized digestive system. Moose are herbivores with a specialized digestive system that allows them to extract nutrients from tough, fibrous plants. They have a four-chambered stomach and can digest up to 40 pounds of plant material per day. Moose are susceptible to a deadly disease called Chronic Wasting Disease (CWD), a neurological disease affecting deer, elk, and moose. It is fatal to infected animals, and there is currently no cure.*

# MOOSE RAGU-GOULASH

**Unlike many other animals, moose are not territorial and do not defend a specific area as their own. Instead, they roam over large areas in search of food and mates. If you want to be successful in hunting, 80% is scouting & tracking, and the other 20% is hunting!**

### SERVING SIZE: 4-6

### INGREDIENTS:

- 1 lb moose meat, diced
- 1 cup onions, chopped
- 1 cup carrots, chopped
- 1 cup parsley root, chopped
- 3 whole garlic cloves
- 2-3 tbsp butter
- 4 cups beef stock
- 1 cup heavy cream
- 1 cup green peas
- ½ cup white wine
- 1 tsp basil
- 1 tbsp parsley leaf
- 1 tbsp flour (optional)
- 1 potato, cooked and mashed (optional)

### DIRECTIONS:

1. Sauté the onions, carrots, parsley root, and garlic cloves in butter on low heat for up to 15 minutes.
2. Add the moose and simmer on low heat for another 30-40 minutes.
3. Add the beef stock and slightly increase the heat to bring it to a boil.
4. Reduce back to low heat and simmer for another 15-20 minutes.
5. Add the heavy cream, green peas, white wine, basil, and parsley leaf.
6. For a thicker stew, stir in the flour or mashed potato.
7. Let simmer for another 10 minutes and remove from the stove.

## FACTS AND STATS:

*The biggest moose ever recorded in the United States was taken by a hunter in November 1994 in the Yukon Flats area of Alaska. The moose had a rack that measured 75 inches (190.5 cm) in width and had a total of 61 points. The moose weighed an estimated 1,800 pounds (816 kg) and stood over 7 feet (2.1 m) tall at the shoulders. The hunter who took the moose, DeWayne Johnston, donated the rack to the Alaska Department of Fish and Game, where it is on display at the department's headquarters in Juneau, Alaska.*

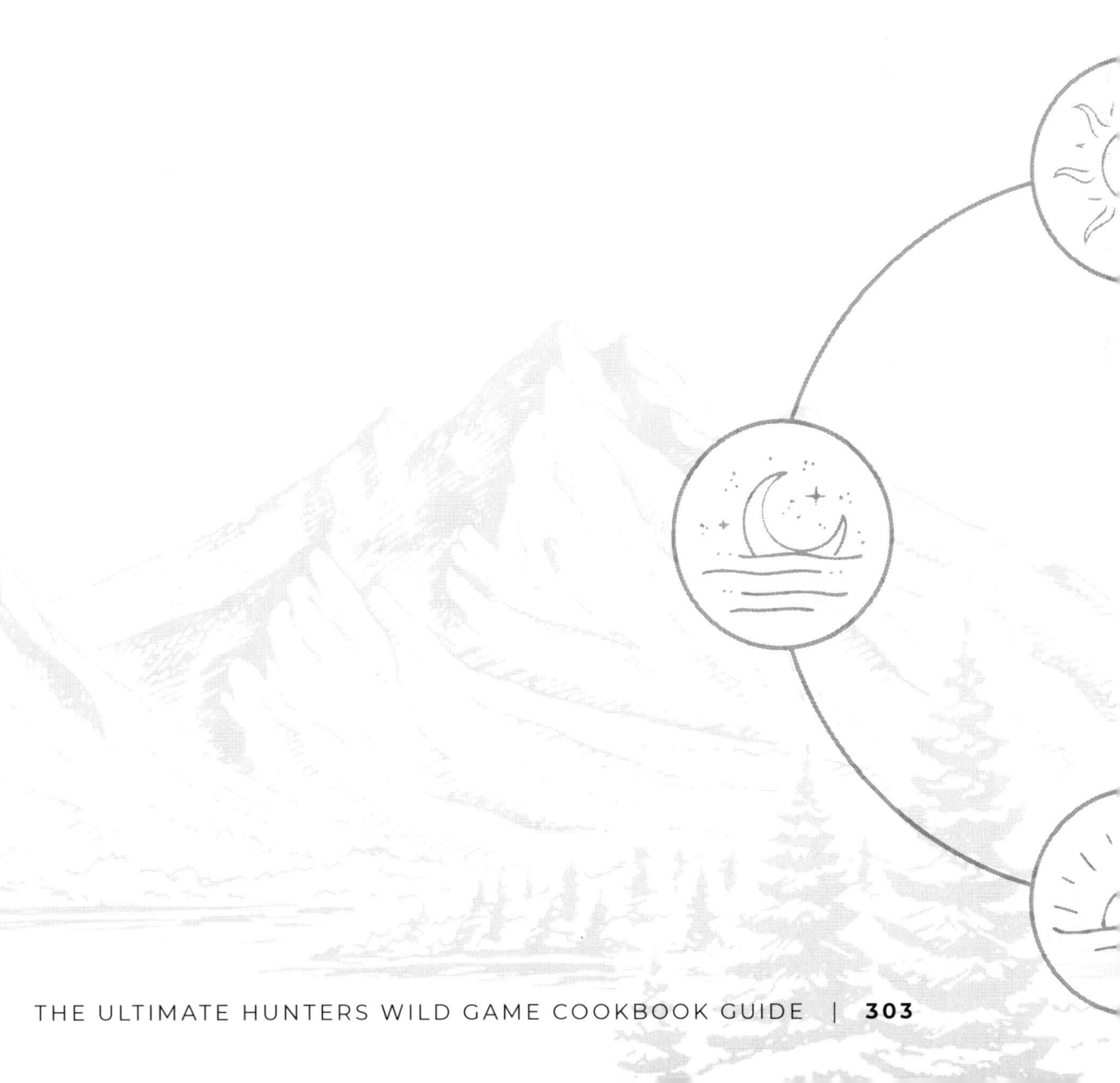

# ALGONQUIN MOOSE STEW

**You can substitute any wild meat with this recipe. You can use turkey, bear, deer, elk, and wild boar. It depends on what you have sitting around the freezer! There are so many delicious dishes you can impress friends with. Their taste buds will be thanking you!**

## SERVING SIZE: 6

## INGREDIENTS:

- 1 lb moose meat, cubed
- 4 cups vegetable broth or water
- 1 cup carrots, chopped
- 1 cup mushrooms, chopped
- 1 cup onions, chopped
- 1 cup red or yellow peppers, chopped
- 1–2 garlic cloves, minced
- 1 tbsp parsley, chopped
- 1 tsp thyme, chopped
- 1–2 tbsp butter
- salt and pepper, to taste

## DIRECTIONS:

1. Heat the frying pan with butter.
2. Add the meat and vegetables.
3. Brown on low-medium heat for up to 15 minutes.
4. Transfer into a cooking pot and add the broth.
5. Bring to a short boil and let simmer for approximately an hour.
6. Add spices 10–15 minutes before the stew is done.

## FACTS AND STATS:

*The biggest moose ever recorded in Canada was taken by a hunter in September 1987 near Favourable Lake, Ontario. The moose had a rack that measured 75.5 inches (191.8 cm) in width and had a total of 51 points. The moose weighed an estimated 1,800 pounds (816 kg) and stood over 7 feet (2.1 m) tall at the shoulders. The hunter who took the moose, Walter J. O'Neil, donated the rack to the Royal Ontario Museum, displayed in the mammal gallery. This is the current world record for the largest antlers on a moose ever recorded.*

# MOOSE MEAT ONE DISH

**You can substitute any wild meat with this recipe. You can use bear, deer, elk, and wild boar. It depends on what you are hunting! It is moose soup for your soul! It is versatile.**

### SERVING SIZE: 4

### INGREDIENTS:

- 1–2 lb moose meat, cubed
- 1 cup beef broth
- 1 can mushroom soup
- ½ cup rice
- 2 tbsp butter
- biscuits, to taste

### DIRECTIONS:

1. Brown the moose meat in butter over medium heat for 10–15 minutes.
2. Add the broth, rice, and mushroom soup, bring to a short boil, and let simmer for another 30–45 minutes or as needed.

## FACTS AND STATS:

*The wilderness north of Nakina has the best moose hunting in Ontario. The population of moose in the region is so high that they receive more adult moose tags than any other area of Ontario. The population of moose in Ontario varies by region and is estimated through periodic surveys conducted by the Ontario Ministry of Natural Resources and Forestry. According to the most recent survey conducted in 2016-2017, the moose population in Ontario was estimated to be approximately 105,000 animals. Most moose in Ontario are found in the northern and central regions of the province, where they inhabit forested areas and wetlands. The population size and distribution of moose in Ontario are carefully managed through hunting regulations and other conservation efforts to ensure the long-term health and sustainability of the species.*

# MOOSE WHISPERS MARVEL FAST FRY

**You can use all assortments of wild game meats from small game, birds, and big game. This recipe has been dedicated to my Northern childhood friend for over thirty years, and many more! "This is the only recipe you need for delicious wild game every single time!"**

- A.J. Saul.

### SERVING SIZE: 4

### INGREDIENTS:

- 1 to 2 lbs of moose or wild game meat of your choice
- 1 stick of real butter
- Pinch of salt (Your discretion.)
- Pinch of pepper (Your discretion.)

### DIRECTIONS:

1. Preheat the stove to medium heat.
2. Melt a stick of real butter in a frying pan.
3. Cut your choice of game meat into thin slices.
4. When butter is melted, put strips of meat in a frying pan with salt & pepper.
5. Cook until golden brown on each side.
6. **NEVER OVERCOOK WILD MEAT!**

## FACTS AND STATS:

*The best place to hunt gigantic moose in Ontario is North Eastern Ontario in WMU 26, 27, 28, 29, 40.*

# GAMMY'S CRAZY LASAGNA

**In the Algonquin Native language, moose means eater of twigs. This recipe is dedicated to my Aunt Suzie. She came up with this fabulous dish! This hearty meal is perfect for a cold northern winter day.**

### SERVING SIZE: 6

### INGREDIENTS:

- 1 ½ lbs moose hamburger
- 1 box of lasagna
- 1 can of stewed tomatoes (Original)
- 1 block or two of your favorite cheese, like cottage cheese, cheddar, or mozzarella
- 1 cup green peppers, chopped
- 1 cup mushrooms, chopped
- 1 cup red onions, chopped
- 1–2 garlic cloves, minced
- salt and pepper, to taste

### DIRECTIONS:

1. Heat the frying pan with butter.
2. Add the meat and vegetables.
3. Brown on low-medium heat for up to 15 minutes.
4. Add a can of stewed tomatoes into a cooking pot.
5. Bring to a boil and let simmer.
6. In another pot, boil water on high-cooking lasagna noodles.
7. When pasta is cooked, and the sauce has been simmering for a bit.
8. In a big casserole dish, layer your lasagna noodles, pasta sauce, and cheese on however your heart desires.
9. Top it off by layering your favorite cheese.
10. Cover and bake for 30–40 minutes at 300 °F.
11. Lick your lips and enjoy the most amazing lasagna!

## FACTS AND STATS:

*Ontario has a well-managed moose hunting program that ensures the sustainability of the species. Hunting regulations are designed to maintain healthy populations while providing hunting opportunities. Moose hunting in Ontario is typically done in remote areas, providing an opportunity for hunters to experience the beauty and wilderness of the province. The hunt can involve trekking through forests, swamps, and lakes, adding to the adventure.*

# MANDY'S MOOSE DEATH ROW SOUP

**Moose meat is lean, high in protein, and low in fat, making it a healthy and tasty option for those who enjoy wild game meat. The meat can also be used in various dishes, including stews, roasts, and sausages. This recipe is in honor of my favorite cousin Mandy.**

### SERVING SIZE: 4

### INGREDIENTS:

- 1 lb moose hamburger
- 1 lb beef hamburger
- 1 box of macaroni
- 6 cups of beef broth
- 1 cup onions, diced
- 1–2 garlic cloves, minced
- 2 cans of stewed tomatoes
- 3 tsp Worcestershire sauce
- 2 tbsp brown sugar
- 1 tsp dried basil
- 1 ½ tsp of steak seasoning
- Salt and pepper

### DIRECTIONS:

1. In a large pan, brown moose/beef hamburger with onions, garlic, steak seasoning, and salt & pepper.
2. In another pot, cook the macaroni.
3. Put 6 cups of beef broth, 3 tsp Worcestershire sauce, and 2 cans of stewed tomatoes in a large pot and cook at medium temperature.
4. When the meat and macaroni are cooked, stir in a large pot for 15 minutes, and bon appetite!

## FACTS AND STATS:

*Moose is my favorite big game animal. As a First Nation Algonquin Native, I have a lot of respect for the majestic moose. That's why I love Canada, my home and native land! Hunting for Greatness will be coming out with its first stuffed animal for the kids, and it will be a moose. Migwetch!*

# CHAPTER 6
# Blissful Bear

Bear is fun to hunt. If you want an adrenaline rush, then hunt bear. Bear fat has many different uses. It is wonderful to cook with. Bear meat is underrated for protein. Bear has a slightly sweet taste but depends on the main diet. Spring and fall bear meat tastes different. Spring bear meat is somewhat less sweet & milder in flavor but is more tender because of the lack of activity during hibernation. Fall bear meat is the sweetest and has the most fat because they are fattening up for winter hibernation. Bear has its unique taste and is a healthy choice if done properly.

### Breakfast
Bear Liver Pate
Bear Breakfast Casserole
Cheesy Arugula Bear Salad
Bear-Stuffed Zucchinis With Cheesy Eggs
Cheesy Bear-Stuffed Paprika Slices

## Lunch
Bear Quiche
Bear Cheese and Veggie Rolls
Light Bear Burgers
Bear Stew
Roasted Bear Risotto
Ground Bear Salad

## Dinner
Bear-Stuffed Paprika Stew
Bear Moussaka
Bear and Bean Stew
Bear Veggie Roast
Bear Steak in Wine Sauce
Bear in White Sauce With Mushrooms
Bear Goulash With Sweet Potato Mash

# BREAKFAST

# BEAR LIVER PATE

Bear meat is a source of protein, iron, and vitamin B12, similar to other types of meat. It is important to note that bear meat may also contain high cholesterol and saturated fat. Bears have been known to carry diseases such as trichinosis, which can be transmitted to humans by consuming undercooked meat. Make sure you cook bear meat thoroughly.

## SERVING SIZE: 4-6

## INGREDIENTS:

- 1 lb bear liver, deveined and chopped
- ½ cup onions, chopped
- ½ cup carrots, chopped
- 3 tbsp sherry
- 3 cups beef stock
- 2-3 tbsp butter
- salt and pepper, to taste
- ½ tsp nutmeg powder
- ½ tsp cinnamon powder

## DIRECTIONS:

1. Sauté the bear liver in beef stock, onions, and carrots for 15-20 minutes.
2. Add sherry and simmer for another 10-15 minutes.
3. Put in a food processor and add cinnamon and nutmeg powder.
4. Process until creamy and transfer onto a container.
5. Leave in the fridge for an hour and serve.

## FACTS AND STATS:

*Three species of bears are found in the US: the American black bear, the grizzly bear, and the polar bear. American black bears are the most common species in North America, with a population of approximately 900,000. Grizzly bears are found in several western states, including Alaska, Montana, and Wyoming, with an estimated population of around 1,500.*

# BEAR BREAKFAST CASSEROLE

**If you are cooking bear meat, it is important to ensure that it reaches a safe internal temperature to kill any potential bacteria or parasites that may be present. The USDA recommends cooking bear meat to an internal temperature of at least 160°F (71°C) to ensure it is safe to eat. You can use a meat thermometer to check the internal temperature of the meat. Handling and cooking bear meat properly is also essential to reduce the risk of foodborne illness. Always follow safe food handling practices, such as thoroughly washing your hands and surfaces and storing and cooking meat at appropriate temperatures.**

## SERVING SIZE: 4-6

## INGREDIENTS:

- 1 lb bear, ground
- 1-2 cups mushrooms, finely chopped
- 1 cup tomatoes, chopped
- 1 cup paprikas, chopped
- 4-5 eggs
- 1 cup heavy cream
- 1 cup cheddar cheese, shredded
- 1 cup flour
- salt and pepper, to taste
- 1 tbsp sweet pepper powder
- ½ tsp nutmeg powder
- 1 tsp cinnamon powder

## DIRECTIONS:

1. Preheat your oven to 350 °F.
2. Brown the ground bear meat in butter for 10-15 minutes.
3. Add tomatoes, paprikas, and mushrooms, and drizzle with sherry.
4. Simmer for 10-15 more minutes.
5. While the ground bear is simmering, start making the casserole batter.
6. In a bowl, break and beat the eggs.
7. Mix in the heavy cream, flour, and cheese.
8. Glaze the bottom of your baking dish with butter and pour half of the batter.
9. Add the meat–veggie filling and pour the second half of the batter.
10. Bake for 15-30 minutes (depending on the depth of your dish) at 400 °F.

## FACTS AND STATS:

*Polar bears are found primarily in Alaska and the Arctic regions and are considered a threatened species due to habitat loss caused by climate change. Bears are omnivores with varied diets, including berries, nuts, grasses, insects, fish, and small mammals. Bears are considered important keystone species, meaning they play a crucial role in maintaining the health and balance of the ecosystem in which they live.*

# CHEESY ARUGULA BEAR SALAD

Bear meat is an excellent protein source, essential for building and repairing muscles and tissues in the body. Bear meat contains vital vitamins and minerals, including iron, zinc, and vitamin B12, necessary for maintaining good health.

## SERVING SIZE: 4-6

## INGREDIENTS:

- 1 lb bear meat, chopped
- 1 cup feta cheese, chopped
- 1 cup cherry tomatoes, quartered
- 1 cup arugula, chopped
- 3–4 bread slices, cubed and toasted
- 2 tbsp olive oil
- 2 tbsp butter
- salt and pepper, to taste
- 1 tbsp lemon juice
- 1 tsp lemon zest
- 1 tsp dill
- 1–2 tbsp sour or heavy cream
- 1 tbsp Parmesan cheese, grated
- 1 tbsp celery leaf, chopped
- 1 tbsp flour
- ½ cup red wine

## DIRECTIONS:

1. Melt and heat the butter in your saucepan.
2. Brown the chopped bear meat for 10 minutes, add wine and flour and simmer for 10–15 more minutes on medium-low heat with frequent stirring.
3. Although the meat should be crispy, ensure it won't burn by drizzling it with ¼ cup water if needed.
4. Grab a salad bowl and mix arugula, feta cheese, toasted bread cubes, and tomatoes.
5. Before the bear meat is finished, mix the salad dressing with olive oil, lemon juice, lemon zest, Parmesan, dill, and celery leaf.
6. Mix in the bear meat with the salad. Remember to drizzle the sauce from your saucepan if any remains after frying.
7. Add the salad dressing and mix well.

## FACTS AND STATS:

*Human-bear conflicts are a significant issue in many parts of the US, with bears often coming into contact with humans due to habitat loss and human encroachment into natural areas. The US has several national parks and protected areas home to bear populations, including Yellowstone National Park, Glacier National Park, and Denali National Park.*

# BEAR-STUFFED ZUCCHINIS WITH CHEESY EGGS

**Consuming bear meat could provide a quick energy boost due to its high protein content. It is important to note that consuming bear meat can also pose health risks due to the potential presence of harmful toxins, such as mercury and lead, which can accumulate in the animal's body over time.**

### SERVING SIZE: 4–6

### INGREDIENTS:

- 4 zucchinis, halved and deseeded to form pits
- 1 lb bear meat, ground
- ½ cup bacon, chopped
- 3 hard-boiled eggs, grated
- 1 cup cream cheese
- 1 tsp garlic powder
- 1 tsp red pepper powder
- 2 tbsp sherry
- ½ tsp cinnamon powder
- ½ tsp nutmeg powder
- 2–3 tbsp butter

### DIRECTIONS:

1. Brown the ground bear meat and bacon in butter for 10–15 minutes.
2. Add sherry, cinnamon powder, and nutmeg powder.
3. Stir and simmer until there's no excess liquid.
4. Mix cream cheese with garlic powder, red pepper powder, and grated eggs and stir well.
5. Fill the zucchini pits with the meat and bake for 20–30 minutes at 350 °F.
6. Top with the cream cheese mixture and serve.

## FACTS AND STATS:

*Hunting bears is legal in some parts of the US, with regulated hunting programs to manage bear populations and reduce conflicts with humans. Bear attacks on humans are relatively rare but can occur, particularly when bears feel threatened or are protecting their cubs or territory. It's worth noting that bear populations and statistics can vary widely across different states and regions of the US, and it's important to consult with local authorities and experts for more detailed information on bear populations, behaviors, and management.*

# CHEESY BEAR-STUFFED PAPRIKA SLICES

Here are the general steps for field dressing a bear:

1. After the bear has been killed, allow time for it to cool down and stiffen up. Approach the bear from behind and be cautious, as the bear may still be alive.

2. Position the bear on its back with its legs facing up. Cut around the anus and genital area and remove these organs. Continue next recipe…

## SERVING SIZE: 4-6

## INGREDIENTS:

- ½ lb bear meat, ground
- 1 cup bacon, finely chopped
- 1 cup cream cheese
- 1 cup Greek yogurt
- ½ cup pickles, chopped
- 2 tbsp vinegar
- 1 tsp garlic, minced
- 1 tsp red pepper powder
- 4 whole bell peppers
- 2 tbsp butter
- Salt and pepper, to taste

## DIRECTIONS:

1. Brown the bear meat and bacon in butter for 10–15 minutes.
2. Mix the meat with Greek yogurt, cream cheese, pickles, vinegar, garlic, and pepper powder in a separate bowl.
3. Cut the caps off the peppers, scrape the inside to create clean pits, and rinse with water.
4. Fill the paprika pits with the bear filling until completely full.
5. Let it cool down in your fridge for an hour, and cut slices with a sharp knife.

## FACTS AND STATS:

*Three species of bears are found in Canada: the black bear, the grizzly bear, and the polar bear. The black bear is Canada's most common bear species, with an estimated population of around 380,000. Grizzly bears are found primarily in western Canada, with an estimated population of approximately 25,000.*

# LUNCH

# BEAR QUICHE

3. Using a sharp knife, make a long cut along the belly of the bear from the anus to the base of the neck. Cut through the skin and muscles, careful not to puncture the organs.

4. Pull the skin and fur away from the body, and remove the internal organs, including the heart, lungs, liver, and kidneys.

5. Remove all the organs and check for any signs of disease or parasites.

6. Rinse the inside of the cavity with cold water to remove any remaining blood or debris.

7. If you plan to transport the bear, you may need to quarter it by cutting it into manageable pieces.

That is a quick overview on field dressing a bear. It's similar to other big game animals.

## SERVING SIZE: 4

## INGREDIENTS:

- 1 lb bear meat, chopped
- 8 whole eggs
- 1 cup spinach, chopped
- ½ cup bell peppers, chopped
- ½ cup onions, chopped
- ½ cup pickles, chopped
- ½ tbsp garlic, minced
- 1 tbsp red pepper powder
- 1 cup cheddar cheese, shredded
- 2 tbsp olive oil
- Salt and pepper, to taste

## DIRECTIONS:

1. Preheat your oven to 350 °F.
2. Heat a frying pan with olive oil and fry the chopped bear meat for 15–20 minutes on low-medium heat.

3. Add drizzles of water as needed.
4. Add vegetables and sauté for another 10–15 minutes. Make sure there's no visible liquid in the pan.
5. In a bowl, break the eggs, whisk, and mix in the cheese.
6. Divide into 4–6 smaller oven dishes.
7. Pour the eggs with Parmesan over the bear meat and vegetables.
8. Bake for 20 minutes or until ready.

### FACTS AND STATS:

*Polar bears are found primarily in the Arctic regions of Canada and are considered a threatened species due to habitat loss caused by climate change. Bear populations and statistics can vary widely across different provinces and regions of Canada, and it's important to consult with local authorities and experts for more detailed information on bear populations, behaviors, and management. Canada has several national parks and protected areas are home to bear populations, including Banff National Park, Jasper National Park, and Algonquin Provincial Park.*

# BEAR CHEESE AND VEGGIE ROLLS

Cooking bear meat can be tricky, as it tends to be relatively lean and can have a strong, gamey flavor. Several methods can be used to prepare bear meat in a tasty and satisfying way. One of the best ways to cook bear meat is to slow-cook it in a crockpot. This will help to tenderize the meat and bring out its natural flavors. Add some vegetables, herbs, and spices for extra flavor.

## SERVING SIZE: 4-6

## INGREDIENTS:

- 1 lb bear meat, chopped
- 1 cup cheddar cheese, shredded
- 1 cup scallions, chopped
- ½ cup sherry
- 3-4 eggs
- 1 cup flour
- 1 tsp baking powder
- 1 tsp nutmeg powder
- 1 tsp cumin powder
- Salt and pepper, to taste
- 1 tsp lemon zest
- ½ tsp ginger powder
- 4 tbsp butter

## DIRECTIONS:

1. Melt 2 tbsp butter in a saucepan and brown the bear meat and scallions for 10–15 minutes.
2. Drizzle with sherry, add nutmeg and cumin powder, and simmer on low heat for another 10 minutes.
3. In a separate bowl, break and beat the eggs. Mix with flour, lemon zest, baking powder, and ginger powder. Mix evenly until there are no lumps.
4. Set aside and grab a larger frying pan. Melt another 2 tbsp butter and spread small amounts of the batter with a ladle.
5. Add a spoonful of the filling to each piece of the batter and roll it over using a regular spoon or any other kitchen tool that works. Ensure to do so while the top layer of the batter is still raw so that the roll can successfully close.
6. Repeat the process until you're all out of the batter and filling.

## FACTS AND STATS:

*Native American tribes throughout North America have long revered bears as powerful and sacred animals, and bears feature prominently in many indigenous myths and legends. European settlers first encountered bears in North America in the early 17th century, with the American black bear being the most common species found in the eastern and southern parts of the continent. In the 19th and early 20th centuries, bears were heavily hunted for their meat, fur, and other products, with populations of some species declining rapidly.*

# LIGHT BEAR BURGERS

Another great option is to roast bear meat in the oven. Marinate the meat beforehand to help tenderize it and add some flavor. Baste the meat regularly with a flavorful sauce to keep it moist. Bear meat can also be grilled over high heat, but be careful not to overcook it, as it can become tough and dry. Marinate the meat to add some flavor beforehand, and grill it to medium rare for the best results.

### SERVING SIZE: 4-6

### INGREDIENTS:

- 1 lb bear meat, ground
- 2-3 tbsp butter
- 2 whole zucchinis, grated
- 1-2 whole eggs
- ½ cup bread crumbs
- ½ cup bacon, chopped
- salt and pepper, to taste
- 1 tbsp red pepper flakes
- ½ tbsp basil
- 2 tbsp heavy cream
- cheddar cheese slices
- 2 tbsp Parmesan cheese, grated
- salad, salsa, or relish of your choice
- buns, halved, as needed
- 2 tbsp sour cream

### DIRECTIONS:

1. Mix the meat, bacon, Parmesan, and seasoning together to make the patties in a bowl.
2. In another bowl, beat the eggs and mix with the heavy cream and meat.
3. Shape the meat into patties.
4. Fry the patties in butter for a couple of minutes on each side.
5. Top the bun halves with sour cream and cheese and fill with the patties.

## FACTS AND STATS:

*Establishing national parks and protected areas in the early 20th century helped preserve and protect bear populations, with many parks becoming important habitats for bears. In the mid-20th century, efforts to reintroduce grizzly bears to parts of their historic range, including Yellowstone National Park, were successful, leading to a gradual recovery of the species in some areas. Human-bear conflicts have been a persistent issue throughout bear management in the US, with bears often coming into contact with humans in urban and suburban areas.*

# BEAR STEW

**Bear meat can be used in stews and casseroles, which will help to tenderize the meat and infuse it with lots of flavors. Add plenty of vegetables and spices to create a hearty, satisfying meal. No matter which cooking method you choose, it's important to cook bear meat thoroughly to avoid any risk of foodborne illness. Use a meat thermometer to ensure that the meat has reached a safe internal temperature of at least 165°F (74°C).**

## SERVING SIZE: 4

## INGREDIENTS:

- 1 lb bear meat, cubed
- 4 cups beef broth
- 2–3 tbsp butter
- ½ cup red wine
- 1 cup carrots, chopped
- 1 cup red onions, chopped
- 1 cup tomato sauce
- 1 cup mushrooms, sliced
- ½ tbsp garlic, minced
- 1 tbsp red pepper powder
- 1 tbsp celery, chopped
- 1 tbsp parsley, chopped

## DIRECTIONS:

1. Brown the bear meat, onions, garlic, and parsley in butter for 15–20 minutes on low-medium heat. Add drizzles of broth as needed.
2. Transfer into a stockpot and add the remaining broth (add more if needed). Bring to a short boil and add tomato sauce.
3. Let simmer for another 45 minutes, and then add the remaining ingredients.
4. Simmer lightly for another 15–20 minutes.

## FACTS AND STATS:

*Bears have played an important role in Canadian history and culture, dating back thousands of years. Bears have long been revered by many Indigenous peoples in Canada, with many tribes viewing bears as powerful and spiritual animals that play a key role in their culture and mythology. European explorers and settlers first encountered bears in Canada in the 16th and 17th centuries, with the American black bear being the most common species in the country's eastern and central parts.*

# ROASTED BEAR RISOTTO

In the 19th and early 20th centuries, bears were heavily hunted for their meat, fur, and other products, leading to a significant decline in the populations of some species. In the mid-20th century, efforts to reintroduce grizzly bears to parts of their historic range, including Banff National Park, were successful, leading to a gradual recovery of the species in some areas.

### SERVING SIZE: 4-6

### INGREDIENTS:

- 1–2 lb bear meat, marinated (the night before)
- 1 cup beef broth
- 1 ½ cups of brown rice
- 1 cup peas
- 1 cup carrots, chopped
- 1 cup onions, chopped
- ½ tbsp turmeric powder
- ½ tbsp red pepper powder
- 2 tbsp butter

**FOR MARINADE**

- ½ cup olive oil
- ¾ cup soy sauce
- ½ cup lemon juice
- 3 garlic cloves, minced
- 1 tbsp celery leaf
- 1 tbsp dill
- ½ cup barbecue sauce

### DIRECTIONS:

1. Mix the marinade ingredients in a bowl and soak diced bear meat. Leave in your fridge to marinate overnight.
2. Preheat the oven to 350 °F.
3. Sauté bear meat, rice, carrots, and onions over medium heat for 10–15 minutes. Add butter and beef broth as needed to avoid sticking.
4. Add spices, bring to a short boil, and let simmer for another 20 minutes.
5. Transfer into a baking dish and roast at 350 °F for 30–45 minutes.

## FACTS AND STATS:

*Today, bears remain an important symbol of Canadian wildlife. They are a key focus of conservation efforts aimed at preserving their habitats and managing human-bear conflicts in a sustainable way. Canada is home to the world's largest population of polar bears, with many of these bears inhabiting the Arctic regions of the country. In recent years, climate change and habitat loss have become significant threats to polar bear populations in Canada and other parts of the world, leading to increased conservation efforts and calls for action to address these issues.*

# GROUND BEAR SALAD

**Before you go bear hunting, ensure you know your area's laws and regulations. This includes obtaining any necessary licenses and permits and following any restrictions on hunting methods or equipment. Scout your hunting area: Spend some time scouting your area to understand the terrain, wildlife, and potential bear habitats. Look for signs of bear activity, such as tracks, scats, and tree claw marks.**

### SERVING SIZE: 4-6

### INGREDIENTS:

- 1 lb bear meat, ground
- 1 cup red wine
- 1 cup tomatoes, chopped
- 1 cup leeks (soaked the night before)
- 3 oz cheese of your choice, ground
- 1 cup onions, chopped
- 1 tbsp garlic, minced
- 1 cup salsa of your choice
- 1 tbsp vinegar
- 1 cup sour cream
- salt and pepper, to taste
- 1 tbsp celery leaf, chopped
- 2 tbsp butter

### DIRECTIONS:

1. Brown the bear meat with leeks and tomatoes in butter for 15–20 minutes on medium heat.
2. Add seasoning and wine.
3. Bring to a boil and let simmer as much as needed until ready.
4. Mix sour cream, vinegar, and cheese in a separate dish for the dressing.
5. Mix the browned meat with the salad dressing.
6. Add your favorite salsa and enjoy!

## FACTS AND STATS:

*Bears have played an essential role in the culture and mythology of many Indigenous peoples in North America, including the Algonquin people. For the Algonquin, bears are viewed as powerful and spiritual animals that embody strength, courage, and wisdom. Bears are seen as protectors and guardians of the forest, symbolizing a strong and healthy ecosystem.*

# DINNER

# BEAR-STUFFED PAPRIKA STEW

Ensure you have appropriate bear hunting gear, including a high-powered rifle or bow, a sturdy backpack, and proper clothing and footwear. It's also a good idea to bring along bear spray for added safety. Bear hunting requires patience and persistence. Spend plenty of time in your hunting area and be prepared to wait for the right opportunity to present itself.

## SERVING SIZE: 4-6

## INGREDIENTS:

- 6-8 large red paprikas
- 1 lb bear meat, ground
- 1 cup onions, chopped
- ½ cup brown rice
- 1 whole potato, sliced
- Salt and pepper, to taste
- 1 tsp cumin powder
- ½ tsp nutmeg powder
- ½ tsp cinnamon powder
- 1 tbsp celery leaf, chopped
- 1 tsp garlic powder
- 2 tbsp butter
- 2-3 cups vegetable stock
- 1 cup tomato sauce
- 1 tbsp flour
- ½ cup wine
- 2 medium-sized tomatoes, slices
- 2 tbsp butter or olive oil

## DIRECTIONS:

1. Brown the onions and bear meat for 5 minutes.
2. Season with salt, pepper, cumin powder, and nutmeg powder, and simmer for 5 more minutes.
3. Wash and drain brown rice through a strainer and mix in with the meat, but don't it cook yet!
4. Cut off the "caps" from the paprikas to separate the stem and remove the inside until you're left with clean pits.
5. Rinse the inside of paprikas with water and fill ¾ with the meat filling.
6. Top with potato or tomato slices.
7. Drizzle some olive oil or slather some butter and arrange paprikas to squeeze them together. If there's space between paprikas that you can't fill, add slices of other vegetables (tomatoes, potatoes, carrots) or bacon.

8. Mix the vegetable stock, tomato sauce, and the remaining seasoning in a separate bowl and stir well.
9. Pour it over the paprikas and cover the pot.
10. Simmer the stuffed paprikas for around 1 ½–2 hours on low heat.
11. Add the red wine 10–15 minutes before it is done, and let it evaporate.
12. You can serve it as soon as the dish cools down.

### FACTS AND STATS:

*The Algonquin natives believe that bears have powerful medicinal properties and that certain parts of the bear (such as the fat or the gall bladder) can be used to treat various illnesses and ailments. Bears are believed to have a strong spiritual presence and are associated with healing, vision, and the ability to communicate with the spirit world.*

# BEAR MOUSSAKA

Always practice good safety habits when walking in the bush. This includes making noise as you move through the woods to avoid surprising a bear and being aware of your surroundings. If you encounter a bear, back away slowly and avoid making eye contact or sudden movements. Remember to respect the bear as a powerful and intelligent animal. Ensure a clean and ethical kill, and use all parts of the animal you can.

### SERVING SIZE: 4–6

### INGREDIENTS:

- 1 lb bear meat, ground
- 2 whole sweet potatoes, sliced
- 3–4 whole tomatoes, sliced
- 1 eggplant, sliced
- 1 cup heavy cream
- 1 cup tomato sauce
- 2–3 tbsp Parmesan cheese, grated
- 2–3 tbsp sour cream
- 1 cup onions, chopped
- ½ cup red wine
- 2–3 tbsp butter
- salt and pepper, to taste
- 1 tsp dill
- 1 tsp garlic powder
- 1 tsp celery leaf

### DIRECTIONS:

1. Heat 2 tbsp butter in a saucepan, brown the onions and ground bear meat for 10–15 minutes.
2. Glaze your baking dish with a tablespoon of butter and line slices of vegetables.
3. Here, you can line one row of potatoes, tomatoes, and eggplant.
4. Add a thin layer of the meat.
5. Repeat the process with all the vegetables and meat.
6. Mix the heavy cream, tomato sauce, wine, Parmesan, and seasoning in a separate bowl.
7. Pour it over the meat and vegetables and bake for 40–50 minutes at 400 °F.

## FACTS AND STATS:

*The Algonquins view bears as highly respected and powerful animals that play an important role in their culture and way of life. Their relationship with bears is revered and respected, with the animal occupying a central place in their mythology and worldview. Bears have also been an important source of food and resources for the Algonquin and are respected as skilled hunters and providers.*

# BEAR AND BEAN STEW

**Spot-and-stock involves locating a bear from a distance and then stalking it on foot to get within shooting range. This technique requires patience, skill, and understanding of bear behavior. Baiting involves setting up a bait station (such as a pile of food) in an area where bears are known to frequent. The hunter then waits at a distance for the bear to come to the bait, providing an opportunity for a shot. You can either hunt from a treestand or a ground blind.**

### SERVING SIZE: 4-6

### INGREDIENTS:

- 1 lb bear meat, diced
- 1–2 oz canned black beans
- ½ cup onions, chopped
- ½ cup carrots, chopped
- ½ cup paprika, chopped
- 1 cup tomato sauce
- 1 tbsp celery leaf, chopped
- 1 tbsp sweet pepper powder
- salt and pepper, to taste
- 4–5 cups vegetable stock

### DIRECTIONS:

1. Brown the bear meat, black beans, and vegetables in butter for 10–15 minutes.
2. Add the vegetable stock and tomato sauce and bring to a boil.
3. Cook for 45 minutes to an hour, and add seasoning before turning off the heat.
4. Remove from heat, let the dish simmer, and cool down, partially covered.

## FACTS AND STATS:

*Here are a few of the top destinations for bear hunting in the USA: Alaska is one of the best places to hunt bears in North America, with healthy populations of both brown bears and black bears. The remote wilderness areas of the state offer a challenging and rewarding hunting experience. Maine is another excellent destination for bear hunting, with a large population of black bears and a well-established hunting culture. The state also offers a long hunting season from August to November.*

# BEAR VEGGIE ROAST

**Still-hunting involves moving slowly and quietly through bear habitat, looking for bears, and taking shots when the opportunity arises. Hound hunting involves using trained dogs to track and tree bears. The hunter follows the dogs and waits for the bear to climb a tree, providing a clear shot.**

### SERVING SIZE: 4-6

### INGREDIENTS:

- 1 lb bear meat, diced
- 1 cup of potatoes, diced
- 1 cup sweet potatoes, diced
- 1 cup carrots, diced
- 1 cup tomato sauce
- 1 cup red wine
- ½ cup bread crumbs
- 1 tbsp celery leaf, chopped
- 1 tsp dill, chopped
- 1 tbsp red pepper powder
- 2 tbsp butter

### DIRECTIONS:

1. Slather the butter on the bottom of your baking dish.
2. Spread the vegetables at the bottom of the dish and then the meat over it.
3. Mix wine, tomato sauce, bread crumbs, and seasoning in a separate bowl.
4. Pour it over the meat and vegetables and roast for 40–50 minutes at 400 °F.

## FACTS AND STATS:

*Wyoming is home to a large population of black and grizzly bears, making it an attractive destination for hunters. The state also has a high success rate for bear hunting, with a large number of bears harvested each year. Montana offers a diverse range of hunting opportunities for both black and grizzly bears, with vast wilderness areas and a long hunting season from September to November. Idaho is home to a significant population of black bears and offers a variety of hunting opportunities, including spot-and-stalk hunting and baiting.*

# BEAR STEAK IN WINE SAUCE

Here are some of the best places to hunt bears in Canada:

**British Columbia is known for its large population of grizzly bears and black bears. The province has vast wilderness areas that offer challenging and rewarding hunting opportunities. Alberta is a great destination for bear hunting, with a large population of black bears and some grizzly bears. The province offers a range of hunting opportunities, from spot-and-stalk hunting to baiting.**

### SERVING SIZE: 4-6

### INGREDIENTS:

- 1 lb bear steaks
- ½ cup wine
- 5-6 potatoes, quartered
- salt and pepper, to taste
- 2 tbsp soy sauce
- 1 tbsp brown sugar
- 1 tsp cinnamon powder
- 1 tsp cumin powder
- 1 tsp nutmeg powder
- 1 tbsp sage
- 1 tsp garlic powder
- 2 tbsp butter
- ½ cup beef stock
- 1 tbsp flour

### DIRECTIONS:

1. Dredge the bear steaks in a mix of sage, cinnamon powder, nutmeg powder, and cumin powder.
2. Melt the butter and brown the steaks for 3-6 minutes on each side. Remove the meat from the pan.
3. Add the wine, beef stock, flour, salt, pepper, and garlic powder to the pan and stir.
4. Add the steaks back to the pan with the sauce and simmer for another 10-15 minutes.
5. Cook the potatoes in a stockpot until soft.
6. Serve the steaks and potatoes covered in sauce.

## FACTS AND STATS:

*Manitoba is known for its large population of black bears and offers a range of hunting opportunities, including spot-and-stalk hunting and baiting. Ontario has a significant population of black bears, making it an attractive destination for hunters. The province also offers a long hunting season from August to October. Quebec is home to a large population of black bears and provides various hunting opportunities, including spot-and-stalk hunting and baiting. Remember that hunting regulations and restrictions vary by province, so it's important to research and ensure you have the necessary licenses, permits, and equipment before embarking on a bear hunting trip in Canada.*

# BEAR IN WHITE SAUCE WITH MUSHROOMS

**Black bears play an essential role in their ecosystem, helping to disperse seeds and control populations of other animals. Black bears have a unique method of communication, including vocalizations, body language, and scent marking. They have a long lifespan and can live up to 30 years in the wild.**

### SERVING SIZE: 4-6

### INGREDIENTS:

- 1 lb bear meat fillets
- 1 cup beef broth
- 2 cups mushrooms, sliced
- 2 cups heavy cream
- 1 cup white wine
- ½ cup sherry
- 1 tbsp honey
- 1 tsp cumin powder
- 1 tsp nutmeg powder
- 1 tsp cinnamon powder
- 2 whole sweet potatoes, quartered
- 2–3 tbsp butter

### DIRECTIONS:

1. Glaze the bear fillets with honey and dredge them into cumin, nutmeg, and cinnamon powder.
2. Heat butter in a pan and fry the fillets on each side for a couple of minutes over low-medium heat.
3. After 10 minutes, drizzle with sherry and simmer until the sherry has cooked down and the meat is done. Take them out and set them aside.
4. Add the remaining ingredients, starting with mushrooms and sweet potatoes, then the heavy cream and white wine.
5. Bring to a gentle boil and simmer on low-medium heat for 15–20 minutes or until done.
6. Place the fillets back into the pan and soak them in the sauce.

## FACTS AND STATS:

*Black bears are not always black. They can also be brown, cinnamon, or white (known as "spirit bears" or Kermode bears). Despite their name, black bears are not always aggressive or dangerous. In fact, they are usually shy and avoid humans. Black bears have an incredible sense of smell, which they use to find food and navigate through their environment. They hibernate in the winter and can survive for several months without eating, drinking, or defecating.*

# BEAR GOULASH WITH SWEET POTATO MASH

If you want to experience the most amazing black bear hunts, you want to call "Saul Outfitters "in Northern Ontario, Canada. The Great Byron Saul has been hunting & trapping for over 30 years with monster black bears. We are talking over 500 + giants. If you want to learn and hunt the Canadian black bear, call Saul @ 1-705-262-3851. You will experience the true North at its finest!

### SERVING SIZE: 4-6

### INGREDIENTS:

- 2 lb bear meat, chopped
- 3 tbsp butter
- Salt and pepper, to taste
- 1 lb onion, chopped
- ½ lb carrots, chopped
- ½ lb parsley root, chopped
- 2 large red paprikas, chopped
- 1 cup red wine
- 1 cup tomato sauce
- 2 bay leaves
- 5 juniper berries
- 2 tsp garlic powder
- 2 whole sweet potatoes, peeled
- 2 whole potatoes, peeled
- 2 tsp cinnamon powder
- 2 tsp nutmeg powder
- 2 tsp cumin powder
- 1 tbsp red pepper powder
- 2 ½ cups beef stock
- ½ cup milk
- 2 tbsp Parmesan cheese, grated

### DIRECTIONS:

1. Melt 2 tbsp butter in a large stockpot and reduce to the lowest heat. Pour in 2 cups of beef stock, onions, parsley, and carrots, and let slowly come to a simmer for 1-½ hours. Stir frequently and keep the lid closed.
2. Add the bear meat and simmer for 40–50 more minutes.
3. Add paprikas, tomato sauce, and the rest of the beef stock and simmer for another 30 minutes.
4. Add the seasoning and juniper berries, and add more beef stock if needed.
5. Simmer for another 15–20 minutes, and add red wine.

6. Simmer for 20 more minutes on low heat and consider the goulash done.
7. Cook the regular and sweet potatoes until soft and mash with 1 tbsp butter and milk.
8. Serve next to the goulash.

### FACTS AND STATS:

*Grizzly bears, also known as North American brown bears, are found in North America, from Alaska to Mexico. They are powerful animals and can weigh up to 1,500 pounds. Grizzly bears have a distinctive hump of muscle on their shoulders, which gives them additional strength for digging, running, and climbing. They are omnivores, and their diet includes roots, berries, nuts, insects, fish, and sometimes larger mammals. Grizzly bears have a great sense of smell and can detect food from miles away. They are excellent swimmers and can swim across rivers and lakes to reach new habitat areas. Grizzly bears have a long lifespan and can live up to 25 years in the wild.*

# CHAPTER 7
# Wonderful Wild Boar

Wild boars are becoming a big problem in many states. They are a pest to farmers and cause a lot of damage & money. They are an invasive species. Thankfully they are a delicious source of protein, with a flavor that is like a cross between beef and pork. Boar meat has a bright-red coloring from the high iron content of a boar's diet. Boars whose diet consists of nuts like acorns and peanuts will tend to have an earthy, nutty taste. Like all wild game, wild boars are prone to parasites and diseases. The best way to prevent those parasites or diseases from ending on the plate is not to damage the boar's digestive organs.

**Breakfast**
Wild Boar Medley
Wild Boar Breakfast Sausage With Pound Cakes
Woody Wild Boar Breakfast Burgers
Wild Boar Grilled Cheese Sandwich
Wild Boar Breakfast Tortillas
Fried Boar in Rice Tarts
Wild Boar and Fried Egg Delight
Wild Boar Breakfast Quiche
Nutty Wild Boar and Mushroom Medley

**Lunch**
Wicked Wild Boar in Mushroom Sauce and Potatoes
Wild Boar Pesto Spaghetti
Hearty Tomato Boar and Bean Stew
Wild Boar Bacon and Sweet Potato Chips
Wilderness Wild Boar Risotto With Mushrooms
Wild Boar Moussaka
Wild Boar Pasta With Cauliflower and Cheese

**Dinner**
Smoky Wild Boar Rib Roast
Wild Boar Risotto Roast
Wild Boar Steak With Sweet Potato Mash
Wild Boar and Pumpkin Pie
Beautiful Boar and Sweet Potato Stew
Cauliflower and Mozzarella Wild Boar Risotto Roast
Wonderful Wild Boar and Sweet Potato Salad

# BREAKFAST

# WILD BOAR MEDLEY

The most tender cuts on a wild boar are the tenderloin, rib back, loin, and striploin, which is also fantastic, slow-roasted, and seared to perfection. Shanks, stew meat, and short ribs are best cooked at low temperatures for long periods of time.

### SERVING SIZE: 4-6

### INGREDIENTS:

- 1 lb boar meat, chopped
- 8 whole eggs
- ½ cup sweet potatoes, chopped
- ½ cup cheddar cheese, shredded
- ½ cup peas
- ½ tbsp garlic, minced
- 2 tbsp olive oil
- salt and pepper, to taste

### DIRECTIONS:

1. Brown the boar meat in olive oil with sweet potatoes, peas, and garlic.
2. In a bowl, whisk the eggs and pour them over the boar.
3. Fry on each side for a couple of minutes and top with cheese once finished.
4. You can serve it with toast, Greek yogurt, and salad if you like!

# FACTS AND STATS:

*Spanish explorers first introduced wild boar, also known as feral pigs or hogs, in the United States in the 1500s. Since then, they have become a prolific invasive species, causing significant damage to crops and native ecosystems and threatening public safety in some areas. Here are some facts and stats about wild boar in the United States: According to the USDA, there are an estimated 6 million wild boar in the United States, and their population is rapidly expanding.*

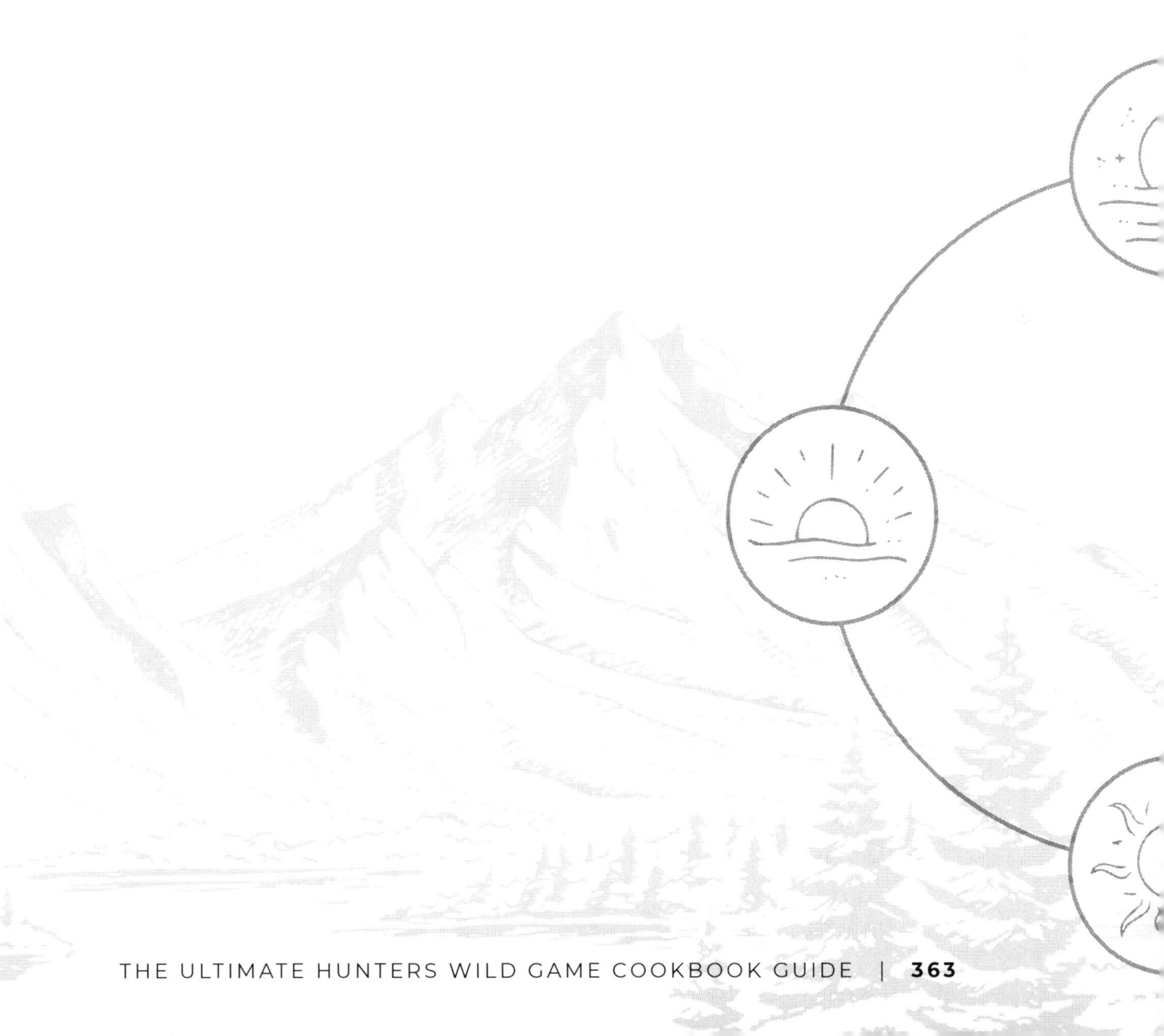

# WILD BOAR BREAKFAST SAUSAGE WITH POUND CAKES

Wild boar meat is a rich source of lean protein, essential for building and repairing muscle tissue and maintaining healthy bones, skin, and other tissues. Compared to commercial pork, wild boar meat is lower in fat and calories, which can help you maintain a healthy weight and reduce your risk of heart disease and other chronic illnesses.

### SERVING SIZE: 4–6

### INGREDIENTS:

- 1 lb boar meat, ground
- 2–3 tbsp butter
- salt and pepper, to taste
- 1 tbsp red pepper flakes
- 1 tbsp white wine
- 3–4 eggs
- 1 ½–2 cups flour
- 1 tbsp brandy
- 1 tbsp orange zest
- 2 tbsp sour cream

### DIRECTIONS:

1. Season the ground boar with salt, pepper, red pepper flakes, and white wine.
2. Shape the meat into sausages.
3. Brown the meat in butter for 10–15 minutes and take off the heat.
4. To make the pound cakes, whisk the eggs and mix with flour, brandy, orange zest, and sour cream.
5. Fry the pound cakes in butter on each side for 2–3 minutes and serve with the boar sausages.

## FACTS AND STATS:

*Wild boar can be found in 39 states across the US, with the highest populations in Texas, Florida, and California. Feral pigs cause an estimated $2.5 billion in damage and control costs annually in the US. Wild boars are extremely intelligent and adaptable and can thrive in various environments, from forests and swamps to suburban neighborhoods. They are omnivorous and eat almost anything, including plants, insects, small animals, and even carrion.*

# WOODY WILD BOAR BREAKFAST BURGERS

**Free from antibiotics and hormones. Wild boar meat is a good source of several essential vitamins and minerals, including iron, zinc, selenium, and vitamin B12, all critical for maintaining optimal health. Unlike commercial pork, which is often treated with antibiotics and growth hormones, wild boar meat is free from these additives, making it a healthier and more natural choice.**

### SERVING SIZE: 4-6

### INGREDIENTS:

- 1 lb boar meat, ground
- 1 tsp garlic powder
- 1 cup onions, chopped
- 1 cup paprikas, chopped
- 1 cup cheddar cheese, grated
- salt and pepper, to taste
- 1 tbsp red pepper flakes
- 1 tsp cumin powder
- 1 tsp ginger powder
- 1 tsp fennel seeds
- 3 tbsp butter
- 12 slices of cheese
- 1 tsp thyme
- ½ tsp fennel seeds
- buns, halved, as needed

### DIRECTIONS:

1. Mix the ground boar meat with garlic powder, onions, paprikas, and cheddar cheese.
2. Season with salt, pepper, red pepper flakes, cumin powder, and ginger powder. You may also add some fennel seeds and thyme.
3. Shape the meat into patties and fry in butter for 3–4 minutes on each side.
4. Next, toast your buns in the toaster or oven.
5. Spread some sour cream on the buns and add a slice of cheese to each bun.
6. Serve the patties between the buns.

## FACTS AND STATS:

*Wild boars are known for their aggressive behavior and can seriously threaten humans, particularly if they feel threatened or cornered. Hunting is often used to control wild boar populations, and there are no bag limits or hunting seasons for feral pigs in many states. Wild boar meat is popular among hunters and can be found in some restaurants and specialty food markets.*

# WILD BOAR GRILLED CHEESE SANDWICH

Wild boar hunting is often used to control populations, which can help prevent damage to crops and native ecosystems, making it a more sustainable option than factory-farmed pork. It's important to note that wild boar meat may also be higher in cholesterol and sodium than some other types of meat, so it's best consumed in moderation as part of a healthy, balanced diet. Additionally, because wild boar is game meat, it should be cooked thoroughly to reduce the risk of foodborne illness.

### SERVING SIZE: 4-6

### INGREDIENTS:

- 1 lb boar meat, sliced
- 3 tbsp butter
- Salt and pepper, to taste
- 1 tbsp barbecue or soy sauce
- slices of bread or buns, as needed
- 10-12 slices of cheese

### DIRECTIONS:

1. Fry the meat in butter for 5-6 minutes on each side. Season with salt and pepper.
2. Toward the end of the frying, add some barbecue sauce or soy sauce. Remove the meat from the pan.
3. Drizzle the slices of bread with some of the juice left in the pan.
4. Add a slice of cheese to each slice of bread and fill it with the meat to make a sandwich.
5. Toast the sandwiches in butter on each side for 1-2 minutes until they are brown and crispy.

## FACTS AND STATS:

*Wild boar are considered a delicacy in some areas and are hunted for their meat and hides. There are concerns that wild boar could potentially spread diseases to domestic pigs and other livestock and could even serve as a reservoir for emerging zoonotic diseases.*

# WILD BOAR BREAKFAST TORTILLAS

Wild boar is a lean and flavorful meat that can be used in various dishes. Here are some of the best cuts of meat on a wild boar. The tenderloin is a long, thin muscle that runs along the boar's spine. It's the most tender and prized cut of wild boar meat and is often compared to filet mignon. It can be roasted or grilled and is best-served medium-rare. The rib rack is a flavorful, meaty cut that can be roasted or grilled. It's best when simmered to ensure it's tender and juicy.

### SERVING SIZE: 4-6

### INGREDIENTS:

- 1 lb boar meat, ground
- 3 tbsp butter
- 1 tbsp chili sauce
- 2 cayenne peppers, minced
- 2 cups tomatoes, chopped
- 1 cup paprikas, chopped
- 1 cup onions, chopped
- 1 cup beef broth
- tortillas, as needed
- 2-3 tbsp sour cream
- 1 cup mayonnaise
- ketchup, to taste
- salsa or relish to taste

### DIRECTIONS:

1. Start by browning the boar meat in butter and chili sauce.
2. Bring to a slow boil and simmer for another 10–15 minutes.
3. Add the cayenne peppers, tomatoes, paprikas, and onions and stir.
4. Pour the beef broth and simmer until the excess liquid evaporates.
5. Heat the tortillas and top them with sour cream, mayonnaise, ketchup, and any other toppings you like.
6. Next, complete the tortilla with your favorite salsa or relish.
7. Add some ground meat to each tortilla and wrap it.

## FACTS AND STATS:

*Wild boars are the ancestors of domestic pigs and are found in Europe, Asia, and Africa. Wild boars have a keen sense of smell and hearing, but their eyesight is relatively poor. Male wild boars are called boars, while females are called sows. Baby wild boars are called piglets. Wild boars are omnivores and eat various foods, including fruits, nuts, roots, insects, and small animals.*

# FRIED BOAR IN RICE TARTS

Texas is known for having a large population of feral hogs, and hunting them is legal year-round on private property. Florida has a large population of feral hogs, and hunting them is allowed on public and private land. There are also many outfitters and hunting ranches that offer guided wild boar hunts. There are also many hunting outfitters and guides available.

### SERVING SIZE: 4-6

### INGREDIENTS:

- 1 lb wild boar meat, sliced
- 3 tbsp butter
- 2-3 cups brown rice
- Salt and pepper, to taste
- 1 tbsp celery leaf, chopped
- 1 tsp garlic powder
- 2 cups sour cream
- 2 cups mushrooms, sliced
- salad, salsa, or relish of your choice

### DIRECTIONS:

1. Soak the brown rice the night before or at least a few hours before cooking.
2. Fry the wild boar slices in butter for 10-15 minutes and season with salt, pepper, celery leaf, and garlic powder.
3. Drain the rice you previously soaked and boil it for 5-10 minutes. The rice should be fluffy and well-cooked.
4. Drain the rice and mix it with sour cream and mushrooms.
5. Shape the rice mixture into tarts and serve wild boar slices on top of them.
6. You can have this dish with your favorite salad, salsa, or relish.

## FACTS AND STATS:

*Wild boars are known for their sharp tusks, up to 6 inches long in males. They use their tusks for defense and to dig for food. Wild boars are social animals and live in groups called sounders. Sounders can include up to 20 individuals, typically made up of females and their young. Wild boars are known for being aggressive, especially when threatened or cornered. It's important to give them plenty of space and avoid approaching them.*

# WILD BOAR AND FRIED EGG DELIGHT

It's difficult to estimate the exact population of wild boars in the United States, as they are considered invasive in many different regions and habitats throughout the country. However, according to the United States Department of Agriculture (USDA), feral swine populations are present in at least 35 states and are estimated to be in the millions.

## SERVING SIZE: 4–6

## INGREDIENTS:

- 1 lb wild boar, diced
- ½ cup red wine
- 1 tbsp soy sauce
- salt and pepper, to taste
- 2 tsp dill
- 1 tsp cumin powder
- 3 tbsp butter
- 1 tbsp honey
- ½ cup cheddar cheese, shredded
- 4–6 eggs

## DIRECTIONS:

1. Dredge the diced wild boar in wine, soy sauce, salt, pepper, dill, and cumin powder.
2. Brown in butter for 10–15 minutes, and then add honey.
3. Let simmer until the liquid from the pan is completely gone, and the meat bites have created a crispy, sticky crust.
4. Heat some more butter in the pan.
5. Once the butter has melted and heated, pour the eggs and let them fry.
6. The mixture will look compound, and if you wish, let the eggs come out rawer, or you can flip the dish so that the other side fries as well.
7. Once the eggs are done, cut them into the number of pieces you want and serve topped with shredded cheese.

## FACTS AND STATS:

*Wild boars are highly adaptable and can live in various habitats, from forests and grasslands to urban areas. Wild boars have been introduced to many parts of the world, including North America, where they are considered an invasive species and a threat to native wildlife and ecosystems. Wild boars are hunted for their meat, which is lean and flavorful, and for sport. Hunting can help control their populations in areas where they are considered a pest.*

# WILD BOAR BREAKFAST QUICHE

Feral swine have been known to cause significant damage to agricultural crops, wildlife habitats, and water sources. They can also carry diseases that can be transmitted to both livestock and humans. As a result, many states have implemented control measures such as hunting, trapping, and fencing to manage feral swine populations. Notably, feral swine are not native to the United States and were introduced by European settlers in the 1500s. They are considered a nuisance species and are not protected under federal law.

### SERVING SIZE: 4-6

### INGREDIENTS:

- 1 lb wild boar meat, ground
- salt and pepper, to taste
- 1 tsp thyme
- 1 tbsp basil
- 1 tsp garlic powder
- bread slices, as needed
- 2 eggs
- 1 cup sour cream
- 1 cup cream cheese
- 1 cup cheddar cheese, grated
- 2 tbsp butter

### DIRECTIONS:

1. Brown the ground boar meat in butter and season with salt, pepper, thyme, basil, and garlic powder.
2. While the meat is browning, make muffin cups from slices of bread. Flatten the bread slices with a rolling pin until firm, and mold them into cups.
3. Bake the quiche cups for 10–15 minutes at 400 °F and let them cool down.
4. Mix the eggs with sour cream and cream cheese in a separate bowl.
5. Once the meat is finished cooking, add it to the bowl and mix everything.
6. Fill the quiche cups with the filling and top with some grated cheddar cheese.
7. Place it back in the baking dish for another 10 minutes at 400 °F.

## FACTS AND STATS:

*Hogzilla: In 2004, a hunter in Georgia claimed to have shot a wild boar that weighed over 1,000 pounds and was over 12 feet long. However, some have questioned the accuracy of these claims and measurements. Pickles: In 2005, a hunter in Alabama shot a wild boar estimated to weigh over 800 pounds. This boar was named Pickles and gained national attention for its size. Monster Pig: In 2007, a group of hunters in Alabama shot a wild boar that they claimed weighed over 1,000 pounds. This boar was nicknamed "Monster Pig" and was later revealed to be a domestic pig that had escaped from a nearby farm.*

# NUTTY WILD BOAR AND MUSHROOM MEDLEY

**California has a significant population of wild pigs; hunting them is allowed on public and private land. However, it's important to note that California has strict hunting regulations, and hunters must obtain a hunting license and follow specific rules. Oklahoma is another state with a significant feral hog population, and hunting them is allowed year-round on both public and private land. Georgia has a large population of wild hogs; hunting them is permitted year-round on public and private land. There are also many hunting outfitters and guides available.**

### SERVING SIZE: 4-6

### INGREDIENTS:

- 2–3 tbsp butter
- 1 lb boar meat, ground
- 1 cup tomatoes, chopped
- 1 cup zucchini, sliced
- 1 cup eggplant, sliced
- 1 cup mushrooms, sliced
- 4–6 eggs
- 1 cup sour cream
- 1 tbsp flour
- salt and pepper, to taste
- 1 tbsp orange zest

### DIRECTIONS:

1. Fry the ground boar meat in butter for 10 minutes.
2. Mix in the chopped tomatoes, zucchini, eggplants, and mushrooms.
3. Fry for 15 more minutes and turn off the heat.
4. In a bowl, whisk the eggs and mix with sour cream, flour, salt, pepper, and orange zest.
5. Pour it over the meat and vegetables and stir-fry until done.

## FACTS AND STATS:

According to a study by the United States Department of Agriculture (USDA), the states with the highest estimated feral swine populations in 2021 are:

1. Texas
2. Florida
3. Georgia
4. California
5. North Carolina
6. Alabama
7. Oklahoma
8. Louisiana
9. South Carolina
10. Mississippi

# LUNCH

# WICKED WILD BOAR IN MUSHROOM SAUCE AND POTATOES

Wild boar meat is generally leaner and more nutritious than meat from domestic pigs. Wild boar is a good source of protein, with around 25-30 grams of protein per 3.5 ounces (100 grams) of meat. Wild boar meat is leaner than pork, with approximately 6-8 grams of fat per 3.5 ounces (100 grams) of meat, compared to around 20-25 grams of fat in pork. Wild boar fat is also higher in monounsaturated fats, considered heart-healthy.

### SERVING SIZE: 4-6

### INGREDIENTS:

- 2–3 tbsp butter
- 1 lb boar meat, ground
- 1 cup parsley, chopped
- 1 cup onions, chopped
- 1 cup carrots, chopped
- 1 cup vegetable stock
- 1 cup mushrooms, sliced
- salt and pepper, to taste
- 1 tbsp celery leaf, chopped
- 1 tsp basil, chopped
- 1 tsp dill, chopped
- 1 cup sour cream
- ½ cup white wine
- 2 lb whole potatoes

### DIRECTIONS:

1. Melt the butter in a frying pan and fry the ground boar for 5–10 minutes.
2. Add parsley, onions, and carrots and slowly simmer for 20–30 minutes while adding drizzles of vegetable stock from time to time to prevent sticking and burning. Stir after adding the rest of the stock.
3. Turn down the heat to the lowest possible and let simmer for another 45 minutes to an hour.
4. Add mushrooms, salt, pepper, celery leaf, dill, basil, sour cream, and white wine toward the end of the cooking. Stir and let simmer for another 10–15 minutes.
5. Cook the potatoes in a separate bowl with skins on them for better flavor.
6. Remove the skins after the potatoes have cooled down and serve with the boar and mushroom sauce.

## FACTS AND STATS:

*Before hunting wild boar, it's essential to familiarize yourself with the area where you will be hunting. Look for signs of wild boar activity, such as tracks, rooting, and wallows, and pay attention to their feeding and bedding areas. Wild boars are most active during dawn and dusk, so these are the best times to hunt them. However, they can also be hunted during the day or night, depending on the hunting regulations in your area.*

# WILD BOAR PESTO SPAGHETTI

Wild boar is a good source of several essential vitamins and minerals, including niacin, thiamin, vitamin B6, vitamin B12, zinc, and selenium. Wild boar meat is relatively low in calories, with around 150-200 calories per 3.5 ounces (100 grams) of meat.

### SERVING SIZE: 4-6

### INGREDIENTS:

- 1 lb boar meat, ground
- 2-3 tbsp butter
- Salt and pepper, to taste
- 1 tsp dill, chopped
- 1 tbsp brandy
- 1 cup basil, chopped
- ½ cup walnuts, crushed
- 1 cup Parmesan cheese, grated
- 2 cups olive oil
- 1 box of spaghetti

### DIRECTIONS:

1. Brown the boar meat in butter.
2. Season with salt, pepper, 1 tsp of basil, and dill, and pour in the brandy.
3. Bring to a boil and simmer for 10-15 minutes.
4. To make the pesto sauce in a separate bowl, combine the rest of the basil, walnuts, Parmesan, salt, and pepper and process them in a food processor for 1-2 minutes. Add the olive oil and process again.
5. Cook the spaghetti as instructed.
6. Mix the pasta with the pesto sauce and meat.

## FACTS AND STATS:

*Hunting wild boar requires specialized equipment, including a powerful rifle or shotgun with the appropriate ammunition, hunting clothes and boots, a hunting knife, and a sturdy backpack for carrying gear. Wild boars have a keen sense of smell and can be easily spooked, so it's crucial to use scent-eliminating products and to approach them quietly and cautiously. Some popular hunting techniques for wild boar include still hunting, baiting, and using hunting dogs.*

# HEARTY TOMATO BOAR AND BEAN STEW

Overall, wild boar meat can be a nutritious and healthy option for those looking for a leaner source of protein. However, it's important to note that the nutritional profile of wild boar can vary depending on a number of factors, including the age and diet of the animal, the specific cut of meat, and how it is prepared.

### SERVING SIZE: 4-6

### INGREDIENTS:

- 1 lb wild boar meat, chopped
- 1 onion, chopped
- 1 carrot, chopped
- 1-2 paprikas, chopped
- 1 cup of black beans
- 10-12 cups of beef stock
- 2-3 tbsp red bell pepper
- 1 cup potatoes, chopped
- 1 cup sweet potatoes, chopped
- 1 cup tomatoes, chopped
- a pinch of salt and pepper
- 1 tsp basil, chopped
- 1 tsp dill, chopped
- 1 tsp thyme, chopped
- 1 tbsp celery leaf, chopped
- 1 cup tomato sauce
- 1 tbsp flour
- salt and pepper, to taste

### DIRECTIONS:

1. Melt the butter in a cooking pot and brown the onions, tomatoes, carrots, and paprikas for 10-15 minutes.
2. Add the boar meat and black beans, stock, boil, and simmer for another 10-15 minutes.
3. Add potatoes, sweet potatoes, flour, and tomato sauce.
4. Bring to another boil and simmer lightly for another 15 minutes.
5. Add salt, pepper, basil, dill, thyme, and celery leaf.

## FACTS AND STATS:

*Hunting wild boar can be a challenging and rewarding experience for those who are prepared and knowledgeable about the animal and the hunting techniques involved. Wild boars can be very dangerous animals, especially when cornered or threatened. Always follow proper safety precautions, such as hunting in a group, wearing bright clothing, and never getting too close to a wounded animal. Hunting regulations for wild boar vary by state and region, so it's important to check the regulations in your area before hunting. Ensure you obtain the necessary permits and follow all hunting rules and guidelines.*

# WILD BOAR BACON AND SWEET POTATO CHIPS

**Here are the general steps for field dressing a wild boar. You will need a sharp knife, a bone saw, and a cleaned area. Ensure the animal is dead before proceeding with field dressing. If not, take appropriate safety measures before handling the animal. Starting at the base of the breastbone, use your knife to make a long incision down the belly of the animal, being careful not to cut into the intestines or other organs. To be continued next recipe…**

### SERVING SIZE: 4-6

### INGREDIENTS:

- 1 lb wild boar bacon
- 2-3 tbsp butter
- salt and pepper, to taste
- 1 tsp dill
- 1 tsp thyme
- 1 tsp cilantro
- ½ cup brandy
- 2 sweet potatoes, peeled and sliced
- salad of your choice
- sour cream, to taste

### DIRECTIONS:

1. Fry the wild boar bacon in butter on each side for 5-6 minutes. Season with salt, pepper, dill, thyme, and cilantro.
2. Pour the brandy over during the last couple of minutes of frying and let it evaporate.
3. Take the meat out of the pan and melt some more butter.
4. Pop in the sweet potato slices and let them fry until crispy.
5. Serve with bacon, your favorite salad, sour cream, or steamed vegetables.

## FACTS AND STATS:

*It is recommended that pregnant women should avoid eating wild boar meat that has not been thoroughly cooked to a safe temperature. The Centers for Disease Control and Prevention (CDC) recommends cooking wild boar meat to an internal temperature of at least 160°F (71°C) to kill any potential bacteria or parasites that may be present.*

# WILDERNESS WILD BOAR RISOTTO WITH MUSHROOMS

Carefully remove the organs, not puncturing the stomach or intestines, as this can contaminate the meat. Set aside the heart and liver for consumption, if desired. Cut through the spine at the base of the skull to remove the head. Use the bone saw to remove the legs at the joints. Rinse the body cavity with clean water and cool the meat as quickly as possible. Wrap the animal in game bags or other protective material and transport it to your desired destination for further processing. That's a quick overview on field dressing wild boar.

## SERVING SIZE: 4-6

## INGREDIENTS:

- 2 cups brown rice
- 1 lb boar meat, chopped
- 3 tbsp butter
- Salt and pepper, to taste
- 1 tsp dill, chopped
- 1 tbsp celery leaf, chopped
- 1 tbsp brandy
- 2-3 cups vegetable stock
- 2 cups mushrooms, sliced

## DIRECTIONS:

1. Soak the brown rice the night before.
2. Fry the boar meat in butter and season with salt, pepper, dill, celery leaf, and brandy for 10-15 minutes.
3. Add 1 cup of vegetable stock.
4. Bring to a boil and simmer for another 10-15 minutes.
5. Add mushrooms, stir, and simmer for a couple of minutes before adding the rice and the rest of the stock.
6. Bring the risotto to a boil and turn off the heat.
7. Preheat your oven to 400 °F, glaze a baking dish with butter, and transfer the risotto.
8. Roast for 15-20 minutes or as needed.

## FACTS AND STATS:

*Baiting involves setting up a bait station to attract wild boars to a specific location. They are using specially trained dogs to track and corner wild boars. Hunters can then take a shot at the animal while it is distracted or immobilized. Once the animal is in range, hunters can take a shot.*

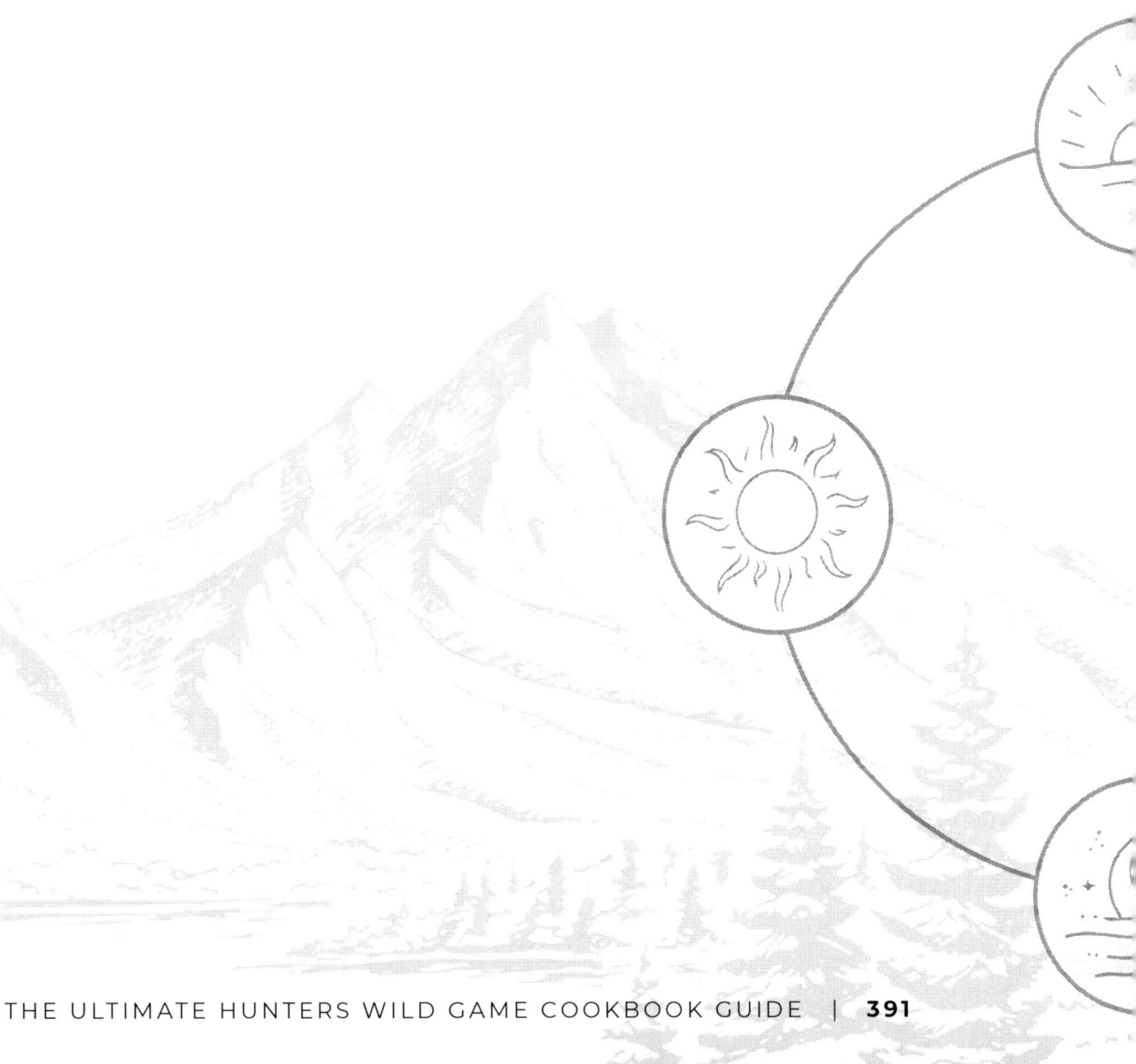

# WILD BOAR MOUSSAKA

**Stalking involves quietly and slowly approaching the animal on foot. Stalking is best done when the animal is active, usually in the early morning or late afternoon. Still-hunting is finding a spot with good visibility and waiting for the animal to come into view. Still-hunting is best done in the early morning or late afternoon when wild boars are most active.**

### SERVING SIZE: 4-6

### INGREDIENTS:

- 1 lb boar meat, ground
- salt and pepper, to taste
- 1 tbsp cilantro
- 1 tsp thyme
- 1 tsp oregano
- 2-3 tbsp butter
- 1 lb potatoes, sliced
- 1 eggplant, sliced
- 2-3 zucchinis, sliced
- 3-4 eggs
- 1 cup sour cream
- 1 cup flour
- 1 tsp lemon zest
- 1 cup mushrooms, sliced
- ½ cup Parmesan, grated
- ½ cup cheddar cheese, grated
- 1 tbsp dill
- 1 tbsp basil

### DIRECTIONS:

1. Brown the ground boar meat in butter and season with salt, pepper, cilantro, thyme, and oregano.
2. Preheat your oven to 400 °F.
3. Glaze a wide baking dish with butter at the bottom and the sides.
4. Layer a row of potatoes, then meat, zucchini, and eggplant.
5. Add another layer of meat and cover with zucchini, eggplant, and potatoes.
6. Whisk the eggs and mix in sour cream, flour, lemon zest, mushrooms, Parmesan and cheddar cheese, dill, and basil.
7. Pour the mixture over the moussaka and allow a couple of minutes for the sauce to settle in the dish.
8. Bake for 30-45 minutes at 400 °F.

## FACTS AND STATS:

*The biggest wild boar ever recorded was shot in 1984 in Alabama, USA. The boar weighed 1,051 pounds (477 kg) and was 9 feet 4 inches (2.84 meters) long. This massive boar was nicknamed "Hogzilla" and became a legendary figure in the hunting world. However, it's worth noting that there have been claims of even larger wild boars shot in other parts of the world, although these claims have not been substantiated.*

# WILD BOAR PASTA WITH CAULIFLOWER AND CHEESE

**Here are some tips on how to cook wild boar. Wild boar can be lean, so it's a good idea to brine the meat to help it retain moisture and flavor. Brining involves soaking the meat in a saltwater solution for several hours before cooking. Marinating can also help add flavor and moisture to wild boar meat. A marinade with acidic ingredients such as vinegar, citrus juice, or wine can also help tenderize the meat.**

### SERVING SIZE: 4-6

### INGREDIENTS:

- 3 cups cauliflower, chopped
- 1 lb boar meat, chopped
- 2-3 tbsp butter
- 2 cups of water
- 1 cup onions, chopped
- 1 cup mushrooms, sliced
- 1 tsp thyme, chopped
- 1 tsp cilantro, chopped
- salt and pepper, to taste
- 1 tsp dill, chopped
- 1 cup sour cream
- 1 cup cheddar cheese, grated
- 1 box of pasta

### DIRECTIONS:

1. Cook the cauliflower for 15-20 minutes in water until soft, set aside, and keep the cooking water.
2. Brown the boar meat with butter, onions, and mushrooms, and season with thyme, cilantro, salt, pepper, and dill.
3. Don't add any liquid until the meat is well cooked.
4. Add the cauliflower with the water to the frying pan.
5. Bring to a boil and simmer more until the water evaporates.
6. Stir frequently to break down all of the cauliflower.
7. Once the sauce has thickened, add sour cream and cheddar cheese.
8. Cook the pasta as instructed and mix it with the sauce.

## FACTS AND STATS:

*The largest wild boar ever recorded and recognized by the Safari Club International (SCI) was shot in 2019 in Turkey. The boar weighed an astonishing 1,100 pounds (498 kg) and had tusks that measured over 14 inches (35.56 cm) each. However, it's worth noting that there have been claims of larger wild boars shot in the past, but they were not officially recognized by organizations such as SCI.*

# DINNER

# SMOKEY WILD BOAR RIB ROAST

Wild boar meat can be tough if not cooked properly, so it's best to cook it low and slow. This can be achieved by roasting, braising, or slow cooking in a crockpot. Wild boar has a distinct flavor that can be enhanced using herbs and spices such as rosemary, thyme, garlic, and black pepper. Wild boar meat is best-served medium-rare to medium, as overcooking can result in tough, dry meat.

### SERVING SIZE: 4-6

### INGREDIENTS:

- 1 lb wild boar ribs
- ½ cup red wine
- 1 tbsp soy sauce
- 1 tsp garlic powder
- 1 tsp dill, chopped
- 1 tbsp celery leaf, chopped
- 1 tbsp sweet pepper powder
- 2-3 tbsp butter
- 1 cup of potatoes, diced
- 1 cup sweet potatoes, diced
- 1 cup cauliflower, chopped
- 1 cup kale, chopped
- 1 cup broccoli, chopped

### DIRECTIONS:

1. Dredge the wild boar ribs in the wine, soy sauce, garlic powder, dill, celery leaf, and sweet pepper powder.
2. Glaze a baking dish with butter and add potatoes, sweet potatoes, cauliflower, broccoli, and kale.
3. Put the ribs over the vegetables and roast for 30-45 minutes at 400 °F.

# FACTS AND STATS:

*Wild boars are omnivorous and have a varied diet that depends on the season and availability of food. Wild boars feed on plants such as roots, tubers, bulbs, acorns, fruits, and berries. They eat insects such as grasshoppers, crickets, beetles, and larvae. Wild boars can hunt and eat small animals such as rodents, reptiles, and birds.*

# WILD BOAR RISOTTO ROAST

The exact population of wild boars in Canada is unknown, but they have been reported in every province except Prince Edward Island. It's estimated that there are tens of thousands of wild boars in Canada. Wild boars can thrive in various habitats, from forests and grasslands to agricultural fields and suburban areas. They are known for their adaptability and can survive in harsh environments.

### SERVING SIZE: 4-6

### INGREDIENTS:

- 1 lb boar meat, cut into small pieces
- 2-3 tbsp butter
- ½ cup white wine
- salt and pepper, to taste
- 1 tbsp celery leaf, chopped
- 1 tsp mustard seeds
- 1 tsp cumin powder
- ½ tsp ginger powder
- 2-3 cups brown rice
- 2 eggs
- 1 cup sour cream
- 1 cup cheddar cheese, grated

### DIRECTIONS:

1. Soak the brown rice the night before.
2. Fry the meat in butter and white wine and season with salt, pepper, celery leaf, mustard seeds, cumin powder, and ginger powder for 10-15 minutes.
3. Drain the rice and add it to the meat.
4. Bring to a boil and simmer for another 10-15 minutes.
5. Preheat your oven to 400 °F.
6. Transfer into a baking dish.
7. Mix the egg in a bowl with sour cream and cheese. Pour it over the rice and meat.
8. Bake for 20-30 minutes at 400 °F.

# FACTS AND STATS:

*Wild boars are known to cause significant damage to the environment, including soil erosion, damage to crops and vegetation, and the destruction of habitat for native wildlife. Wild boars can cause extensive damage to agricultural crops, including corn, wheat, and soybeans. They also pose a threat to livestock by spreading disease.*

# WILD BOAR STEAK WITH SWEET POTATO MASH

Wild boars are a popular game animal in Canada; hunting them is legal in most provinces. However, some provinces have restricted hunting to control their population. In Canada, there are ongoing efforts to control the population of wild boars, including hunting, trapping, and sterilization programs. However, their ability to reproduce quickly and adapt to new environments makes control efforts challenging.

### SERVING SIZE: 4-6

### INGREDIENTS:

- 2-3 tbsp butter
- 1 lb wild boar steaks
- ½ cup brandy
- salt and pepper, to taste
- 1 tsp cumin powder
- ½ tsp ginger powder
- 1 tsp orange zest
- 2 cups bread crumbs
- 2 cups potatoes, diced
- 2 cups sweet potatoes, diced
- 1 cup of milk
- 1 cup Parmesan cheese, grated

### DIRECTIONS:

1. Glaze a baking dish with butter.
2. Dredge the wild boar steaks in brandy and seasoning consisting of salt, pepper, cumin powder, ginger powder, orange zest, and bread crumbs.
3. Bake in your oven for 20-30 minutes at 400 °F.
4. While the meat is baking, cook the potatoes and sweet potatoes in a stockpot until tender and drain.
5. Mash and add the milk, butter, and Parmesan cheese.
6. Keep mashing and stirring until there are no lumps.
7. Serve with the steaks.

## FACTS AND STATS:

*Wild boars have a high reproductive rate, with females capable of producing several litters of piglets each year. This makes their populations challenging to control and can contribute to their invasive status in certain areas. Wild boar meat is a popular culinary ingredient in many cultures and is prized for its lean, flavorful meat. It can be prepared in various ways, including roasting, grilling, or slow-cooking.*

# WILD BOAR AND PUMPKIN PIE

Wild boars are social animals and live in groups called sounders. Sounders can consist of several females and their young and a few males. They communicate with each other through a variety of vocalizations and body language. They have sharp tusks and can cause severe injuries to humans or other animals.

### SERVING SIZE: 4–6

### INGREDIENTS:

- 2–3 tbsp butter
- 1 lb boar meat, ground
- 1 cup mushrooms, sliced
- 1 cup sour cream
- ½ lb pumpkin flesh
- 1 tsp cinnamon powder
- ½ tsp ginger powder
- 1 tsp orange zest
- 1 pie crust

### DIRECTIONS:

1. Brown the boar meat with mushrooms in butter for 10–15 minutes.
2. Add the sour cream, stir, and let simmer for another 10 minutes.
3. Cook the pumpkin flesh for about 10 minutes, add to the meat, and stir well.
4. Add some cinnamon powder, ginger powder, and orange zest and mix.
5. Glaze your baking dish with butter at the bottom and the sides and spread the pie crust.
6. Add the meat filling and top with another layer of the pie crust.
7. Bake for 20–30 minutes at 400 °F.

## FACTS AND STATS:

*Wild boars are brilliant animals and are known for their problem-solving skills. They can remember the locations of food and water sources and navigate complex terrain. Wild boars are fascinating animals with complex social behaviors and surprising levels of intelligence. While they can pose challenges as an invasive species, they are also valuable game animal and culinary ingredient.*

# BEAUTIFUL BOAR AND SWEET POTATO STEW

Wild boar populations in Canada are generally found in the provinces of Alberta, Saskatchewan, Manitoba, and British Columbia. However, it's important to note that hunting wild boar in Canada is tightly regulated, and many areas have specific rules and regulations regarding hunting seasons, licenses, and other requirements.

### SERVING SIZE: 4-6

### INGREDIENTS:

- 1 lb boar meat, cubed
- 1 cup sweet potatoes, cubed
- 1 cup red onions, chopped
- 1 tbsp garlic, minced
- 1 cup carrots, chopped
- 1 tbsp red pepper powder
- 1 tbsp mustard seeds
- ½ cup wine or beer
- 4 cups beef broth or water
- 2 tbsp butter

### DIRECTIONS:

1. Brown the boar in butter in a skillet over medium heat. Add drizzles of broth as needed.
2. Move into a stockpot after 10–15 minutes.
3. Pour the broth and bring it to a short boil. Add the remaining ingredients except for the wine/beer and seasoning, leaving the herbs at the last 10 minutes of cooking.
4. Simmer for another 45 minutes and season.
5. Add wine or beer.
6. Let simmer for 10–15 minutes more.

## FACTS AND STATS:

*The coloration of wild boars can vary depending on the species and geographic location. However, wild boars generally have a dark brown or black coat with lighter-colored underparts. Some wild boars may also have distinctive markings on their body or legs, such as stripes or spots. The coloration and markings can help camouflage the animal in its natural environment and protect it from predators. In some cases, domesticated pigs that have escaped or been released into the wild may also interbreed with wild boars, resulting in hybrid animals with various colors and markings.*

# CAULIFLOWER AND MOZZARELLA WILD BOAR RISOTTO ROAST

Here are some tips for protecting yourself. If you spot a wild boar in the wild, try to keep your distance and avoid approaching it. These animals can be unpredictable, and you don't want to provoke an attack. If you come across a wild boar and are not hunting them, make noise and try to appear larger by holding your arms above your head or opening a jacket. This can help to intimidate the animal and discourage it from approaching.

### SERVING SIZE: 4–6

### INGREDIENTS:

- 1–2 lb boar meat, chopped
- 1 cup vegetable broth
- ½ cup white wine
- 1 ½ cups brown rice
- 2 cups cauliflower, chopped
- 1 cup carrots, chopped
- 1 cup onions, chopped
- ½ tbsp celery leaf, chopped
- ½ tbsp dill, chopped
- ½ tbsp turmeric powder
- 1 tbsp garlic, minced
- 1 tbsp mustard
- 7.5 oz mozzarella cheese, chopped
- 2 tbsp butter
- Salt and pepper, to taste

### DIRECTIONS:

1. Preheat your oven to 350 °F.
2. Sauté the boar meat in butter and a drizzle of vegetable broth with rice, cauliflower, carrots, onions, mozzarella, and garlic over low heat for 20–30 minutes.
3. Stir frequently to keep the mozzarella from sticking.
4. After a short boil, add the mustard, seasoning, and wine, and let simmer for another 10–20 minutes.
5. Season with salt and pepper to taste.
6. Roast in a large baking dish at 350 °F for 45 minutes or as needed.

## FACTS AND STATS:

*Suppose the wild boar begins to charge or approach you. Back away slowly and try to maintain eye contact. Do not turn your back on the animal or run; this can trigger a chase response. Climb a tree or seek higher ground to escape the animal's reach. If you carry a firearm, use it as a last resort to protect yourself. Aim for the head or vital organs to ensure a quick and humane kill. It's always best to avoid encountering a wild boar if possible. Keep your distance, make noise, and remain aware of your surroundings to prevent potential conflicts.*

# WONDERFUL WILD BOAR AND SWEET POTATO SALAD

The giant wild boars in the world are generally found in Europe and Asia, where the species originated. Some of the largest boars ever recorded have come from these regions. However, it's worth noting that wild boars can be found worldwide and vary in size depending on the specific subspecies and region.

### SERVING SIZE: 4–6

### INGREDIENTS:

- 1 lb wild boar meat, ground
- 4 cups sweet potatoes, chopped
- 1 cup onions, chopped
- 1 cup zucchini, sliced
- 1 cup eggplant, sliced
- 3 oz Parmesan cheese, ground
- 1 cup salsa of your choice
- 1 tbsp lemon juice
- ½ cup white wine
- 1 cup mayonnaise
- 1 cup plain yogurt
- 1 tbsp sesame seeds, toasted
- 1 tbsp celery leaf, chopped
- salt and pepper, to taste
- 1 tbsp dill
- 3 tbsp olive oil

### DIRECTIONS:

1. Brown the boar meat, white wine, onions, sweet potatoes, zucchini, and eggplant in olive oil for 15–20 minutes.
2. Add Parmesan, sesame seeds, celery leaf, dill, salt, pepper, and a drizzle of water, and stir-fry for another 10 minutes.
3. Mix the salad dressing with yogurt, mayo, and lemon juice.
4. Grab a salad bowl.
5. Transfer the meat and veggie salad and top with the dressing.

## FACTS AND STATS:

*Russia is known for having some of the largest wild boars in the world. Other countries with significant populations of large wild boars include Germany, Italy, and Spain in Europe, as well as parts of Asia such as China, Korea, and Japan. However, it's important to remember that the size of a wild boar can vary widely based on genetics, diet, and environmental factors.*

# CHAPTER 8
# Goodness Game Fish

Fishing is the second best thing I love doing outdoors, next to hunting. Catching fish doesn't usually work out all the time, but it is pure joy when you are. I want to try spearfishing in the ocean one day. Freshwater fish has more delicate meat than saltwater. Freshwater fish do not have the same flavors as saltwater fish. Freshwater fish has a slightly sweet flavor, which makes it an excellent choice for anyone who doesn't like a "fishy" taste. Saltwater fish is a much stronger taste than freshwater. Saltwater makes them have a briny flavor. Salmon are anadromous, meaning they live part of their lives in fresh and saltwater.

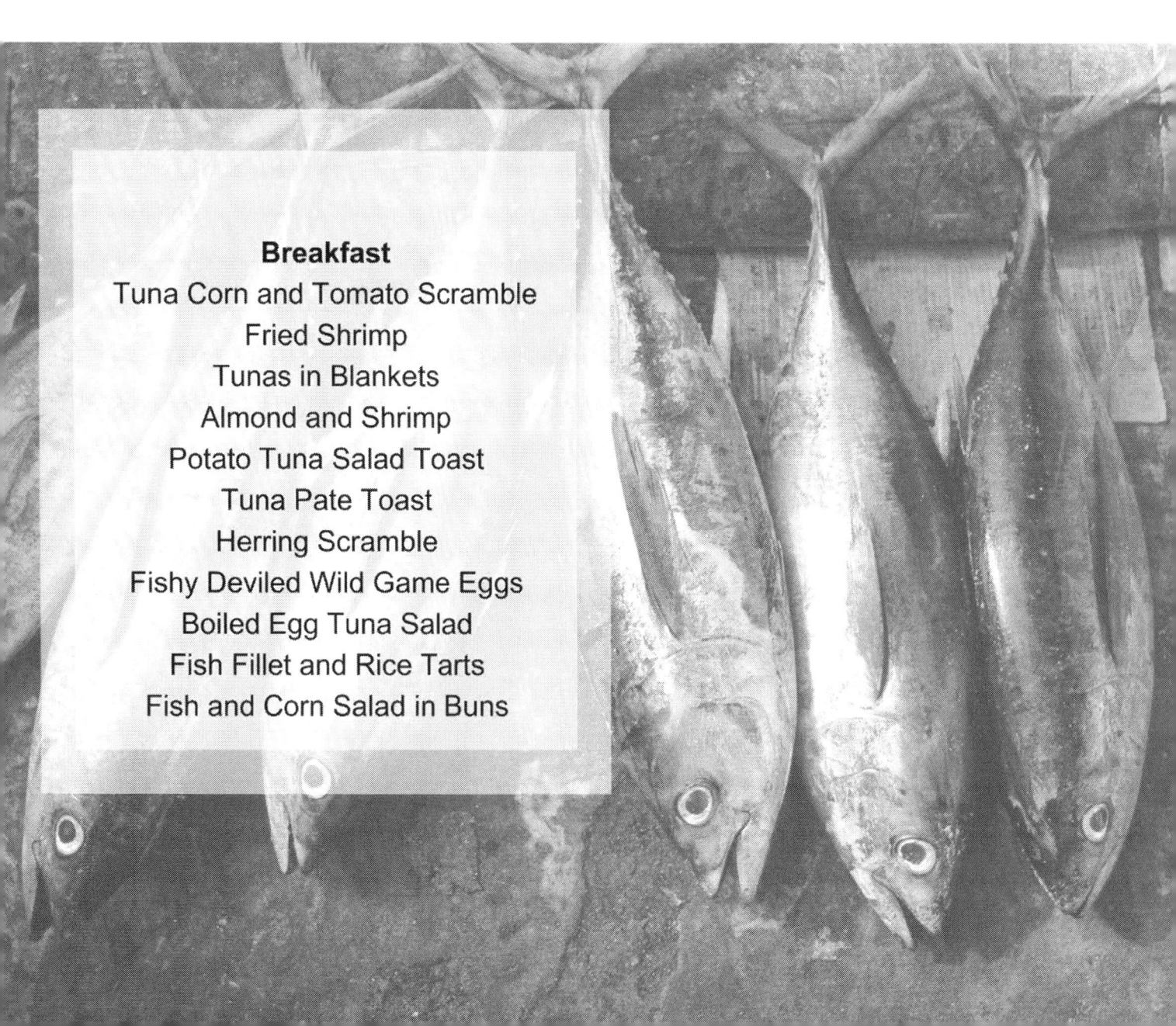

**Breakfast**
Tuna Corn and Tomato Scramble
Fried Shrimp
Tunas in Blankets
Almond and Shrimp
Potato Tuna Salad Toast
Tuna Pate Toast
Herring Scramble
Fishy Deviled Wild Game Eggs
Boiled Egg Tuna Salad
Fish Fillet and Rice Tarts
Fish and Corn Salad in Buns

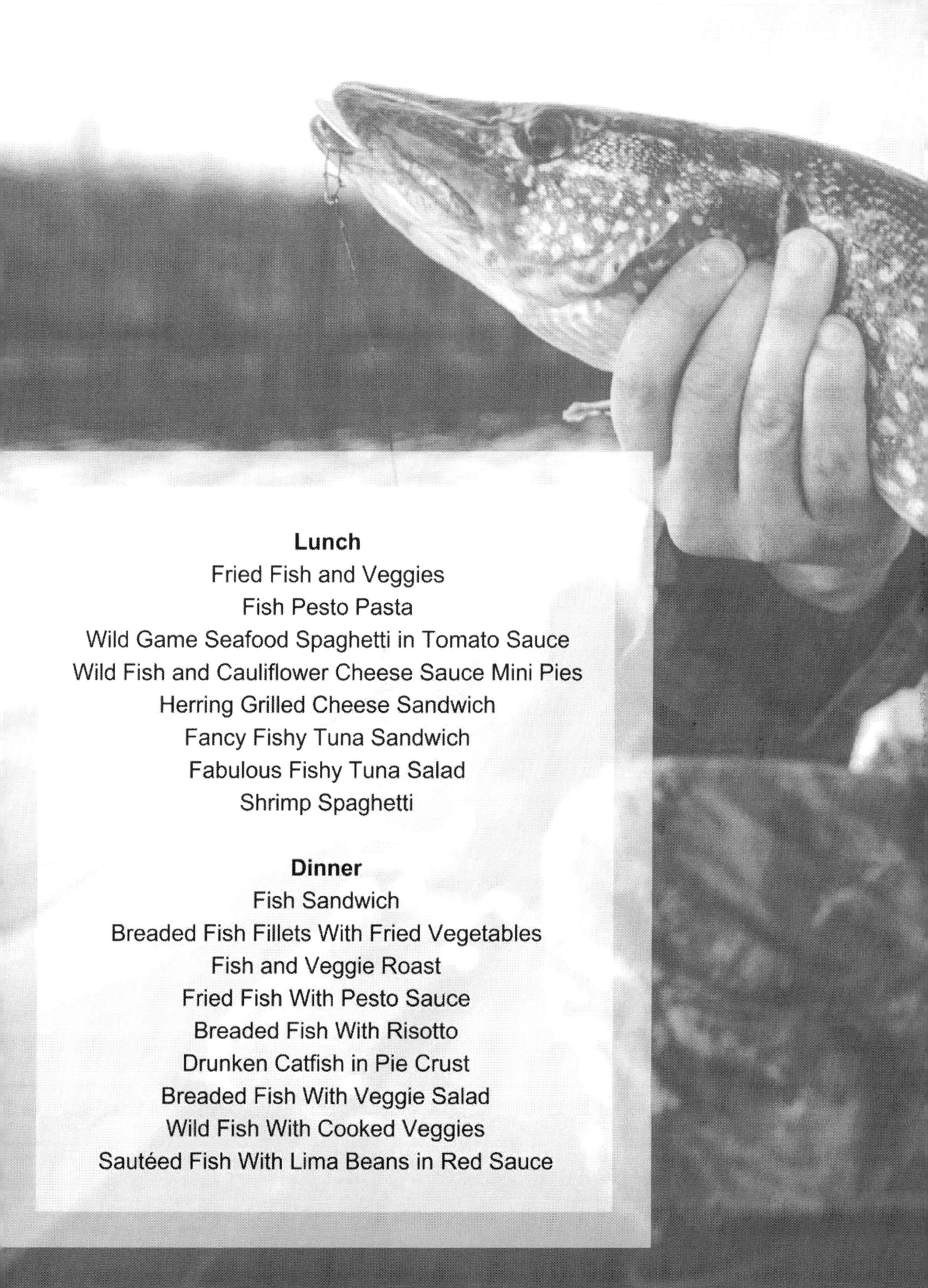

## Lunch
Fried Fish and Veggies
Fish Pesto Pasta
Wild Game Seafood Spaghetti in Tomato Sauce
Wild Fish and Cauliflower Cheese Sauce Mini Pies
Herring Grilled Cheese Sandwich
Fancy Fishy Tuna Sandwich
Fabulous Fishy Tuna Salad
Shrimp Spaghetti

## Dinner
Fish Sandwich
Breaded Fish Fillets With Fried Vegetables
Fish and Veggie Roast
Fried Fish With Pesto Sauce
Breaded Fish With Risotto
Drunken Catfish in Pie Crust
Breaded Fish With Veggie Salad
Wild Fish With Cooked Veggies
Sautéed Fish With Lima Beans in Red Sauce

# BREAKFAST

# TUNA CORN AND TOMATO SCRAMBLE

Tuna fish is a good source of protein, vitamins, and minerals and has several health benefits. Tuna is a good source of omega-3 fatty acids, which are beneficial for heart health and may help to reduce inflammation in the body. Tuna is a rich source of protein, which is essential for building and repairing tissues in the body.

### SERVING SIZE: 4

### INGREDIENTS:

- 1 lb tuna, chopped
- 8 whole eggs
- ½ cup corn kernels, cooked
- ½ cup tomato puree
- ½ cup onions, chopped
- ½ cup cheese, shredded
- ½ tbsp garlic, minced
- 2 tbsp olive oil
- Salt and pepper, to taste

### DIRECTIONS:

1. Heat a frying pan with olive oil on medium heat.
2. Fry the tuna with corn, onions, and garlic for 5–10 minutes.
3. Break the eggs in a bowl, pour the tomato puree, and whisk.
4. Pour the eggs over the tuna, top with cheese, and season to taste.

## FACTS AND STATS:

*Tuna is one of the most commercially valuable fish in the world. It is second only to the Alaska pollock regarding global fishery production. Several different tuna species include bluefin, yellowfin, skipjack, and albacore. Bluefin tuna is considered the most prized and expensive tuna species.*

# FRIED SHRIMP

Shrimp are a rich source of protein, vitamins, and minerals. They are also low in calories and fat, making them a healthy food choice. Shrimp is low in calories, with about 84 calories per 3-ounce serving. This makes it a good choice for people to watch their calorie intake. Shrimp is a good source of protein, with about 18 grams of protein per 3-ounce serving. Protein is essential for building and repairing tissues in the body. Shrimp is low in fat, with about 1 gram of fat per 3-ounce serving. This makes it a good choice for people watching their fat intake.

### SERVING SIZE: 4-6

### INGREDIENTS:

- 1 lb shrimp, peeled and deveined
- 1 egg
- 1 cup flour
- 2 tbsp cornstarch
- ¼ tsp baking soda or baking powder
- 1 cup water or beer
- olive oil, as needed

### DIRECTIONS:

1. Mix all dry ingredients in a bowl.
2. Add the egg and water or beer to create the batter.
3. Dredge the shrimp in the batter. Let them soak for a while so that the batter sticks better.
4. Fry evenly on each side in olive oil.

## FACTS AND STATS:

*Shrimp are decapod crustaceans, which means they have 10 legs. They are closely related to crabs and lobsters. Shrimp are found in saltwater and freshwater habitats, including oceans, rivers, and lakes. There are over 2,000 species of shrimp, ranging in size from tiny, freshwater species to larger, ocean-dwelling species. The most popular shrimp species are white, brown, and pink shrimp.*

# TUNAS IN BLANKETS

The omega-3 fatty acids in tuna may reduce the risk of heart disease by lowering triglyceride levels, reducing blood pressure, and improving blood vessel function. Some studies have suggested that eating tuna may help to reduce the risk of certain types of cancer, such as breast and colon cancer.

## SERVING SIZE: 4–6

### INGREDIENTS:

- 6 tuna fillets
- 1 egg
- 1 cup flour
- ½ tbsp celery
- ½ tbsp dill, chopped
- 1 tsp garlic powder
- 2 tbsp cornstarch
- ¼ tsp baking soda or baking powder
- 1 cup water or beer
- 2 tbsp lemon juice
- olive oil, as needed

### DIRECTIONS:

1. Mix the batter ingredients (egg, flour, water or beer, cornstarch, baking soda or powder, and garlic powder) in a bowl.
2. Soak the tuna in the batter. Let sit for 10–15 minutes.
3. Fry the tuna fillets in olive oil for up to 5 minutes on each side.

## FACTS AND STATS:

*Tuna are migratory fish that can travel thousands of miles during their lifetime. Some tuna species have been known to migrate from the Atlantic Ocean to the Mediterranean Sea and back again. Tuna are some of the fastest-swimming fish in the ocean, capable of reaching up to 45 miles per hour. Tuna are carnivorous and primarily feed on smaller fish and squid. The flesh of tuna is typically pink to dark red and has a firm texture and rich flavor.*

# ALMOND AND SHRIMP

Shrimp is a good source of several vitamins and minerals, including vitamin B12, iron, and selenium. Vitamin B12 is essential for nerve function and red blood cell production, while the iron is vital for the formation of red blood cells. Selenium is an antioxidant that may help to protect against oxidative damage. Shrimp is low in carbohydrates, with about 1 gram of carbohydrates per 3-ounce serving. This makes it a good choice for people watching their carbohydrate intake, such as those on a low-carb or ketogenic diet.

### SERVING SIZE: 4

### INGREDIENTS:

- 9 oz shrimp, peeled and deveined
- 1 cup almond flour (or as needed)
- 5 tbsp cream cheese
- 1 tbsp Parmesan, ground
- 1 tsp celery, chopped
- 1 tsp oregano, chopped
- 1 tsp rosemary, chopped
- 1 tsp garlic powder
- 1 tbsp lemon juice
- ½ cup white wine (or as needed)
- 4 cups sweet potatoes, cubed
- olive oil, as needed

### DIRECTIONS:

1. To make the batter, grab a salad bowl and add all ingredients together except for the shrimp and sweet potatoes.
2. Soak the shrimp in the batter and let sit while you're frying the sweet potatoes.
3. Fry the shrimp in olive oil until ready.

## FACTS AND STATS:

*Shrimp is one of the most popular seafood items in the world. They are the most-consumed seafood in the United States. Shrimp are a rich source of protein, vitamins, and minerals. They are also low in calories and fat, making them a healthy food choice. Shrimp farming, also known as aquaculture, is the fastest-growing sector of the seafood industry.*

# POTATO TUNA SALAD TOAST

The omega-3 fatty acids in tuna also help to improve cognitive function and reduce the risk of age-related cognitive decline. Tuna is a good source of vitamin D, which is essential for bone health and immune system function.

## SERVING SIZE: 4-6

## INGREDIENTS:

- 1 lb tuna, cleansed and chopped
- 1-2 tbsp butter
- salt and pepper, to taste
- 1 tsp dill, chopped
- 1 tsp cilantro, chopped
- 4 medium-sized potatoes
- 1 onion, sliced
- 2 tbsp sour cream
- 1 tbsp olive oil
- 1 tbsp lemon juice
- bread slices or buns, as needed

## DIRECTIONS:

1. Fry tuna in butter for 1 minute and season it with salt, pepper, dill, and cilantro.
2. Boil potatoes with skins on in a separate pot, remove skins once they have cooled down, and cut them into small pieces.
3. Mix the onion slices with potatoes, sour cream, tuna, a drizzle of olive oil, and lemon juice.
4. Serve the salad between halved buns or slices of bread, and enjoy this for breakfast.

## FACTS AND STATS:

*Tuna are apex predators in the ocean and play an important role in maintaining the balance of the marine ecosystem. Overfishing and illegal fishing practices have led to declining tuna populations worldwide. As a result, many conservation organizations are working to promote sustainable tuna fishing practices. Tuna can be found in many different types of cuisine around the world, including sushi, sashimi, and tuna steaks.*

# TUNA PATE TOAST

It's worth noting that while tuna can be a healthy part of a balanced diet, it's also important to be mindful of the potential risks of consuming too much tuna due to mercury contamination. It's recommended that pregnant women and young children limit their intake of certain types of tuna to reduce their mercury exposure.

### SERVING SIZE: 4–6

### INGREDIENTS:

- 1 lb tuna, cleansed and chopped
- 1 tbsp white wine
- salt and pepper, to taste
- 1 tsp dill, chopped
- 1 tsp garlic powder
- a pinch of ginger powder
- 1 cup carrots, sliced and cooked
- slices of toast, as needed
- 1 tsp cumin powder

### DIRECTIONS:

1. Fry tuna in butter and white wine briefly for 1–2 minutes.
2. Transfer it from the frying pan to a food processor and add salt, pepper, dill, garlic powder, ginger powder, cumin powder, and cooked carrots.
3. Process all together to create the pate.
4. Transfer the pate from the food processor to a plate and enjoy the pate on slices of toast.

## FACTS AND STATS:

*The largest bluefin tuna ever recorded weighed 1,496 pounds (680 kg). Ken Fraser caught it off Nova Scotia, Canada in 1979. The fish was caught using a rod and reel, and it took Fraser over 3.5 hours to reel it in. The bluefin tuna measured 12 feet and 3 inches in length and had a girth of 8 feet and 1 inch. This catch remains one of the largest fish ever caught on a rod and reel, and it was a record-breaking catch at the time. It's worth noting that bluefin tuna populations have declined significantly since the 1970s, and many conservation organizations are working to promote sustainable fishing practices to help protect this species.*

# HERRING SCRAMBLE

Herring is a type of small, oily fish rich in nutrients and can provide several health benefits. Herring is a good source of several vitamins and minerals, including vitamin D, B12, selenium, and phosphorus. Vitamin D is essential for bone health and immune function, while vitamin B12 is vital for nerve and red blood cell production. Selenium is an antioxidant that may help to protect against oxidative damage, and phosphorus is important for bone and teeth health.

### SERVING SIZE: 4-6

### INGREDIENTS:

- 1 lb herring, cleansed and chopped
- 1 tbsp butter
- salt and pepper, to taste
- 1 tsp cilantro, chopped
- 1 tsp dill, chopped
- 1 tbsp celery leaf, chopped
- 3-4 eggs
- 1 tbsp flour
- 2-3 tbsp sour cream
- 1 tsp lemon zest
- 1 tbsp lemon juice
- ½ cup cheddar cheese, grated

### DIRECTIONS:

1. Fry the herring in butter for a couple of minutes.
2. Season with salt, pepper, cilantro, dill, and celery leaf.
3. Whisk the eggs and add flour, sour cream, lemon zest, and lemon juice. Mix all together, and pour into the pan.
4. Cook until done and serve sprinkled with cheddar cheese.

## FACTS AND STATS:

*Herring are known for their distinctive silver color, and their streamlined body shape helps them swim quickly through the water. Herring has a unique reproductive system in which females release their eggs into the water, and males release their sperm to fertilize them. The fertilized eggs hatch into larvae, which drift with the ocean currents until they reach their juvenile stage. The herring fishery is one of the world's oldest and most important fisheries. It has been a significant part of the economy and culture of many coastal communities for centuries.*

# FISHY DEVILED WILD GAME EGGS

Fish is just healthy meat, no matter how you look at it! Freshwater fish, such as salmon and trout, are rich in omega-3 fatty acids, which are important for heart health and may help reduce inflammation. Freshwater fish are a good source of several vitamins and minerals, including vitamin D, vitamin B12, selenium, and phosphorus. Vitamin D is essential for bone health and immune function, while vitamin B12 is important for nerve function and red blood cell production. Selenium is an antioxidant that may help to protect against oxidative damage, and phosphorus is important for bone and teeth health.

### SERVING SIZE: 4-6

### INGREDIENTS:

- 8–12 eggs
- ½ lb game fish, chopped
- 1 tbsp butter
- Salt and pepper, to taste
- 1 tsp cilantro, chopped
- 1 tsp thyme, chopped
- ½ tsp ginger powder
- 1 tsp garlic powder
- 2–3 tbsp sour cream
- 1 tbsp lemon juice
- ½ tsp lemon zest

### DIRECTIONS:

1. Cook 6–8 eggs and peel the shells.
2. Cut the eggs in half and take out the egg yolks.
3. Fry the fish in butter and season with salt, pepper, cilantro, thyme, ginger powder, and garlic powder.
4. Mix the fried tuna in a bowl with egg yolks and sour cream. Stir and mash well. Add some lemon zest and lemon juice.
5. Stuff the egg whites with the filling and let them sit in your fridge for 15–20 minutes to cool down.

## FACTS AND STATS:

*Over 40,000 freshwater fish species worldwide, making them the most diverse vertebrates on Earth. The largest freshwater fish in the world is the arapaima, which can grow up to 10 feet long and weigh over 400 pounds. Freshwater fish are found in many habitats, including rivers, lakes, ponds, and wetlands. Some freshwater fish species, such as the electric eel and the electric catfish, can produce electric shocks for defense and prey capture.*

# BOILED EGG TUNA SALAD

Here are some general good practices for cleaning a tuna. Rinse the tuna under cold water and pat it dry with paper towels. Lay it on a clean, flat surface, like a cutting board, with the belly facing up. Use a sharp knife to cut off the head and tail of the tuna. Discard them or use them for other purposes. Starting at the head end of the tuna, make a shallow incision along the spine using a sharp knife. Be careful not to cut too deep; you want to avoid cutting through the bones. Use the knife tip to cut along the ribs on one side of the spine, starting from the head end and working toward the tail. Keep the knife as close to the bones as possible to avoid wasting meat. To be continued on the next recipe…

### SERVING SIZE: 4-6

### INGREDIENTS:

- 1 lb tuna, chopped
- 1 tbsp butter
- Salt and pepper, to taste
- 1 tsp dill, chopped
- 1 tsp basil, chopped
- 1 tsp mint, chopped
- 8–12 eggs, hard-boiled and peeled
- 3–4 slices of bread, cubed and toast
- 1 tbsp white wine
- 1 tbsp lemon juice
- 1 tbsp Parmesan cheese, grated
- 1 tbsp sour cream

### DIRECTIONS:

1. Fry tuna in butter and season with salt, pepper, dill, basil, and mint. Take off the heat after a couple of minutes and pour in a salad bowl.
2. Slice the eggs and mix with tuna. Add the toasted bread cubes.
3. Mix the salad dressing with wine, lemon juice, Parmesan, and sour cream.
4. Mix the dressing with the salad and serve.

## FACTS AND STATS:

*Bluefin tuna are highly migratory and can be found in various parts of the world, including the Mediterranean Sea, the Atlantic Ocean, the Pacific Ocean, and the Indian Ocean. Some popular locations for bluefin tuna fishing include the waters off the coast of Cape Cod, Massachusetts. The Gulf of Mexico, the waters around Prince Edward Island, Canada, and the waters off the coast of Japan.*

# FISH FILLET AND RICE TARTS

Once you've cut along the ribs on one side, use the knife to lift the fillet away from the bones, separating it from the spine. Repeat the process on the other side of the tuna to remove the other fillet. To remove the skin from the fillets, carefully place the fillet skin-side down on the cutting board and use a sharp knife to separate the skin from the meat. Start at one end and work down the fillet, keeping the blade close to the skin. Use a sharp filet knife to trim any remaining bones, fat, or other unwanted parts from the fillet. Rinse the fillet under cold water and pat it dry with paper towels. Now you have two fillets of tuna that you can use for cooking or freezing for later use. Always use a sharp filet knife, and be careful when filleting a tuna to avoid injury or lost fingers! Always cut away from you, friends!

### SERVING SIZE: 4-6

### INGREDIENTS:

- 2 cups brown rice
- 2 tbsp butter
- 1 lb game fish fillets
- salt and pepper, to taste
- ½ tsp ginger powder
- 2 tsp dill, chopped
- 1 tbsp cream cheese
- 1 tbsp cheddar cheese, shredded
- 1 tbsp white wine
- 1 tbsp lemon juice

### DIRECTIONS:

1. Simmer the brown rice for 15–20 minutes.
2. Stir frequently so that the rice doesn't stick.
3. Fry the fillets in butter on each side for 1–2 minutes and season with salt, pepper, ginger powder, and 1 tsp dill. Once done, set it aside on a plate.
4. Mix the cooked rice with cream cheese and 1 tsp dill. Shape the rice mixture into logs, ensuring they're the same size as the fillets.
5. Place the fillets on top of the shaped rice.
6. Make a dressing out of cream cheese, cheddar cheese, white wine, and lemon juice.
7. Drizzle over the tarts.

## FACTS AND STATS:

*Tuna are migratory fish, so it's important to know where and when they will most likely be found. Research the best locations and times of year to catch tuna in your area. Tuna can be very strong and tough, so having the right gear is crucial. Choose a rod and reel that is strong enough to handle the weight and power of a tuna, as well as a sturdy line and a variety of lures or bait. Look for signs of tuna, such as birds diving or fish jumping. Tuna often swim in schools, so if you see one tuna, there are likely more nearby.*

# FISH AND CORN SALAD IN BUNS

Yellowfin tuna are commonly found in tropical and subtropical waters around the world. Some popular locations for yellowfin tuna fishing include the Gulf of Mexico, the waters around Panama, the waters off the coast of Hawaii, and the waters around South Africa and Australia. Albacore tuna are typically found in colder waters and can be caught off the coasts of California, Oregon, Washington, and British Columbia. They are also commonly found in the Atlantic Ocean and the Mediterranean Sea.

### SERVING SIZE: 4-6

### INGREDIENTS:

- 1 tbsp sour cream
- 1 tbsp cream cheese
- 1 tbsp Parmesan cheese, grated
- 1 cup scallions, sliced
- 1 cup corn kernels
- 2 tsp dill, chopped
- Salt and pepper, to taste
- 1 lb game fish, sliced
- 1 tbsp butter
- buns or slices of bread, as needed

### DIRECTIONS:

1. Mix the sour cream, cream cheese, Parmesan cheese, scallions, corn, dill, salt, and pepper in a salad bowl. Mix well until you've achieved a creamy texture.
2. Fry the fish for 1–2 minutes in butter.
3. Mix with the salad and serve between the buns.

## FACTS AND STATS:

*Tuna can be caught using various techniques, including trolling, casting, jigging, and chunking. Experiment with different approaches to see what works best for the tuna in your area. When you feel a tug on your line, setting the hook quickly and firmly prevents the tuna from getting away. Tuna are known for their strength and speed, so using the right technique to reel them in is important. Keep the line tight and pump and reel to bring the tuna closer to the boat.*

# LUNCH

# FRIED FISH AND VEGGIES

It's worth noting that the health benefits of eating freshwater fish can vary depending on the species and how the fish is prepared. Some freshwater fish species may contain higher levels of contaminants like mercury, which can be harmful to health when consumed in large amounts. It's important to choose fish that are low in contaminants and to cook fish in a healthy way, such as baking, grilling, or broiling, to avoid adding extra fat and calories.

### SERVING SIZE: 4-6

### INGREDIENTS:

- 1 lb game fish fillets
- 2–3 tbsp butter
- 1 cup sweet potatoes, grated
- 1 cup carrots, grated
- 1 cup broccoli, chopped
- 1 cup kale, chopped
- 1 cup cauliflower, chopped
- salt and pepper, to taste
- 1 tbsp dried mint
- ½ tsp ginger powder
- ½ cup white wine
- bread slices, as needed
- 1–2 tbsp cream cheese
- grated Parmesan cheese, as needed
- 2 tbsp sour cream

### DIRECTIONS:

1. Fry the fish fillets in butter along with sweet potatoes, carrots, broccoli, kale, and cauliflower.
2. Season with salt, pepper, mint, and ginger powder.
3. Once cooked, sprinkle it with a cup of white wine and stir-fry long enough for the wine to evaporate.
4. You can serve it with slices of bread, sour cream, cream cheese, and grated Parmesan.

## FACTS AND STATS:

*Some freshwater fish species, such as the lungfish and the mudskipper, are adapted to breathe air and can survive out of water for extended periods. The most popular freshwater fish species for human consumption include carp, tilapia, trout, and catfish. Many freshwater fish species are important for recreational fishing and highly valued for their sport and trophy potential. Freshwater fish are essential to many ecosystems and play a key role in nutrient cycling and energy flow.*

# FISH PESTO PASTA

**Some studies have suggested that eating fish may help to reduce the risk of cognitive decline and dementia in older adults. Always cook fish until it reaches an internal temperature of 145°F (63°C) to ensure it is safe to eat. Grilling is a great way to cook fish because it imparts a smoky flavor and crispy texture. Brush the fish with oil and seasonings, and grill over high heat for a few minutes on each side until cooked. Baking fish in the oven is a simple and healthy way to cook fish. Season the fish with herbs and spices, and bake in a preheated oven until cooked. Delicious!**

### SERVING SIZE: 4-6

### INGREDIENTS:

- 2 cups fresh basil, chopped
- 1 cup Parmesan cheese, grated
- 2 tbsp cream cheese
- 1-2 tbsp olive oil
- salt and pepper, to taste
- 1 tsp dill, chopped
- 1 tsp lemon zest
- 1 tbsp lemon juice
- 1 lb game fish, deboned and chopped
- 1 box of macaroni or spaghetti
- 1 tbsp butter

### DIRECTIONS:

1. Start by making your pesto sauce. Mix basil, Parmesan, cream cheese, olive oil, salt, pepper, and dill and run it through a food processor for a minute.
2. Add lemon zest and lemon juice and mix thoroughly.
3. Cook the pasta as instructed.
4. While the pasta is cooking, fry the pieces of fish in butter.
5. Combine the pasta, pesto sauce, and fish and mix.

## FACTS AND STATS:

*Bigeye tuna are found in tropical and subtropical waters around the world. Still, they are most commonly caught in the waters around Hawaii, the Gulf of Mexico, and the waters off the coast of Australia and New Zealand. Remember always to follow local fishing regulations and guidelines and to practice responsible fishing techniques to help preserve the tuna population for future generations.*

# WILD GAME SEAFOOD SPAGHETTI IN TOMATO SAUCE

**Poaching is a gentle cooking method ideal for delicate fish like cod or halibut. Pan-frying is a great way to cook thin fish fillets like sole or tilapia. Coat the fish in seasoned flour or breadcrumbs, and fry in a hot pan with oil until crispy and golden brown. Heat a flavorful liquid, such as broth or wine, and simmer the fish in the liquid until cooked through.**

## SERVING SIZE: 4-6

## INGREDIENTS:

- 3 garlic cloves, minced
- 1 cup carrots, grated
- 2 cups tomatoes, cooked and crushed
- ½ cup red wine
- 1 tsp dill, chopped
- 1 tbsp celery leaf, chopped
- 1 cup heavy cream
- 1 lb game fish, deboned and sliced
- 1 tbsp Parmesan cheese, grated
- 1 box of macaroni or spaghetti

## DIRECTIONS:

1. Brown the garlic and carrots in butter until the carrots are tender.
2. Add the tomatoes, red wine, dill, celery leaf, and heavy cream.
3. Bring to a boil and let simmer for 5-10 minutes or until you've achieved a thick sauce.
4. Pop in the fish and simmer for another 1-2 minutes.
5. Once done, mix with Parmesan.
6. Cook the pasta and mix it with the sauce.

## FACTS AND STATS:

The Florida Everglades is home to various freshwater fish species, including largemouth bass, peacock bass, and snook. The region is known for its extensive network of waterways and backcountry, providing plenty of opportunities for anglers to explore. Florida, Lake Okeechobee is one of the largest freshwater lakes in the U.S., covering more than 730 square miles. It is home to various fish species, including largemouth bass, crappie, and bluegill.

# WILD FISH AND CAULIFLOWER CHEESE SAUCE MINI PIES

**Steaming is a healthy and easy way to cook fish without adding extra fat. Place the fish in a steamer basket over simmering water, and cook until opaque and flaky. Always cook fish until it reaches an internal temperature of 145°F (63°C) to ensure it is safe to eat.**

## SERVING SIZE: 4-6

## INGREDIENTS:

- ½ lb cauliflower, chopped
- 1 tbsp butter
- 1 cup of milk
- 1 tbsp flour
- 2 tbsp Parmesan cheese
- 1 lb game fish, deboned and chopped
- Salt and pepper, to taste
- 1 tsp dill, chopped
- 1 pie crust
- 1 tsp ginger powder

## DIRECTIONS:

1. Cook the cauliflower in a pot covered with water for a couple of minutes until tender.
2. Take the cauliflower out of the pot and mash it in a frying pan with butter.
3. Add milk and flour. Bring to a boil and stir for a minute.
4. Add Parmesan cheese and bring again to a boil and take off the heat.
5. Stir and mix thoroughly with the cauliflower.
6. Fry the chunks of fish for a couple of minutes in butter and season with salt, pepper, dill, and ginger powder.
7. Mix with the cheese sauce and cauliflower.
8. Spread the pie crust, cut it into squares of the desired size, and wrap the fish filling in the dough.
9. Glaze the bottom and sides of your baking dish with some butter.
10. Line the mini pies and bake for 10 minutes at 400 °F.

## FACTS AND STATS:

*Lake Fork is a popular destination for bass fishing and has produced many record-breaking largemouth bass. The lake also has a healthy population of catfish and crappie. Lake Champlain is a large freshwater lake located on the border of Vermont and New York. It is home to various fish species, including lake trout, landlocked salmon, and walleye. The Kenai River is a world-renowned destination for salmon fishing, with runs of king, sockeye, coho, and pink salmon. The river is also home to rainbow trout, Dolly Varden, and other species.*

# HERRING GRILLED CHEESE SANDWICH

**Herring is a small, fast-growing fish low in mercury, making it safer than larger, predatory fish like tuna and swordfish. The omega-3 fatty acids found in herring may help to reduce inflammation in the body, which can help to lower the risk of chronic diseases like arthritis, heart disease, and cancer. The omega-3 fatty acids found in herring may help to improve brain function and protect against cognitive decline. Omega-3s may improve memory, attention, and overall cognitive function.**

### SERVING SIZE: 4

### INGREDIENTS:

- 9 oz cooked herring, flaked
- 1 tbsp cream cheese
- 1 tsp Parmesan cheese, ground
- 1 tsp tomato puree
- 1 tbsp dill
- 1 tsp garlic powder
- 1 tbsp olive oil
- 2 tbsp butter
- arugula, to taste
- slices of bread

### DIRECTIONS:

1. Combine herring flakes, tomato puree, cream cheese, Parmesan, olive oil, arugula, dill, and garlic.
2. Take a slice of bread and spread a good amount of the mixture. Top with another slice of bread.
3. In a frying pan, grill the sandwiches in butter for a couple of minutes on each side until the bread has browned.

## FACTS AND STATS:

*Herring is a popular food fish that is commonly pickled, smoked, or canned in recipes. Herring are a key part of many traditional dishes in countries like Norway, Sweden, and the Netherlands. For example, herring is often served pickled with onions and sour cream in Sweden.*

# FANCY FISHY TUNA SANDWICH

Most saltwater fish are low in saturated fat, which is a type of fat that can increase cholesterol levels and increase the risk of heart disease. Saltwater fish are also a great source of protein, which is essential for building and repairing tissues in the body. Protein also helps to keep you feeling full and satisfied after meals.

## SERVING SIZE: 4

## INGREDIENTS:

- 2 cans (6 oz) tuna
- 3 oz cooked herring, flaked
- 5 tbsp mayonnaise
- lettuce leaves, as needed
- buns, as needed

## DIRECTIONS:

1. Grab a bowl and mix tuna, herring, and mayo.
2. Serve on buns, top with lettuce, and make a sandwich.

## FACTS AND STATS:

*There are over 28,000 species of saltwater fish in the world, and they inhabit every ocean and sea on the planet. The largest saltwater fish is the whale shark, which can grow up to 40 feet long and weigh over 20 tons. The lionfish is a venomous saltwater fish native to the Indo-Pacific region but has become an invasive species in parts of the Caribbean and Atlantic.*

# FABULOUS FISHY TUNA SALAD

This is a unique quick, simple, delicious fish salad. It's different from what you are picturing right now. Give it a chance and read on!

### SERVING SIZE: 4

### INGREDIENTS:

- 6 oz tuna, canned
- 3 oz dry macaroni
- ½ cup tomato sauce
- 1 tbsp lemon juice
- 1 tbsp olive oil
- 2 tbsp Parmesan, ground
- 1 tsp oregano, chopped
- 1 tsp dill, chopped
- 1 tsp thyme, chopped
- Salt and pepper, to taste

### DIRECTIONS:

1. Cook the macaroni according to package instructions.
2. Mix all the remaining ingredients in a salad bowl.
3. Pop in the macaroni, mix well, and enjoy!

## FACTS AND STATS:

*On May 24, spring down at Blanche River, Ontario, and you can smash right offshore beautiful pan-size walleye. In the same area, you can get whitefish & smelts.*

# SHRIMP SPAGHETTI

**Shrimp is also a source of cholesterol, with about 189 milligrams of cholesterol per 3-ounce serving. Additionally, shrimp is relatively low in saturated fat, a more significant contributor to high cholesterol levels. However, research suggests that dietary cholesterol may not significantly impact blood cholesterol levels as was once thought.**

### SERVING SIZE: 4-6

### INGREDIENTS:

- 6 oz shrimp
- 2-4 oz dry spaghetti
- 3 cups pesto sauce
- 2 tbsp butter
- Salt and pepper, to taste
- 1 tsp garlic powder
- ½ cup white wine
- 1 tbsp lemon juice
- 1 box of spaghetti

### DIRECTIONS:

1. Fry the shrimp in butter for 5-10 minutes.
2. Add the white wine and some water if needed, and sauté for a few more minutes.
3. Mix in the pesto sauce and seasoning, stir, and set aside.
4. Cook the spaghetti and mix it with the shrimp and pesto sauce.

## FACTS AND STATS:

*Shrimp are essential to the food chain, serving as prey for many larger fish and other marine animals. In some cultures, eating shrimp with heads still attached is considered bad luck. The largest shrimp ever recorded was a giant tiger prawn that measured over 16 inches long and weighed more than 1 pound.*

# DINNER

# FISH SANDWICH

**Saltwater fish species, such as salmon and eels, are born in freshwater rivers but spend most of their lives in the ocean before returning to their birthplace to spawn. Saltwater fish are vital to many coastal communities and provide an important food source and livelihood for millions of people worldwide. The saltwater fish industry is a multi-billion dollar global market, with countries like Japan, China, and the United States among the largest producers and consumers of seafood.**

### SERVING SIZE: 4-6

### INGREDIENTS:

- 1 lb game fish fillets
- ½ cup white wine
- 1 tbsp lemon juice
- 1 tbsp olive oil
- 1 tsp garlic powder
- 1 tsp dill, chopped
- 1 tbsp celery leaf, chopped
- bread slices, as needed
- 2 tbsp Parmesan cheese, grated
- 2 tbsp butter
- 1-2 tbsp sour cream

### DIRECTIONS:

1. Combine white wine, lemon juice, olive oil, garlic powder, dill, and celery leaf for the mixture.
2. Prepare some bread slices, drizzle them with the mixture, and top with butter or sour cream.
3. In a pan, fry the fish fillets in butter for a couple of minutes.
4. Transfer the fillets from the frying pan to the bread slices.
5. Drizzle with marinade, sprinkle with Parmesan cheese, and then top with another slice of bread to create a sandwich.

## FACTS AND STATS:

*Ontario is known for its great lakes and many rivers, which provide excellent opportunities for catching species like bass, trout, and walleye. British Columbia has many beautiful lakes and rivers, home to various fish species, including salmon, steelhead, and rainbow trout. Quebec is known for its beautiful scenery and many lakes and rivers, which provide opportunities for catching species like brook trout, pike, and walleye.*

# BREADED FISH FILLETS WITH FRIED VEGETABLES

**Alberta has many pristine lakes and rivers, home to species like rainbow trout, brown trout, and northern pike. Manitoba is known for its world-class fishing for species like lake trout, northern pike, and walleye in its many lakes and rivers. Saskatchewan has many lakes and rivers, which provide opportunities for catching species like northern pike, walleye, and lake trout.**

### SERVING SIZE: 4-6

### INGREDIENTS:

- 1 lb game fish fillets
- 4 eggs
- 1 cup onions, chopped
- 2 tbsp sour cream
- salt and pepper, to taste
- 1 tsp lemon zest
- 1 tbsp lemon juice
- 2 cups bread crumbs
- 3-4 tbsp butter
- 2-3 whole garlic cloves
- 1 cup carrots, sliced
- 1 cup potato, diced
- 1 cup sweet potato, diced
- 1 cup broccoli, chopped

### DIRECTIONS:

1. Break the eggs and whisk them.
2. Mix with sour cream and add salt, pepper, lemon zest, and lemon juice.
3. Soak the fillets in the egg mixture and dredge them in bread crumbs.
4. Fry in butter on each side for 2-3 minutes to create a firm crust.
5. Take out of the pan, melt more butter, and stir-fry garlic, onions, carrots, potato, sweet potato, and broccoli until tender.
6. Serve next to the fillets.

## FACTS AND STATS:

*Choose the right fishing equipment based on the type of fish you want to catch and the fishing location. You'll need a fishing rod, reel, fishing line, hooks, sinkers, and bait or lures. Look for areas where freshwater fish are known to gather, such as near underwater structures, in deep pools, or near the edges of weed beds. Consult with local fishing guides or ask for recommendations from local bait and tackle shops.*

# FISH AND VEGGIE ROAST

Choose the appropriate bait or lure for the fish you're trying to catch. Some popular baits for freshwater fish include worms, minnows, and insect larvae. Lures can also be practical and come in various shapes and sizes. Once you've selected your bait or lure and identified a good fishing spot, cast your line into the water. Pay attention to the water's depth and speed, and adjust your cast accordingly. Fishing requires patience and persistence. Wait for a fish to bite; don't be discouraged if it takes time. Be prepared to wait for extended periods of time, and use the time to relax and enjoy the natural surroundings.

### SERVING SIZE: 4-6

### INGREDIENTS:

- 2 tbsp butter
- 1 cup potatoes, diced
- 1 cup onions, sliced
- 1 tbsp mustard
- 1 tbsp sour cream
- 1 tbsp white wine
- 2 tbsp cheddar cheese, grated
- 1 lb game fish fillets

### DIRECTIONS:

1. Glaze the bottom of a baking dish with butter and pour the chopped vegetables.
2. Mix the mustard, sour cream, white wine, and cheddar cheese in a separate bowl to create a marinade.
3. Drizzle the vegetables with only a quarter of the marinade and roast for 15–20 minutes at 400 °F.
4. Dredge the fish fillets in the marinade and let them sit while the veggies are roasting.
5. Add the fish fillets to the baking dish and pour the rest of the marinade.
6. Roast for another 10 minutes.

## FACTS AND STATS:

*When you feel a tug on your line, quickly reel in the slack and give a sharp tug on the line to set the hook in the fish's mouth. Once you've set the hook, reel in your catch carefully. Avoid jerky movements that could cause the fish to escape, and use a net or your hands to remove the hook from the fish's mouth safely. Always follow local fishing regulations and guidelines, including catch limits and size restrictions. Return any fish that do not meet the regulations back to the water unharmed.*

# FRIED FISH WITH PESTO SAUCE

The population of freshwater fish in the USA varies depending on the species and location. However, according to the U.S. Fish and Wildlife Service's 2016 National Fishing, Hunting, and Wildlife-Associated Recreation Survey, an estimated 36.5 million freshwater anglers in the United States caught approximately 2.2 billion fish in 2016.

## SERVING SIZE: 4–6

## INGREDIENTS:

- 1 lb game fish fillets
- 3–4 eggs
- 1 cup of milk
- 1 cup flour
- 2 ½ cups sour cream
- 1 tbsp Dijon mustard
- 1 tsp lemon zest
- 1 tbsp lemon juice
- 2 tbsp butter
- 1 cup basil, chopped
- 1 tbsp vinegar
- ½ cup walnuts, chopped
- 1 tbsp Parmesan cheese, grated

## DIRECTIONS:

1. In a bowl, whisk the eggs and mix with milk, flour, 1 tbsp sour cream, Dijon mustard, lemon zest, and lemon juice.
2. Dredge the fish pieces in the batter and sit for 5–10 minutes.
3. Fry in butter until crispy.
4. To make the pesto, process basil, the rest of the sour cream, vinegar, walnuts, and Parmesan in a bowl using a food processor.
5. Serve the fried fish with the pesto.

## FACTS AND STATS:

*The freshwater fish population in Canada is diverse and abundant, with numerous species found in lakes, rivers, and streams across the country. According to Fisheries and Oceans Canada, some of Canada's most commonly caught freshwater fish species include walleye, pike, bass, trout, and salmon. Canada's total freshwater fish population is challenging to estimate as it varies by region and species and is influenced by factors such as habitat quality, water temperature, and fishing pressure. However, Fisheries and Oceans Canada conducts regular assessments and monitoring of fish populations in various water bodies to inform management and conservation efforts.*

# BREADED FISH WITH RISOTTO

**Fishing requires patience and persistence. If you're not planning to keep the fish you catch, practice catch and release to help conserve fish populations. Handle the fish carefully, remove the hook gently, and release the fish back into the water as quickly as possible. Be prepared to wait for extended periods of time, and use the time to observe the water and surroundings. Look for areas where fish will likely gather, such as near underwater structures or deep pools.**

### SERVING SIZE: 4-6

### INGREDIENTS:

- 1 lb game fish fillets
- 3 eggs
- 1 cup vegetable broth
- 2 cups bread crumbs
- 2 cups brown rice, soaked
- 1 cup onions, chopped
- 1 cup carrots, chopped
- 1 tsp dill, chopped
- 1 tsp cumin powder
- ½ tsp ginger powder
- 2 garlic cloves, minced
- 2 tbsp butter

### DIRECTIONS:

1. Soak the fish fillets in whisked eggs and then in bread crumbs.
2. Fry the fillets with the rice in the frying pan and mix in the onions, carrots, dill, cumin powder, ginger powder, and garlic.
3. Stir and add vegetable broth.
4. Bring to a boil and let simmer for 10–15 minutes until cooked and serve.

## FACTS AND STATS:

*Freshwater fish are sensitive to changes in water temperature, clarity, and flow. Pay attention to the weather and water conditions, and adjust your fishing strategy accordingly. For example, fish may be more active during overcast or rainy weather or in areas with cooler or warmer water temperatures. Different species of freshwater fish have other feeding habits and preferences. Choose the right bait or lure for the fish you're trying to catch. Live bait, such as worms, minnows, or insects, can be effective for many species, while lures can also be effective and come in various shapes and sizes.*

# DRUNKEN CATFISH IN PIE CRUST

Catfish is relatively low in calories, with approximately 120-150 calories per 3.5 ounces (100 gram) serving, depending on the cooking method. This makes it a good option for those trying to manage their weight or maintain a healthy diet. Catfish is a versatile fish that can be prepared in various ways, such as grilled, fried, baked, or sautéed. It is also widely available and relatively affordable, making it a convenient and budget-friendly option for many people.

### SERVING SIZE: 4-6

### INGREDIENTS:

- 1 lb game catfish, filleted
- ½ cup white wine
- 1 tsp garlic powder
- 1 tbsp lemon juice
- 1 tbsp olive oil
- 1 tsp dill, chopped
- 1 tbsp celery leaf, chopped
- 1 pie crust
- 1 egg
- 3 tbsp sour cream
- 1 tbsp Dijon mustard
- 1 tbsp flour

### DIRECTIONS:

1. Combine white wine, garlic powder, lemon juice, olive oil, dill, and celery leaf to make the marinade.
2. Marinate the catfish for 15–20 minutes.
3. Spread the pie crust and top it with a mixture of egg and 1 tbsp sour cream.
4. Take the fish out of the marinade and set them aside.
5. Add flour, the rest of the sour cream, and Dijon mustard to the remaining marinade.
6. In a pot, pour the marinade, boil, and stir. Remove from heat.
7. Spread the marinade over the pie crust.
8. Place the fish in the middle of the crust and wrap it in the dough.
9. Bake for 20–30 minutes at 400 °F.

## FACTS AND STATS:

*Catfish are a diverse group of fish that belong to the order Siluriformes. There are over 3,000 species of catfish. Catfish can be found all over the world. Catfish are found in freshwater habitats around the globe, including in rivers, lakes, and ponds. Some species of catfish can grow to enormous sizes like the Mekong giant catfish, which is found in Southeast Asia, is one of the largest freshwater fish in the world and can grow to over 9 feet (2.7 meters) in length and weigh up to 660 pounds (300 kg).*

# BREADED FISH WITH VEGGIE SALAD

**Catfish are a popular bait fish for anglers and are used to catch a variety of other fish species, including bass, walleye, and pike. Catfish farming, also known as aquaculture, is a growing industry worldwide. In the United States, catfish is the largest aquaculture industry, with over 300 million pounds of catfish produced each year.**

### SERVING SIZE: 4-6

### INGREDIENTS:

- 3-4 eggs
- 1 tbsp sour cream
- 1 tbsp Dijon mustard
- salt and pepper, to taste
- 2 tsp dill, chopped
- 1 tbsp celery leaf, chopped
- 1 lb game fish fillets
- 2 cups bread crumbs
- 2-3 tbsp butter
- 1 tbsp vinegar
- 1 cup Greek yogurt
- 1 tsp garlic powder
- 2-3 carrots, grated
- 2-3 apples, grated
- 1 sweet potato, grated
- 1-2 beets, grated

### DIRECTIONS:

1. In a bowl, break the eggs and mix them with sour cream, Dijon mustard, salt, pepper, 1 tsp dill, and celery leaf.
2. Soak the fish in the mixture and sit for a couple of minutes.
3. Dredge the fish in bread crumbs and fry in butter for 4-5 minutes on each side. Once done, set it aside.
4. Mix the vinegar, Greek yogurt, 1 tsp dill, garlic powder, and celery leaf in another bowl to create the salad dressing.
5. Then add the carrots, apples, sweet potato, and beets to the dressing and mix well.
6. Serve the fish fillets with the salad.

## FACTS AND STATS:

*Catfish are a popular food fish in many parts of the world known for their mild, slightly sweet flavor. Some species of catfish, such as the walking catfish, can breathe air and survive out of water for extended periods. The current record for the largest catfish caught in the United States is a blue catfish caught in Virginia's Kerr Lake in 2011. The catfish weighed 143 pounds and measured 57 inches long, breaking the previous record for the largest catfish caught in the U.S. by nearly 20 pounds. However, it's worth noting that catfish can be found in many different bodies of water throughout the U.S. There may be other impressive catches that have yet to make it into the record books. The current record for the largest channel catfish caught in Canada is a 58-pound specimen caught in the Red River in Manitoba, while the record for the largest blue catfish caught in Canada is a 91-pound fish caught in the St. Lawrence River in Quebec.*

# WILD FISH WITH COOKED VEGGIES

**Walleye are one of the most popular game fish in North America and are highly prized by anglers for their challenging fighting abilities and delicious flavor. Walleye are highly prized for their firm, white flesh, and mild, sweet taste. They are often prepared by frying, baking, or grilling.**

### SERVING SIZE: 4-6

### INGREDIENTS:

- 3-4 eggs
- 1 cup flour
- salt and pepper, to taste
- 1 tsp garlic powder
- 1 tsp orange zest
- 1 tsp dill, chopped
- 1 tsp cilantro, chopped
- 1 tsp basil, chopped
- 1 lb game fish, sliced
- 1 cup potatoes, diced
- 1 cup sweet potatoes, diced
- 1 cup carrots, sliced
- 2 tbsp butter

### DIRECTIONS:

1. Dredge the fish slices in a mixture of eggs, flour, salt, pepper, garlic powder, orange zest, dill, cilantro, and basil.
2. Fry the fish in butter for a couple of minutes or until crispy.
3. In a separate pot, cook the potatoes, sweet potatoes, and carrots until tender.
4. Take out of the pot and drain.
5. Serve next to the fish.

## FACTS AND STATS:

*Walleye are found in various freshwater habitats throughout North America, including lakes, rivers, and reservoirs. Walleye are top-level predators that feed on smaller fish and eat insects, crayfish, and other aquatic invertebrates. Walleye have large, reflective eyes that allow them to see well in low-light conditions, making them especially active at dawn and dusk.*

# SAUTÉED FISH WITH LIMA BEANS IN RED SAUCE

While the average size of a walleye is around 14-18 inches, they can grow much larger. The world record for the largest walleye caught is 22 pounds in Ontario, Canada, in 1960. Various factors can affect walleye populations, including changes in water temperature and quality, overfishing, and habitat loss. Walleye are an essential part of many ecosystems.

### SERVING SIZE: 4-6

### INGREDIENTS:

- 1 can of lima beans
- 1 lb game fish, deboned and sliced
- 1 onion, sliced
- 1 cup carrots, sliced
- 1 cup paprikas, sliced
- 1 cup tomatoes, sliced
- Salt and pepper, to taste
- 1 tsp dill
- 1 tbsp lemon juice
- ½ cup white wine
- 1 cup vegetable broth

### DIRECTIONS:

1. In a pan, fry the lima beans in butter for 1–2 minutes.
2. Add the fish and vegetable broth to the pan. Bring to a boil and let simmer for another couple of minutes.
3. Add the onion, carrots, paprikas, and tomatoes.
4. When the vegetables have softened, add white wine and cook for another 5–10 minutes.
5. Season with salt, pepper, dill, and lemon juice.

## FACTS AND STATS:

*Here are some of the best places to catch walleye in Ontario. Lake of the Woods is a massive lake on the Manitoba-Ontario border and is renowned for Its excellent walleye fishing, with countless bays, islands, and reefs to explore. Georgian Bay is this large Bay on Lake Huron and is home to a healthy walleye population, with many excellent fishing locations accessible by boat. Bay of Quinte is another large bay on Lake Ontario known for its trophy-sized walleye, with many professional fishing guides offering their services. Lac Seul is a large, remote lake in northwestern Ontario. Lake Nipissing is a large lake in central Ontario known for its excellent walleye fishing, with many boat launches and fishing access points available to the public. French River is a historic waterway in northeastern Ontario and is a popular destination for walleye anglers, with many areas accessible by boat or kayak.*

# GRANDPA'S EASY FISH BATTER

This works with all kinds of fish. I have used partridge, grouse, goose, and shrimp. You can use a shallow pan with oil if you need a deep-fryer to fry fish in. This method entails a little more patience!

### SERVING SIZE: 4-6

- 6 Fish fillets
- 1 Cup of flour
- 1 Egg
- 2 Tablespoons of cornstarch for thickening
- ¼ Baking soda & Baking powder
- ¼ Tablespoon of salt
- 1 Cup of water or 1 can of beer

### DIRECTIONS:

1. Mix all ingredients in a bowl. Whisk until desired thickness.
2. Add 1 cup of water or beer if you got one to spare.
3. Soak fish fillets or bird fillets in the mixture. The longer you soak thicker the batter stays on.
4. Deep fry or frying pan with oil your wild game meat for one delicious dish!

## FACTS AND STATS:

*Grandpa's Easy Fish Batter has to be perfected a couple of times before you nail the thickness. You want it sticky but not thick. If you run into this situation, use cornstarch for thickener, a little bit at a time, whisking thoroughly, or beer/water for thinning. You decide your fate!*

# COOK WILD GAME & GET EDUCATED!

Cook every popular wild game with confidence! Over 200+ recipes for breakfast, lunch, and dinner to satisfy your taste buds. Quick and easy recipes!

Simply by leaving your honest review of this book on Amazon, you will help other readers find the information they're looking for. Together, we can make sure more people are realizing their cooking ambitions – and doing so safely.

I can't thank you enough for your support. Cooking is a basic human skill, and it's beginning to die out in the modern world. Together, we can make sure that doesn't happen.

>>> **Click here to leave your review on Amazon.**

https://www.amazon.com/Simple-Hunting-Guide-Beginners-Tracking/dp/B09BGM1TB5/ref=sr_1_2?crid=3M6XR16NKQ5JP&keywords=Pat+gatz&qid=1681430095&sprefix=pat+gatz%2Caps%2C303&sr=8-2

# CONCLUSION

Great job learning how to make fresh wild game recipes! In this book, you learn how to cook all sorts of wild game. You now know how to cook squirrels, muskrats, bears, elk, moose, deer, fish, and boar. In many ways, cooking game meat is similar to making any other dish: You start with boiling, frying, or sautéing, and you prepare side dishes that you like. If you're making a salad, tarts, or roast, various toppings can enhance the flavor.

Yet game cooking is different in many critical ways. Let's sum them up so that you can create your recipes from scratch or personalize those given in this book.

*Marinating.* Wild game can have a strong flavor that only suits some's taste. Marinating can help, and I always recommend soaking the meat in a marinade the night before. Marinating can help dissolve some strong flavors that some people find unappealing. There are many different marinades that you can make if you understand the structure of a marinade and use the ingredients that serve the intended purpose. An oily or creamy compound, like olive oil, butter, and Dijon mustard, enhances the flavor while softening and dissolving some of the compounds in the meat. That way, the flavor is friendlier to an average palate. You also need a sour or acidic ingredient in your marinade, like vinegar, orange juice, or lemon juice. These components soften the meat, make cooking easier, and alter the smell and flavor. Spices like salt, pepper, and herbs not only improve the flavor but can also enhance the natural taste of the meat.

*Seasoning.* Pay close attention to which seasoning *goes* with the type of game you're cooking. The taste of the herb should complement the flavor. This means it should be mild enough not to overwhelm a dish yet strong enough to enhance the taste. In this book, you learn that your pantry will need copious amounts of

- celery leaf
- garlic powder
- ginger powder
- cumin powder

- orange and orange zest
- lemon and lemon zest
- salt and pepper
- nutmeg
- cinnamon
- cilantro
- basil
- thyme
- mint
- and any other herbs you like

Now, you can go ahead and stock your pantry so that you don't have to go out and purchase the seasoning each time you're cooking.

*All that dairy.* Aside from stocking your pantry with herbs, it would be wise to equip your fridge with some nice

- Parmesan cheese
- cheddar cheese
- cream cheese
- sour cream
- heavy cream
- butter (and a lot of it)
- Greek yogurt

The dairy in the recipes serves the purpose of "lightening up" the dish and making it sweeter. It also helps add volume to your toppings, batter, and sauces without using seasonings. Cheeses and creams will only taste the food very little, likely to make a meal more satiating without making it feel heavy.

*Stock, honey, bread, and pie crust.* I frequently use premade pie crust. Why make you roll out dough when you don't have to? You can use pie crust to make pies and easily prepare fancy-looking dishes that would otherwise take much longer to make. Flattening bread with a rolling pin is an incredible hack to make dough when you don't feel like making it from scratch. Flattened bread is easily molded into the needed shapes, and making it will take only a few minutes. Using stock instead of water is wise to enhance the flavor or make the meal more satiating without increasing the amount of food (calories). Adding liquid to fried meat and roasted dishes makes the meal more tender yet crispy and not overly "cooked." Glazing your meat with honey when frying, roasting, or baking also adds flavor and the kind of crispness you'd otherwise achieve only with higher temperatures or longer cooking. It is a helpful hack to keep the meat crispy on the outside and tender on the inside. Don't worry, your meal won't taste like your cookbook pages stuck together, and you made half pie and half dessert. Honey blends with meat just fine and won't taste too sweet.

*Fruit and game meat?* Sure! Don't be afraid of experimenting with game meat and fruit sauces. I aimed to bridge the gap between the flavors by making sauces with stock and sour or heavy cream. These "buffer" ingredients help you balance out flavors and get the best of both worlds. If you're passionate about cooking game meat, buy some frozen berries or canned applesauce. Canned fruit sauces are a great way to be more creative and make a more elaborate meal without much extra effort.

The Hunters Wild Game Cookbook Guide - 200+ Mouth-Watering Recipes to Master the Art of Cooking Popular North American Animals with Facts and Stats is the ultimate solution for anyone looking to elevate their game cooking skills. Whether you're a seasoned hunter or an adventurous foodie, this book will take you on a culinary journey that's both informative and delicious.

Are you tired of the same old recipes and want to try something new and exciting? Do you want to impress your friends and family with your wild game cooking skills? Are you looking to learn about the nutritional benefits of game meat and how to cook it to perfection? If you answered yes to any of these questions, then The Hunters Wild Game Cookbook Guide is the book for you.

Did you know that game meat is a healthier alternative to traditional meats such as beef and pork? It's lower in fat and calories, higher in protein, and free from antibiotics and hormones. Additionally, game meat is more sustainable and environmentally friendly, as it's often harvested from wild populations that are managed for conservation purposes.

Stereotypical situations where this book would come in handy include:

1. You've just come back from a successful hunting trip, but you have no idea how to cook the game meat you've harvested.
2. You want to impress your friends and family with a unique and delicious meal, but you don't know where to start.
3. You're interested in the nutritional benefits of game meat but don't know how to incorporate it into your diet.

But what if you're concerned about the gamey taste that's often associated with game meat? Don't worry! The Hunters Wild Game Cookbook Guide includes tips and tricks for removing the gamey taste and enhancing the meat's natural flavors.

Here are some of the key benefits of this book:

- Over 200 mouth-watering recipes that cover a wide range of North American game animals such as deer, elk, bear, rabbit, and more.
- Tips and tricks for preparing, cooking, and storing game meat to ensure maximum flavor and freshness.
- Information about the various North American game animals, including their natural habitats, hunting regulations, and conservation efforts.

But what about the cost of game meat and the availability of certain species? The Hunters Wild Game Cookbook Guide includes recipes for both common and less common game animals, so you can choose the recipes that best suit your budget and availability.

And what if you're concerned about the complexity of the recipes? Rest assured that this book includes recipes for all skill levels, from beginner to advanced, so you can find the perfect recipe to match your cooking expertise.

In conclusion, The Hunters Wild Game Cookbook Guide - 200+ Mouth-Watering Recipes to Master the Art of Cooking Popular North American Animals with Facts and Stats is the perfect book for anyone looking to expand their culinary horizons and explore the world of game meat. With its informative and easy-to-follow recipes, this book is a must-have for any adventurous cook. So don't wait any longer, start cooking like a pro!

# REFERENCES

Amazon. (n.d.-a). *Eat My Meat: A beginners field dressing guide for small game by Pat Gatz.* https://www.amazon.com/EAT-MY-MEAT-BEGINNERS-DRESSING/dp/B09HRW83P8

Amazon. (n.d.-b). *The simple hunting guide: Beginners quick start into the sport with ease - tracking, scouting, and survival skills by Pat Gatz.* https://www.amazon.com/Simple-Hunting-Guide-Beginners-Tracking/dp/B09BGM1TB5

Foote, R., & Blaze, K. (2010). *Wild game recipes and laughs: A collection of recipes and cartoons for hunters.* Wheatmark, Inc.

Tidball, K. G., Tidball, M. M., & Curtis, P. D. (2022). *Locally procured wild game culinary trends in the U.S.: A study of the ruffed grouse as entrée and accompanying nutritional analysis.* Frontiers in Sustainable Food Systems, 6, 200.

# HUNTING FOR GREATNESS COMMUNITY!
## COME DISCOVER THE MOST VALUABLE HUNTING COMMUNITY!

www.facebook.com/groups/www.huntingsecrets

# OTHER BOOKS YOU'LL LOVE!

"Hunt to Live, Live to Hunt!"
First Nation Algonquin Native
Little Eagle

ONE-OF-A-KIND #1 BEGINNERS HUNTING GUIDE

# THE SIMPLE HUNTING GUIDE

BEGINNERS QUICK START INTO THE SPORT WITH EASE
TRACKING, SCOUTING AND SURVIVAL SKILLS

**PAT GATZ**

# OTHER BOOKS YOU'LL LOVE!

**A BEGINNERS FIELD DRESSING GUIDE FOR SMALL GAME**

## EAT MY MEAT

### PAT GATZ

Made in United States
Troutdale, OR
09/23/2023